ONE MAN'S CRUSADE

BY

DR. ALHASAN SISAWO CEESAY, MD

© 2017 by Dr. Alhasan Sisawo Ceesay, MD

All rights reserved. No part from this book may be reproduced in any form without written permission from the publisher, except by a reviewer who may quote passages in a review to be printed in a newspaper or magazine.

FIRST PRINTING

PUBLISH KUNSA.COM

INSCRIBED TO

My parents, wife and children, Friends, Friends of Manding charitable trust, Colchester, UK and Alpena, Michigan, USA; and the downtrodden

Glory achieved in bringing relief to communities is heavenly. It is patriotic duty of each person to lift lives of people we relate to or share this planet with. None is more deserving of our hearts and energy than beleaguered villagers who through no fault of theirs wallow in squalid life among plenty. Patients and hard work by dreamers yields marvellous rewards

Dr. Alhasan S. Ceesay, MD

PREFACE AND ACKNOWLEDGMENTS

This work reveals tip of the ice-berg regarding determination and effort to literally unilaterally bring medical aid and healthcare delivery to Northern part of rural Gambia. It is a trailer blazer of hard work intermingled with the most challenging immigration problem marred by foot-dragging beurucratic ineptness.

Incident I came across early in my boyhood days, 1954, reinforced my determination to be part of bringing solution to Gambia's healthcare delivery problem. At the time villagers walk on foot for well over a hundred miles seeking medical service to only find empty shelved dispensaries and no doctor to attend them or their loved ones.

Gambia's healthcare was in shambles; delivered by understaffed and ill-equipped Health Centres operated by dispensers and Nurse Midwives. I had to take the bull by the horns and dedicate my life to providing medical service to rural Gambia, as long as I lived, through NGO Manding Medical Centre I founded at Njawara village since 1993.

At this juncture I remain the lone wolf running the NGO and will carry on to the end of my earthly life. The Centre has treated free more than 9000 villagers. The centre needs all and any help one can give or for groups able to be part of a good humanitarian cause to needy villagers.

Hence feast your eyes on the following pages while I let in few sentimental acknowledgements. First, I am profoundly grateful to my wife and daughters for persevering through thick and thin with me in this most difficult adventure of providing medical aid to rural Gambia. I also express profound gratitude to the numerous friends who were persistent in encouraging me to publish my story to give heart to other dreamers like me.

Special thanks to my wife and children for persevering and persisting through thick and thin of my adventure to bring medical aid to villagers and children. I am deeply grateful to Mrs. Lorna Robinson, Dr. Laurel Spooner, Dr. Barbra Murray, Dr. Phil Murray, Dr. Richard Spooner, Dr. Linda Malhon-Daly, Dr. Angela Stull and Lloyds law firm, Atique Rheman, Keba Sanneh, Matida Sanneh, Roheyata Sey-Corr, Yamarie Sey, Fatou Isata Ceesay, Ganem Al-Hadied, Muhamad Adam, Abdualah Shahim, Asiya Qadri, Sulayman Bojang, Kofi Awudo, Binta Ceesay, Ahmed Nizami, Kostas Miliotis, Bishop Coleman McGehee jr, Rita Riggs, Neville Brown, Rowan Sheddon, Ebrahima Bojang, Ebrahima Jaiteh, Daryl Gasson, Eliza Jones, Monica Sanchez, Penny West, Dr. Nelson Herron, Faisal Alin, Abdinnisir, Noora Sugulle, Yusuf Ali, Ndumbe Gaye, Hussein K. Alavi and staff of both Long Sight and Hulme Libaries, Ms. A. Harter, Mr. Charlie Jones, and all their colleagues at the Home office. Bravo for doing good job at a difficult post. Also I am immensely thankful to illustrious lawyer Ousainu Darboe, Eliza Jones, Dr. Richard Murray, Dr. Malkaight Singh, Cloyd Ramsey, Howard Riggs, Rita Riggs,

Dr. Charles Egli, Dr. Cooper Milner, Dr. Nelson Herron, Deidre O'Leary, Margaret Cruise, Bill Cruise, Alison Cruise, Dr. Eunice Kahan, Dr. Betzabi Alison-Prager, Henry Valli, Fr. John Milner, Homer Sheppard, Geraldine Sheppard, Dr. Lamin J. Sise, Dr. Sulayman S. Nyang, Bishops Masson & Coleman McGhee of the Episcopal Diocese of Michigan, Detroit, the Ceesay Committee Diocese of Michigan, Lois R. Leonard, Rev. Walter White, Rev Hugh White, Patricia Koblynski, Mayors: Carol Shafto and John Gimllet, Alpena city Council, Ishfaque Ahmed, Imran Khurum Ahmed, Abdinnisir Hassan, Faisal Alin, Noora Sugulle, Solicitor Kemo Ceesay, Ida Ceesay, Mike Tijan, Yusuf Ali, and numerous others whose names are not mention but not forgotten.

Many thanks to my brothers and sisters who encouraged me complete this work throughout these hard working months and years. I write to raise money for the building of a village hospital at Njawara, Gambia. It is my hope that you would be inspired to join our dream of providing medical aid and service to Gambian villagers and children.

I write to raise awareness of a need to support the building a hospital at Manding Medical Centre, Njawara village the Gambia, West Africa. Purchasing this book or donating in cash or kind would help bring our dream to fruition of Manding Medical Centre for a much needed healthcare delivery and hope to villagers, especially children who frequently die prematurely from childhood diseases because of lack of medical service. Together we can catch a dream for the villager and children. Log onto:

www.friendsofmandinggambimed.btck.co.uk; or www.publishkunsa.com to learn more about our self-help village health project Manding Medical Centre at Njawara Lower Badibou District, NBD, The Gambia, West Africa.

Portions of proceed from sale of this work go to support goals of Manding Medical Centre. In addition it will in due course offer scholarships to rural candidates wishing to read for a medical or an agricultural degree and return to serve in rural Gambia.

Dr. Alhasan Sisawo Ceesay, MD

Chapter 1

The humanitarian Ethos

The first thing any heart pleads with God is to be given power of endurance, love and tolerance. The heart start beating from time it is formed to the trillionth minute of its life. Nothing is as efficient and enduring as the heart which keeps it's secrete deep in its four chambers. The heart is where our inner most secrets lurk. In the heart dwells the milk of human kindness.

No wonder it is commonly heard folks challenging others to have a heart. Kind people and philanthropists are said to have a big heart. However, in some this is the home of treachery and darkness as portrayed by dictators and inhuman action in battle. The heart is the vehicle of love and emotion.

Empathy makes us tolerant and bonds this with a committed heart. Women become pregnant multiple times because of loving hearts our mothers possess. No heart no love says the romantic pilgrim. Without the heart the rest of the organs are certain to die sooner than later. Poets serenade the heart by comparing it with angels on our side.

No wonder, I a poor village boy from humble background was able to venture to climb mount ambitious to bring modern healthcare delivery to villagers in rural Gambia.

The path was very challenging, lonely, and educative above all; however I persevered pain and unimaginable destitute for my people. The strength of a crusader comes from sheer steely will to achieve goal one is convinced of its benefits to mankind.

A lot of the journey has already been documented in earlier works of mine. However here is a synipet for those who did not chance to read about my life. I am of a humble farmer's background and was born at Njawara village in the North Bank region of the Gambia. I had my Primary School education at Kinte Kunda, then Armitage High School, ending up as a registered nurse at the Royal Victoria Hospital, Banjul, before embarking to the USA on my medical degree quest.

I graduated from the American University School of Medicine in Montserrat, West Indies, in 1992 and returned to the Gambia to serve and to start setting up a self-help village health NGO Manding Medical Centre. The Gambia Government and the Badibou local authority register NGO Manding Medical Centre. The centre has treated more than 9000 patients free. I am currently a medical officer at the Royal at the Royal Victoria Hospital on study leave. It is my hope that this work will inspire others and bring much needy help to providing medical service to rural Gambia.

Ambition for the villager as well as improvement of my medical skill led me make, to date, the most trying venture of my life as it incurred my family and I very sad tale to narrate later. Ambition makes us aim higher heights that pierce the sky. Grip ambition has over us is demonstrated by passion it fires in us. One gets restless and feels the wall crashing upon one in the event of not answering the call of mighty ambition.

The ambitious mostly dream of success and thinks of higher achievements in hope of bringing relief, hope and something with which to help our fellow beings. Ambition is not selfish for it seeks to improve individuals and society. Ambition is made of sterner stuff than any of our goals. It pushes us to the brink of breaking in lieu of and in pursuit of success. Its effect overrides our life and forces us to aspire to be the best out of the best. It makes us champions among the best there is in competing.

The other side of ambition leads solders to turn monsters to their people as in over throwing of legitimate elected civil government just to meet or satisfy their lust for power. All politicians yearn to someday become heads of state of their respective countries. And the over ambitious student strives not only to be the best but the most renowned professor later on. The opera singer and Ballerinas all yearn to be the best in their field or theatricals performance. The literally ambitious wants to leave you work which when one opens the first page is just unable to stop reading until one gets to the end of the book or thesis.

The mountaineers never stop conquering extreme high mountains. Ambition directs us to certain set of values where we spend our energies to conquer or achieve our goal. Researchers are tirelessly seeking to find out cause and effect of disease or inventing things that enhances life such as drugs to cure diseases and cancers, electricity and light bulbs, bicycles, cars, trains, planes, Ocean liners, space crafts and submarines just to name a few products of ambitious people.

Ambition enables the scholar to excel beyond the best competitor. This work examines the effect of ambition in our lives. It shows how it moulded and propelled my medical aspirations for the villager which gave birth to Manding Medical Centre at Njawara village, Lower Badibou District, in the North Bank of the Gambia.

Chapter 2

CHASING TIME TO CATCH A DREAM

It is said that time and tides waits for no man. For me I have been chasing elusive time from time immemorial. The chase started at birth when I stopped breathing in the first hour of my life. In those precious minutes and hours to follow time left me behind and I was declared none existent and was to be buried first thing in the morning.

I woke up before dawn and have been chasing time since February 14th, 1942 to the present time. My peers in other villages started schooling at the age of 5 years and I started primary school at the raw age of 12 years old. And I enrolled at college at the age of 22 years. I graduated from medical school at age 50. There has always been this huge gap between time and when things happen for me.

I wish there was a way I can reverse or stop time so that all delays in my life would level up with elapsed time. All my peers have grown grey or have complete white hairs or totally bald but I look like some 28 year old lad and as fit as a 16 years old athletic kid, even though I never ceased chasing after time. Time for that precious priceless record of history has not arrived for me.

William Shakespeare said of time thus: "Come what comes May. Time and the hour runs through the roughest day." For me it kept flying and irreversibly so. Friends console me by telling me; "Your time will come." In desperation I ask when? Time cares less for it will tick with or without us. Hence, it is my duty to catch up and do well to live footprints worth following when my time comes. Navigating through the valleys and gorges strewn at us on life's path is a nightmare. I came to England just to do the PLAB and MRCP degree in medicine and return to my home land in the shortest possible time.

This time would not allow as I unknowingly fell into the deepest gorge of visa and job problems. I arrived as a visitor and hence more of tourist than student status. The Home Office's refusal to change my status to student left me in limbo and a destitute. This made it difficult to pass the PLAB because of being torn between hunger and struggling to find help to send money to feed my equally beleaguered wife and three daughters. I became catechetic and weak that even the arch angels of death and hell would feel sad and sorry upon meeting me. Again time and tide refused to wait for Dr. Ceesay. All my compatriots got through the PLAB because they had monetary help enabling them to pay for PLAB review courses. For me I had to feed from the surface of my teeth while I chased time to take my exams under very difficult circumstances that would drown most people.

Time was far ahead and I needed to catch up before it becomes too late for me and my dream for the Gambia. Let me reiterate that the greatest of all faults is to be conscious of none. Hence, time would have not slipped from my fingers had I taken a moment or two to seek for student visa while at the British Embassy in the Gambia. Anyhow hind sight is always too wise as I later learnt from bitter experience. Despite this long and hash experience, I never gave up and things happened at a surprising and lightening speed for the arrival of a new dawn in my life and goal for the Gambia.

Alasan Mbalo woth mum Famatanding Ceesay

Chapter 3

THE PARADOXICAL SCHISMS

Back in Africa life is simply or mostly of an agricultural or rural type. It usually starts with education and guidance from parents, initiation, which connotes the day one, is circumcised or inducted into manhood/womanhood, and finally the individual's return to our maker and reunion with our ancestors in the world beyond.

For sojourners like me, it's the beginning of endless challenges and changes we have to adapt to quickly for our survival. Life becomes an endless long hours, 16 or more hours a day, of work with the earning paid to schools, universities, landlords and sending whatever is left to family back in Africa for their sustainers. It is full of surprises and unfamiliar behaviours, customs, and outcomes.

First the weather one encounters unravels in four seasons; spring and summer being the most tolerable but autumn and bone chilling winters are for Eskimos not warm blooded Africans. Winter curdles my blood and frizzes every bit of me no matter the number of thermal layers I manage to put on. Thanks to technology and kindness of the people over in these frigid places I survived my wintry days in Europe and America.

Paradoxically, the expression of freedom and degree to which it is adhered to far exceeded my imagination and expectations. One of the most surprising paradoxes or schism was being castigated when I attempted to settle a simple dispute between husband and wife friends of mine. In Africa and most places one can give genuine counsel to warring factors for them to resort to reconciliation instead of being at each other's throat over trivial matters mostly emanating from misunderstanding or failing to listen to the other's point of view.

Let me reiterate what St. Francis of the Franciscan order in Assis, Rome, eloquently admonished us regarding incidence as above. He said, "Where there is discord, May we bring harmony; where is error, may we bring truth, where there is doubt may we bring faith. And where there is despair, may we bring hope." A dear friend made matters worse for me, by repeatedly asking that I consider moving out of his premises.

The demands made on December 5th, 2000, May 30th, 2001, and again on August 11th, 2001were painful experiences. However the July 13th, 2001 order to relocate from his place was the last straw that made me move. Can you imagine how difficult it was for me to hear that from a friend? I quote, "You have to move any where you can relocate."

This brought endless tears of remorse running down my chicks. It came a year after my wife returned to Gambia living me in solitude and un-employed. There was still no sign of a financial relief by means of acquiring a temporal job until after my being registered with the GMC. Joblessness cum intolerable circumstances catapulted me to Manchester City in the North West region of the UK. Life did not turn out all roses for me in Manchester. It was a struggle against failures! No pass, No job and no money or peace of mind.

My plan to serve as a nurse in UK, until the time I could get my GMC registration, was set a terrible blow when the Overseas Nurses Association stopped processing my request for assistance because the NHS has ceased accepting nurses from regions like mine. NHS feared draining the health personnel of developing countries by accepting nurse and doctors from underdeveloped countries. What a farce!

In the same vein the very people can go to our countries and shamelessly pick up our gold, diamonds and other mineral wealth without a second thought to poverty their pilfering was doing to the so called developing country. To make matters worse, if not very grim for me, the Home Secretary announced in April 2006 that from that time hence forth the NHS will only give training priority to UK and EU doctors.

Such pronouncements left self-sponsors like me in limbo as we have to fight harder in other to get training placement in teaching hospitals. This tantamount to a stab from the back from an institute we relied upon. This announcement ignored efforts people like me have been putting in to help improve our medical skills we wish to serve our people back in our countries. The current state of affairs along with my age nudged me into devoting the rest of my life building Manding Medical Centre to a fully functional health unit serving the Gambia.

L-R: Alasan Mbalo Jr, Famata (mum) and Alasan Mbalo Sr.

Chapter 4

MANNA NEVER CAME TO ME FROM HEAVEN

I am among few doctors whose life retrograded to the level of living on exactly £5 (five pounds) a week on a nine hours seven days shoe selling job. The hundred and five pounds weekly earning this slave life brought was split £50 for rent, the other £50 goes towards paying loans I took to pay for my exams, my children's school fees and sustenance of my family back in the Gambia. Oh! I had a paradoxical raise in salary of £1a day which propped up my income to £16/day.

It was disheartening time for me. It was a nightmare neither member of the family will ever forget. Most painful for me were the times when my daughters ask for shoes or other things their peers have and I had to come out clean and explain that daddy was, even though I would like them have their requests, at no monetary position to provide such items at that time. I would promise to do my best to get it for them as soon as feasible.

I can hear them cry before putting the telephone down or simply passing it to their mother to talk to me. I do not wish my worst enemy to have to go through such experience or be embedded in hell on earth as my life was. I love my family and missed being with them.

Mean while for those who know me, my state was pitiful. Most would ask "Doctor, what on earth are you doing in a shoe shop and not by the patient's bedside?" I simply reply this is what fate has for me at the moment and I have to feed my family back home. The next day one or two would return to the shop with offering of £2, £5, or £10 for me to send to my children. Yes, I was literally turned out into a silent street beggar and my pride was trampled to the lowest earthly level.

At the end of the day I return to my flat with a heavy heart knowing that I had nothing to eat but two slices of bread with sardine sandwiched in-between. After this kingly meal I try to study for as long as my wondering mind would let me. The ringing of the telephone brings palpitation and anxiety to me.

I fear whether our landlord, back in Gambia, has not gotten impatient with my family or if food has ran out because of uncontrolled daily high prices of food commodities in the Gambia. My wife and I use to pray, over the phone, for relief and yet we both know and agreed that life could be worst if I failed my villagers and Manding Medical Centre. So we bit the bullet and continue trying to get more awareness on the good cause Manding medical Centre would bring to the children and villagers.

There are those who think that my enduring such painful experience was predicated on sheer stupidity on my part. For family, especially my wife and I, it was a worthy self-sacrifice for humanity. Life, as ordained, did change for the better and my daughters' education was never set back by the above financial limbo I endured while in the UK. This is further propounded upon in the following chapter titled, Failure conquered amid roadblocks. Tears do not solve difficult moments like these dark days. Only faith and hard work solves small economic pains as I encountered.

Late: Omar Baba Sallah Ceesay, RIP

Chapter 5

Climbing Mount Ambitious

Mount Ambitious is the steepest challenge one can face for it never let go and nudges one to push for successful end of one's objective. It makes one feel the wall crumbling over oneself on any attempt to drop or be lazy about the goal. Mount Ambition never let us down but drowns us in thrill that the heart at times can hardly take. It is a miracle as to how lonely crusaders survived such drills of desire amid improbabilities.

Many a dreamer's projects are normally classed as either white elephants or worse laughable mission impossible. The story of the Wrights brothers and of recent, Hillary Blood, all point out that sceptics and fears of man can be overcome through full commitment to a goal. Did Christopher Columbus become scared sailing across the mighty Atlantic ocean in the Nina, Pinta and the Santa Maria?

This work is just about archiving the impossible that, I almost singlehandedly brought Manding Medical Centre at Njawara, the Gambia into a full fledge operating hospital that serves both citizen and none-citizens. The path led to deep and many painful experiences. It is tale of relentlessness and of people coming together to bring Manding Medical Centre into reality.

I have never lost sight and determination since its inception in my mind to bring medical aid and service to beleaguered villagers that travel miles to ill-equipped and under stocked dispensaries and health centres. I did it because of sheer shortage of doctors and health facilities to rural Gambia and being convinced that it is the right of the villager and the right thing for my people.

This work is about being a positive contributing member of society no matter where you may find yourself. It tries to shed reason why we need ignite the spirit and embers of giving not only to illuminate an others' life but to remove dark and despondent moments from those needy hearts. In so doing we let hope and light triumph over darkness and hence allow peace to transcend earth.

Very inspirational characters are presented in hope of motivating you to do good causes waiting for your mark. In the mean time allow me express profound gratitude to my wife and children for bearing and persevering patiently through with me in thick and thin during my drive to bring medical aid and service to villagers. It is a mission by a simple person determined to heed his people's call. Project Manding Medical Centre is to provide medical aid to Gambian villagers.

All humans make mistakes or are capable of making one. The difference in outcome of our errors is being able to accept that we erred and to learn from them to make better judgments next time. Some say my mistake was refusing to stay in the village mould and that I was too ambitious if not a grandiose psychopath pursuing Western ideals.

So far, I have been able to assail through most criticisms and completed university education despite it all. Some say I should not have left America to study medicine at the A. M. Dogliotti, school of medicine in Monrovia, Liberia, West Africa or even attend the American university of the Caribbean at Montserrat in the West Indies.

Friends have on many occasions asked why I did not seek the Green card while a student in America or apply for the United Kingdom citizenship during my clinical clerkship rotation at Colchester, Essex.

My response then and even today is that I refrained from such a course because I love Africa and there is no place I rather be other than the Gambia. More over our people need our services more than any other place.

I love helping villagers and would do just that with my life in the time that God gave me on planet earth. In addition I am certain to fulfil my goal, with help of Manding Medical Centre, of providing medical aid to the villager.

The end result of, dear reader, that error, if it be one, was it turned me into the doctor I am today for the villagers and the needy. The road to that lofty end was long and difficult and at times too slippery and steep to walk on. It was strewed with stagnation, starvation, and destitutionous life.

Hope you will agree that the end result was worth the means for family and country. It is no fanfare or path for the weak and none persistent person. I suffered tremendously since my arrival in the UK, the so-called land of honey and milk of Europe.

I faced series of evictions from flats, had been threatened with CCJ actions and a host of collection agents vying to lay hands on anything belonging to me to recoup money owed to either the RBS or BT. Life in this state was nerving, shameful and painful.

The mistake, which lead to this disheartening state, was that I came to the UK on a visitor's visa. The Home Office's refusal to reclassify my visa to a student visa landed me into hell on earth.

Some asked if the struggle was worth the pain and dehumanization state I found myself at. My response had always been a resounding yes with a challenge for doubters to meet me in the Gambia upon my completing certification with the GMC three years hence.

On my way home, I had two fellows discussing about me. The other said that I was wrong in not listening as well as obeying my father's wish that I become a farmer instead of being immersed in some foreign ideology and system. The sensible one retorted by asking why they were the in UK and not farming in the Gambia.

He told his companion that Dr. Ceesay was spending himself for the future good of all Gambians for if his medical center catches on it would be added valuable medical service to the Gambia and the Badibus in particular.

I met some Gambian at the Alexandra Park and they too suggested that I think of returning since life had been nothing but a downward spiral for me since my coming to the UK.

I reminded them that if mountain climbers were scared of the height they wish conquered or mistakes others made in their attempts to climb those mountains, we would never assailed Mount Everest.

A mistake is a necessary lesson to learn from and to humble ourselves from the belief of being infallible. Our mistakes are eye openers to bigger gains. They may at first be bitter to swallow but if we learn from them we gain a lot of insight in future plans.

Difficulty is the orchestra of life. No human ever lived without having gone through moments he wished never happened even if it were his or her worse enemy. My passion to bring modern medical aid to Gambian villagers catapulted me to the UK in 2000 to bring NGO: Manding Medical Centre at Njawara to attention of the international community in our fund raising drive to build the Centre's hospital.

I had planned to also do a postgraduate course in medicine before returning to serve the villagers. Well, man proposes and God disposes as exemplified by my unbelievable experience in the sojourn for Gambian villagers. This work chronicles my experience since 1998 through 20014.

It is tale of people coming together to bring dream Manding Medical Centre into reality for rural Gambia. It reveals my determination to provide medical service to villagers because it is the right for my people. My life is a simple mission to heed to call for much needed medical service to rural Gambia.

Healthcare delivery never existed for Gambian farmers and reason why the prevalence of bygone diseases. Despite all the painful experience I ran through in life, I still deeply believe in my convictions and will do whatever needed correction strong enough to hold me committed to provision of medical aid to the villager regardless of how short my life may turn out. If the Manding Medical Centre and all it now provide the Gambia was a mistake then I pray to make a billion more similar sincere mistakes for mankind.

It is said to err is human and to forgive divine. I hope those could not see beyond the tip of their noses could forgive me for refusing to stay in the village mould and pursue to the hilt what I believe to be worthy end for the Gambia, villagers and the downtrodden.

I am no angel and like you I am full of human imperfections. The difference between my critics and I is that I am a dreamer who never gives up dreaming and I am always ready to see the dreams come true to a positive beneficial reality for all of us.

This is my way of leaving footprints on the sand of time so that beleaguered Gambians can muster courage and work for the development of the region. It is my hope that Manding Medical Centre continues to be the template its today for generations to come.

Let us learn from our mistakes and have the foresight and fortitude to turn them into something positive for all. Grandpa Bajoja advised that we have courage to accept our faults and fortitude to correct them for the good of all. The world is not always our making but we must make the best of it.

Our destiny is caved seventy five percent by us and twenty five percent by sheer luck. Since the latter is of rare gift one must buck up and role sleeves to not only build a worthy rewarding life but one nobly shared. My date with Gambia is nothing less than bringing a much needed healthcare delivery to rural Gambia.

Njawara Basic School being visited by Alpena Community College students, May, 2005

Chapter 6

Road Blocks and slippages

This chapter unveils how myth became reality. In ancient times when only Gods, Angels, Ghosts, Witches or Goblins and birds were the only one known to have gift of flight; the Wrights brother took it upon themselves to prove such believe to be wrong and mythical. They set the stage to prove that men can also touch the skies and return safely to home base earth.

The Rights were accused of being witches, magicians and of outright insane in trying to emulate birds. Ambition kept them working hard on their goal until their astonishing of man on the day their glider flew into air soaring above man and earth. This feat set others not only to try but the tool was replicated and improved to time when a dare devil took a solo fight across the mighty expanse of the Atlantic Ocean and landed safely in Europe.

From the Rights brothers' ambitious experiment man became accepted as a 'bird without wings' as he too with help of marvellous engineering can fly like a bird. Today, thanks to ambition and feat set by the Right brothers, thousands upon thousands if not millions of planes ply through the blues skies to and fro to America and any corner of the world.

Planes have shortened travel time, especially during the days of the supersonic plane which crosses the Atlantic in maximum time of just two hours.

We raise our hats in gratitude for gift the ambitious Right brothers left us with. No wonder we now have dare devils like Uri Gagarin, Noël Armstrong and many more astronauts that the right brothers' effort gave birth to in our generation.

Sail boats like the Nina, Pinto and the Santa Maria took well more than six months to cross the Atlantic to its American coast. Today with better built study ships hundreds of thousands of people sail the mighty Ocean seeking leisure experience over the waters. Again ambitious daring sailors like Christopher Columbus and pirates set the trail in ancient times.

It is one thing to float in challenging of the tempestuous Atlantic waves but travel beneath like submarines do was not dreamt of until in the later part of the 18th century. Man toyed with idea of being not only able to dive to the depths of the mighty seas but to travel within them with bleitant impunity.

Again mighty ambition got its way for man to now remain submerged in the dark belle of the oceans for months at a time and be anywhere undetected. If microscopes were a wonder then today's Hobble telescopes are as unique and tantalizing as during the first flight man ever made it across the Atlantic or space.

We now are privileged with visual capacity that the ancient believed belongs to Gods and not sinning men. With these telescopes we now see distance unthinkable and they have helped us derive great knowledge about space.

Ambition cloaks our successes and pushes us to frontiers never dreamt of until today. Ambition made man the most advanced animal living on planet earth. The instrument behind these feats is passion and determination.

The call is neither fetish nor mysticism but a strong desire and conviction to achieve a goal in the hope that people will benefit from it. No, there is usually no telephone call from the powers above or a ghost whispering to us about our passion.

It is just a plane and pure humble feeling deeper than that, for it is reality backed by unshakable conviction that remains in us until the accomplishment of our goal and beyond it. Yes, my friends, the call, our passion and stance or dream for our people is stronger than the self.

The walls tend to cave on me any time I try to forgo my dream of providing medical aid to villagers and the down trodden. Passion feels the void in life and without it the choir of life becomes deafening instead of melodious. We do what we passionately believe is worthy cause with an eventual reward to humanity.

No successful man or woman ever dreamt of failing. The challenge to succeed becomes a passionate and personal challenge marked by unflinching determination unrivaled by any other at the time.

I am completely committed to the enriching and enhancing the quality of life for people. My mystic drive is to reach out and help the needy i.e. villagers and the down trodden.

It's the joy of my heart and total being. Sir Hilary Blood's drive to conquer Mount Everest is less passionate in comparison to my desire and believes that one can bring medical aid to the doors of the villager.

Hence, I created Manding Medical Centre, a health NGO at Njawara village, Lower Badibou, the Gambia, which involved local authority and all villages in the region and provides medical aid free to the region. Many were initially tinged with trepidations as to what the future of this white elephant of mine would turn out.

I mustered courage around mockery and laughter from skeptics knowing it to be infectious and pressed or without ever looking back word or believing failure could be my lot. The good that comes out of fighting for what one believes in or aim for community has nothing equal to it.

Pursuing or pushing for Manding Medical Centre was like sailing through stormy waters to be free or flying high in the sky like the fearless Hawk for my villagers in Gambia.

I tease critics by telling them small-minded people make only small gains in life. Fear of the future paralysis us and leads to no future. My dream NGO, Manding Medical Centre has blossomed to a fully recognized health organization not only by the Gambia but also to my delight and relief by British American and soon by Spanish friends. The center is today a recognized charitable trust in the United Kingdom and America.

In addition, helping the center raise funs is the newly formed Badibou Cultural Dancers. We await completion of processing of our P-1 visas to travel to Alpena Michigan, USA on a fun raising tour for the building of the children's unit.

Manding medical center became a strong desire for me to achieve as far back as in 1953. It became a mission etched in the sky for me when I came across a husband who lost his two year old boy along with a pregnant wife for lack of much needed medical aid or personnel. From that day on I prayed to be part among those bringing relief to such beleaguered families.

Ambition not being domain of the timid or weak led to many Erie paths for my family and me. Thanks to God the center has membership nearing thirty thousand villagers who are enthused and happy to be part of such a humanitarian venture for the villager and the Gambia.

Alas, reader, Louis May Alcott said, Far away there in the sunshine are my highest aspirations. I may reach them, but I can look up and see their beauty, believe in them and try to follow their lead.

Indeed this is where the call leads, a vision not fetish or mystical in nature. Is it not true that obstacles are those frightful things we see when we take our eyes off our goal or call. No hillock or crisis ruffles my feathers and the match toward providing medical aid to villagers.

The bounds or scope and extend of my determination to bring medical aid to villagers is immeasurable. This strong urge emanated in me since primary school whence I vowed to be part of the solution to the Gambia's medical personnel and or service shortage. It flows in my veins like the great Amazon River and its sister River Gambia.

The call is not blind but does consume the endowed. It makes one overly determined to scale the top where most failed. It is the good that comes out of fighting for what one believes in which may be at the time oblivious to others.

It is a force that stands a certain lofty peak that endows dreamers to explore its height. The call urges us never to yield our goals, our love for life and humanity. The call blinds and blunts our emotion that sways us from it.

The call leaves us restless and ever determined to achieve our goal. The call is a rare gift a few have or can meet its challenges of poverty, oblivion stagnation and destitutions life that one has to traverse before reaching its achievement. The call is sacrifice of the self for others and generation not pat homed by one's peers.

The call opens our eyes to lofty peaks or heights a few dream of in their lives. It makes one not afraid of the morrow judging you, and that your words shall be witness before its judgment and testimony before its justice. The call makes one better as well as does what shall be proclaimed before people in days to come.

The call makes one certain that life has something worth revealing and sharing to propel progress and social cohesion. The call makes us risk the day for all to learn from it and move to better and rewarding future.

The call makes each day specific thrill that leads to that exhilarating moment of victory for mankind. The call is a hard challenge worth pursuing. The Pell Mel towards a better medical service for the villager is a worthwhile cause to enshrine my life with.

Dudou Sisawo Ceesay, elder brother, Njawara

Chapter 7

Never a white Elephant

Fear is ancient enemy of success so refuse to fail because fear of your mission turn out into a mythical white elephant. To bring the Golden Fleece one must learn from must work hard and learn from mistakes incurred during the adventure to the unknown.

In summary my life was welcomed to this Garden of Eden at Njawara village, Lower Badibou District, the Gambia in 1946. My twin partner's early departure from earth was my first experience with solitude and cruel chilly hand of death.

I recalled touching his cold face and vowing to punish one that so cruelly took my true friend. Years later, after a brief Almudo life at a roving Madrasa, I despite disapproval of my father and his friends, I enrolled myself at Kinte Kunda Primary School in 1953 to gain Western education that few villagers dream to have privilege of.

From Kinte Kunda I went to do my High School stint at Armitage boarding School from 1957 t0 1961; some one hundred and seventy five miles away from Kinre Kunda. At the end of my schooling at Armitage I enrolled at the Royal Victoria Hospital School of Nursing to be trained as male nurse at the Royal Victoria Hospital, Bathurst, later known as Banjul, Gambia.

I completed the training with a State Registered Nursing Certificate. I severed the Gambia until 1967 when I travelled to Alpena, Michigan, USA to start my pre-med courses for entry to medical school. I had no scholarship but with help of the city and staff of the community college I earned my first degree.

I earned an Associates of Arts degree in biology from Alpena Community college in 1969 and transferred to Olivet College, Olivet, Michigan where I completed the B.SC degree in biological sciences 1971.

My harbinger of impending residency permit problem reared its ugly head right after Olivet to cause me proceed to do another two years program at Michigan Tech. University, Houghton where I eventually earned the M. Sc. Degree in biology December 1973. Bad luck forced me to enrol to do a PhD program in biology at Howard University in Washington DC 1974.

After three years at the program It became claret that a PhD degree would put the last nail coffin of my drive to read for a medical degree. Hence, I regretfully dropped that approach and started medical school at the Italian A. M. Dogliotti School of Medicine at the University of Liberia 1979.

Again, African instability reined in unexpectedly in 1980 through military coup led by Sergeant Samuel K. Doe and seventeen other none commissioned men.

Here was a rude awakening for shortly after the coup all institutes of learning were closed till further notice. I weather the waiting time but in one my return trips from the City of Monrovia, I was accosted by drunk military patrol who threw me at the back of their jip like sack of rotten potatoes where I met other arrested foreigners. Luckily my head was saved from injury.

My thoughts were that it was all a dream and it will resolve moment the officers knew that I was a medical student returning to the medical school campus fifty metres away from where I was picked for curfew violation. We were kicked and eventually frisked for valuables. People had their monies, watches, passports and or anything the drunken officers felt worth their fancy.

In brief a senior office came by dawn to give command on what to do with the detainees. Luckily the fellow recognised me and asked, "Hey, Gambia man, what the hell are you doing here?"

I too made him out and shook his hand while claiming innocence and that I never broke the law but was picked on my way back to the campus. I told him his junior men would not listen but instead hauled insults at us 'foreigners' guilty of helping President William Tolbert's regime.

I pleaded for all fifteen men in my predicament and we were freed after a heated argument in the vernacular between junior officers making me belief that the end might not be far away for us.

The only thing that kept our lives safe was the presence of the senior officer. He ordered that we be taken to Monrovia and booked but to be freed on condition we are never caught violating the curfew.

Again, life has dealt another blow to my medical dreams and now I have to watch my steps because the military boys have marked me. I stayed until reopening of the school and just at the beginning of my third year at medical school hell broke in Gambia, my home country, with disgruntled police force along with some civilian attempted overthrow of President Dawda Jawara's government in 1981.

The Gambia over reacted and band the Movement for justice in Africa (MOJA) which I was a member in the Liberian branch. To cut a long story I went into hiding until when my American Good Samaritan helped with an air ticket to return to the USA in 982.

Ramsey helped me apply for Asylum, which was give green light waiting signature or decision of vice President George Bush, sr. State department sent him recommendation to approve by the District Director of Naturalisation and Nationality Service at Detroit, Michgan in 1984. President in reply to Bishop Mcgehee of Detroit's appeal told him that he had reviewed the recommendation and the State Department would contact us. That never happened causing me to go through the Applet Court Appeal system.

Wheels of justice turned very slow and I lost a $42,000 scholarship to attend Louisville University School of Medicine in Kentucky, USA. It would be two more difficult years staying at the Marinas Inn where alcoholics and rehabilitating drug addicts roomed.

This was great revelation in my life about people. I survived to finally restart medical schooling at the American University of the Caribbean, Plymouth in Montserrat British West Indies.

I did two and half tears of the pre-clinic classes before proceeding to the United Kingdom to do the clinical at Essex County Hospital in Colchester Essex from 1990 through 1992 before returning to Montserrat to be conferred with the MD degree 1n 1993.

Chapter 8
Hurricane Hugo September 16, 1989.
The Day Hell Broke Loose

For readers who do not know, a hurricane is a tropical cyclone with winds of 74 miles per hour or greater and are usually accompanied by torrential rain, thunder and lightening, never heard or seen, that sometimes move into temperate latitudes such as the Caribbean zones.

A year prior to hurricane Hugo neighbouring Jamaican was devastated by hurricane Gilbert. Most Montserrantian never expected or experienced winds stronger than 60 miles per hour and only reads or hear about the terrible thing Gilbert did to Jamaica.

This was all rudely changed by 11.45 p.m. on Saturday September 16th, 1989. This day gave Montserrat and its neighbouring islands a rude awakening and a taste of her first hurricane in fifty years. The first was in 1660, the second in 1928 and now hurricane Hugo in 1989.

This wild bestial wind of September 16, 1989 blew mad all night with a fury that destroyed all of Monsterrat to pieces. Ninety percent of the homes had their roofs blow away with the high tide that swept the Island.

Things were smashed or smithereens while the thunder and lightning blazed with vengeance. One could at one time hear the cows, sheep and other domesticated animals frenziedly and frantically running to their doom as the wind and rain built up vehemently.

Mine and wife's life became threatened and at serious risk when a flying galvanized sheet left us at the mercy of wind and rain and flying tree trunks with galvanized sheets from nearby buildings. As matters got out of hand we knelt and fervently prayed for our lives and survival of everyone on the path of this monstrous wind.

The hurricane must have poured at least 5 to 15 inches of rain on the island in less than ten minutes on top of the destructive bellows of wind. It was until Sunday, September 17, 1989, that the wind slowed down to forty miles per hour.

And by 1.00 P.M. people were able to or dared to venture out and survey the damage left behind by hurricane Hugo. Only thirteen elderly people became casualties of the hurricane and the whole nation lay in twisted rubbles. All I saw near my place were metal and concrete inter-twined and blown to some far away location or ditches.

Fallen trees, tables, telephone poles, galvanized sheets and all of these in a meshwork of cables and parts of roofs from buildings blocked roads to what were left of the university campus. Upon daring to venture to the campus I saw a small Hiroshima of Japan. Everything just looked like after the dropping of the Atomic Bomb. Thank God no student died or got injured.

The students held on well but were very frightened. There was no pandemonium. It was as if everyone was partly spellbound or sedated for the scenery was too calm and orderly. Some demanded immediate evacuation while others just wondered about in a daze. The few who were in control of themselves helped gather the remaining food supplies and water.

Everyone stayed in the first floors of the dormitories since the roofs of all second floors were no longer there or safe shelter for anyone as they were inhabitable waterlogged rooms. Monday saw a lot of student meetings and the Dean came in to alley our fears and to let us know that efforts were being made to get in touch with the outside world.

Yes, Montserrat was completely isolated from mankind during the first two days of the aftermath of hurricane Hugo. By Tuesday, September 18, 1989, most of the students had enough of the encounter to their necks.

All they kept asking was when they will be able to leave Montserrat. With this, rumors ran wild on the grounds of the ruined campus.

The once showcase of Montserrat was now reduced to rubbles and twisted galvanized sheets all over the places. It was not until Wednesday September 19, 1989, that we had a glimpse of the outside world in the form of a British Frigate, HMS Alacrity, which docked at Montserrat.

One of her helicopters flew over to survey the island and then headed to Antigua perhaps in consultation with the British and American Embrasures and consulates. Later that day more planes flew over us but none dropped anything or came down.

The helicopter landed men from the Frigate and these went to work, setting up communication centers and helping the government and the governor of Montserrat. Everyone tried to recover as much as possible of his or her retrievable belongings.

The British sailors helped to clear the feeder roads and the ship served as lifeline to the rest of the world.

At the campus we cleared the tennis court and made a helicopter-landing path. It worked, for in one overpass flight of the helicopter the pilot saw the big cross with a circle around it.

He circled the campus twice and flew back to the ship. After a long half an hour later he came directly and hovered for a while before heading to the temporal landing ground the students had prepared. The huge helicopter landed smoothly and frightened and eager students swamped the pilot.

Being an experience fellow he asked his co-pilot to take off and leave him on the ground with the students. The rush tampered immediately as the metal bird too off and hovered over campus. All of us wanted to touch the gentleman and thank him for bringing hope to our hearts.

He spent roughly twenty minutes with the students discussed with the staff and likewise the student government before being flown back to the ship where he relayed our messages to the American Consulate in Antigua. That very day, the American vice councilor, Steve Vanhuness, reported to the campus. Yes, and yes again, America does take care of its own in time of crisis like this one.

Steve spoke with Dr. Paul Tien, president and owner of the university, and with the student government and then left for his base in Antigua. The campus settled while diplomatic maneuvers took place between Antigua and Washington, D.C. The general student body was expecting a word or two from the consulate but no matter how uneasy life was for them they must wait for Washington's directives on how to relief or evacuate them from the Island.

Meanwhile several lists of students by name, nationality and home addresses were constantly being compiled and prepared for possible evacuation. The Consular returned the next day with word from the state department that a plane was on the way to take only American and Canadian students to the United States at a cost of $178 per student.

By Friday, September 23, 1989, most of the students were ferried to Antigua by a British Coast Guard ship that brought supplies to Montserrat. Only the staff, a few students, my wife Fatou Koma and I were left on Campus. The American Consulate refused to evacuate Fatou and I because we were not American or Canadian according to

Mr. Steve Vagueness, vice-consular at the U.S. Consulate in Antigua. I broke down and tried to contact the Gambia High Commission in London on several times but was unable to get through for scarcity of International lines at the time.

  I tried the next day but could not get anywhere with the telephones, which sapped the little money left in my account. This left Fatou and I in more financial precariousness. At this time I started worrying about Fatou and wanted help to return her home until life returns to normal.

It was just plain risky for her to remain on the island. People believing that the university would never open its doors again came looting at night. At one time I had to stand my grounds from rouges wanting to break in the makeshift room Fatou and I used while trying to sort things out. It was pathetic and shame how adversity reduces some men to less than animals.

At this stage I never cared what the Gambia may or may not do to me all I wanted was and safe place for the lady who gave so much of herself to me. And now not only mine but her life is at risk from attack by night hooligans.

A sympathetic, Mr. K. Cotter and all at the Command Centre need be praised for their hard work and kindness. They were very helpful and sympathetic about my plight. For the first time and in mall my travels I felt like an orphan stranded and marooned in a tiny island in the middle of the Atlantic Ocean.

It felt scary but as usual, I left my fate in God's hands and at the same time prayed for His forgiveness, mercy and guidance over Fatou Koma and this nightmare.

  Fatou Koma-Ceesay turned to be much stronger and steadfaster than I credited her.

It was during one these depressed moments that Professor Steve Deschner and his wife Derby came to my help. I had already had a difficult night with looters who thought that the school would not open for years. On hindsight, it was a very tough night that Fatou and I had prepared our minds for death on a desolate Island.

It was difficult trying to remain sane in situations like this and at the same time protect my wife from molestation and fortune hunters of hurricane Hugo. Dr. Deschner spoke to me and offered to talk to one Miss Gayle Baumgardner at the Condominiums with regards to her sheltering my wife and I until a more safe state or place could be found for us.

Meanwhile one of the last American students to leave the island, Dean Mcfinning offered his car for me to sell and use the money to buy air ticket for my wife to fly to Gambia or Guinea Conakry. A word or act of encouragement during difficult times or failures is worth more than a dictionary of praises after a success.

Miss Gayle Baumgardner, a former Peace Corps volunteer, now resident in Montserrat, turned out to be another of those rare breed of kindness. Upon being told of our predicament at the campus by Dr. Deschner, she accepted to lodge us at the Shamrock villa and out of her kind-heartedness she loaned me money to buy air ticket for Fatou Koma-Ceesay to fly to the Gambia until the improvement of the situation.

I would reimburse her by working for her and helping her clean the mesh hurricane Hugo left behind at the condominium complexes. We were overwhelmed by her generousness and noble act for a humane cause. My wife and I shall ever be obliged and most grateful to her.

I am personally profoundly grateful to Miss Gale Baumgardner.

A friend in need is a friend indeed. Gayle's participation was a touch of an angel's hand from heaven. With this understanding reached. Drs Deschner and Ronda Cooper helped me transport my books, and little belongings left with us to the condominium. Drs. Deschner and Cooper continued to show great interest in us and we are indebted to both for time and help they gave us.

On hindsight, everyone on the Island agreed that it was wicked to leave us stranded on the island while other students were taken out to America. Gayle and I went to town and bought Fatou her ticket to freedom. Fatou Koma, who lightens my spirit, had to leave for the Gambia after two weeks of stay at the condominiums with me.

So we flew to Barbados to the British High Commission for her to secure a transit visa via London on her way to the Gambia. This done we headed for Barbados International Airport. There, Fatou began to shed tears uncontrollably. I tried to square up my shoulders, stepped back a little and in a voice choked with love and emotion said, I wished I were going with you to Africa.

My eyes were full of mist and deep down I was crying and yet praising God for saving our lives and for relieving my wife from the difficulties that lay ahead in the coming days at Montserrat. Very soon the PA announced the boarding for BA flight to Heathrow, London.

Fatou Koma was jus able to hug me and say, "Good luck and good bye Dr. Ceesay." And she disappeared into the boarding queues for British Airways flight 259 heading for Heathrow, London. My studied composure cracked as I watched the plane disappear into the clouds with my heart and the only woman I loved.

Fatou Koma brings joy to me like a child's first exposure to magic. When I hear her speak it is always positive and she speaks with candour and humour. Fatou is a delight to be with. It is feeling I never felt until I came across her. Oh, no, no do not rashly conclude my feeling for to be that of an infatuation love. No that fades while ours sprouts daily and full of joy. Fatou Koma is love and gift from God to me. You can laugh at me if you wish but this how I feel about her and she feels the same or more about me.

Now that my Fatou Koma-Ceesay was gone I embarked on bracing myself for the task of getting out of Montserrat and completing my pre-clinic courses. I was in Montesrrat the next day and in solitude lonelier than the grave.

A word or two about Miss Gayle Baumgardner would now befit the saga of my current life after hurricane Hugo. Gayle had, according to friends, devoted all her life to teaching and sharing her day with others. She is nicknamed the mother Theresa of Montserrat.

Like a missionary she was literally known by almost everyone and was always helping the needy. Gayle was a giving heart that yearns and beckons people to allow her hem lighten their burdens just as inscribed at Liberty Island. Gayle seems to say, "Come to with your laden hearts. I shall do my best to lighten your load."

Miss Gale Baumgardner was unique, for at the condominiums she was duped, "Primary Manager" for she knew everything about the place and how to get problems solved quickly better than the then designated manager of a place. All one had to do was to ask Gayle about something relating to the condominium and the answer would spew out as if it is from a well organized computer. Gayle knows where to find things better than any on the grounds.

Rain or dry this heart of gold is on the move helping others. When asked, Gayle where next? She would calmly and with a broad smile, reply, "I was just going to visit an old friend and help restore so and so thing for him or her."

Gayle works from dawn to dusk with a capacity unique only to Gayle Baumgardner. Having worked with her and as well as observed her, I at times wished I had a way of keeping her rested just for twenty four hours a week. But rest makes her miserable as she once told me.

I do not want that to happen to her for boredom would mean suicide for her. It will be too anguishing an experience for this princess of Montserrat. Gayle Baumgardner was a jack-of-all-trades, teacher, carpenter, a junk sales person, and above all, a devoted philanthropist. My Miss Gayle Baumgardner like mother Theresa was a living example of sharing and caring in the literal sense of the word.

This angel was happiest when helping others and restless if not engaged in some form of work. She was true and truest of the most holy workaholic. I hope this short synopsis gave a bird's eye view of the lady of Montserrat.

Meanwhile the Deschners, Derby and Steve, became interested in helping me go to the USA as we became more and more acquainted with each other. Dr. Ronda Cooper arrange my meeting with the Skeletal staff who were about to depart for America to join the rest of the students at the Wayland Baptist University in Plainview, Texas, left on the Island.

They tried all they could to travel with me but again visa and money problem blocked that effort in my behalf. Hence it was agreed that I stay with Gayle Baumgardner and my exam papers would be sent periodically to an official to proctor while I take the exam.

Time came when the Deschners and other teachers had to leave. We had developed strong bonds and they too will soon be away from me. I thank God for making them care and they became the lifeline between the University in Texas and I in hurricane ravaged Montserrat.

They made certain that all the agreed arrangements concerning my exams were carried out in time by the administration of the medical school. The Deschners also solicited funds for me while in America so that I can complete payment of my fees to the American University of the Caribbean.

It is said that our genetic endowment may well limit our heights and intelligence which we can attain, but it is our environment and experiences, which determines to what extent our potential can be reached or realized. Hence, their agreeing to keep the channels of communication open while at Texas was indeed a benevolent act for which I was most grateful to this very day.

This gracious couple, despite delays and unforeseen complications, left their doors and hearts open to me. They relayed requests and messages to the Dean and professors while AUC piggy bags at Wayland Baptist University.

Fatou and I certainly look forward to the day we can gather all these immaculate wingless lovely angels at our villages and the banks of the River Gambia where my villagers will be able to serenade and thank them for helping me fulfill my dream of providing needed medical aid to the villager.

It was during this sad and lonely time that another blow was dealt to me. News reached me from the defunct Ceesay Committee at Diocese of Michigan that my angel, Mrs. Patricia Koblyski had died. Pat, as everyone calls her, was the Refugee coordinator for the Diocese of Michigan in Detroit, and the first person I spoke to upon arriving at the Diocese center.

She devoted her life to helping people and became my best friend and confidant. She along with Lois R. Leonard fought very hard for me during our discussions and had always come up with brilliant ideas on how to go about bringing a solution to my crisis. She brought lots of positive help to me and I will never forget the kindness and love she showed me before her cancer took her away from me.

I knew chemotherapy was not a miracle cure but that she would succumb so early took us all by surprise. I cried for more than four days, being unable to stop my tears welling whenever I think about Pat Koblyski and kindness she represented to me.

The feeling still persist in my heart. Could you imagine she cried along with me on the first day I met her and told her about my experience with the INS? I sent the following letter to Bishop McGehee and Diocesan Newspaper, The Record.

C/O Miss Gayle Baumgardner
The Condominiums
Plymouth, Montserrat
West Indies

In loving memory of Mrs. Patricia Koblynski
Diocese of Michigan

Dear Editor,

I wish through your paper to express sympathy and sincere condolence to Mr. Bob Koblyski, his family and the Diocese of Michigan for the untimely lost of our dear friend and Sister Mrs. Patricia Koblyski. The departure of some leaves us bewildered, shocked and flushed. We ask why at this time dear God? Mrs. Patricia Koblyski is now gleefully resting in the right hands of our maker. We will miss her. For me, a part of me went along with her.

She was a good friend and a true Christian heart that was dedicated to all of us God's children. Four years ago she cried with me and at that same time helped to wipe my tears. She gave hope of freedom and assistance to me and to entire villagers several thousand miles away.

Patricia Koblyski knew none of them but like the rest of you she more than any was dedicated in seeing that we all breathe the air in peace and walk together side by side in freedom on mother earth.

Patricia thanks a million for having lived a full Christian life and for all of us. Our profound gratitude and ineptness goes to you for being our Good Samaritan. The only befitting legacy I have for you and my villagers is returning to serve rural Gambia and especially the villager you fought for during these last minutes of a full Christian and a wonderful life of giving to others. We will never, never forget you and May your soul rest in eternal peace by the right hand side of the Almighty God. Amen!!

Your everlasting Friend

Alhasan S. Ceesay

With Fatou Koma-Ceesay back in the Gambia I continued my scourged or blighted life at the condominiums. I stayed in Montserrat like an orphan working all day and studying up to 1.30 A.M every night for four good months before being join the rest of the students at the Wayland Baptist University in Plainview, Texas. In that interim I chanced to make a lot of friends at the condominiums.

Most rewarding of all was the bond that developed between Rudolf and Sophie Kurt; retired German couples who had come to make this nation island their home away from home. The rumor about a marooned American University of the Caribbean's student on the island needing urgent help spread in town and around the business community like a wild fire making me even more embarrassed to go to town. So on December 19, 1989, I decided to take a break from my studies and be with Rudolf and his wife Sophie Kurt for a chat before they retire for the night. I will come back to this day later.

Dr. Alhasan Ceesay holding Africa

Hassan Bah and his father **Mr. Abdoulie Bah 1998**

Chapter 9
The search for a Sponsor

The death of Mrs. Patricia Koblyski left me devastated and concerned. She meant a lot to me and her sincerity and determination to free me was unsurpassed by any other member of the Ceesay Support Committee. Her death was indeed a tragic loss to my villagers and I.

We pray and mourn her passing. Mrs. Lois R. Leonard's statement summed up my feeling about Patricia A. Koblyski when she wrote, "It still seems terribly strange to go in that building (meaning the Diocese) and not see Pat Koblyski." I missed her very much. Her death ushered in pain and a sense of great loss for me.

May she rest in peace with God in heaven. Patricia Kolinsky was one of those who fought vehemently against the intentions of Richard Smith effort to stop my going to the Caribbean. Instead, Richard wanted me to do nursing because we fail to see eye to eye on most points he raised during our meetings.

It was as though he felt a black should not challenge ideas he tabled. This became great snarl between us with Lois enjoy the tug of war going on between Richard and I. Still determined to stop my getting help from the Diocese Richard managed to get himself selected to pay a surprise visit to AUC medical school in Plymouth, Montserrat, West Indies.

He was eager come and check on my performance and to use any negative aspect of it to derail me. He now had the opportunity because some of the staff like David Breidenbach was not happy with me.

This was Richard's chance to drown me into oblivion to the bottom of the Atlantic Ocean. Hence on December 1, 1987, I received a departmental notice from Dr. G. F. Breidenbach, assistant dean of the school telling me that Richard would be on campus shortly. The memo ushered an ominous sign of anxiety akin to surveying the forest before walking among the trees.

It exacerbated the paroxysm that caused a retrogressive dream for me. It brought all the arguments we had fresh in my mind. It was a Delphien memo that foretold a bleak future for medical education and aspirations.

The memo simply read, "A Mr. Richard Smith, who apparently is one of your sponsors, will be on Montserrat and AUC on December 11, 1987. He will be meeting me 9.00 AM. Please let me know where you will be contacted between 9.30 and 11.30 A. M on that day.

I met Breidenbach the same afternoon to let him know where I would be on said day of Richards visit to the campus. I was not happy meeting the man who fought against my coming to AUC for he had expressed such opinion too many times during our debate about alternative route to relieve of my torturous INS experience.

Richard cared little about time it would take for my INS Appeal Board appeal to come through. Age and time were not going to wait for me. Richard Smith did not care about stressed my life went through in the past fours of exile in skid row America.

He might have construed a drug rehabilitation center to be a palace for an African like me. He did not care about the rebound effects of being constantly turned down by the INS would have on me nor what it meant living with addicts and former convicts at Ledyard. All Richard Smith cared was to reverse the decision, which sent me to Montserrat in the first place. This being his primary intention, chagrined Richard Smith showed up on campus on December 4, 1987. I had gone to town to mail letters that day. He was only able to meet my ach enemy Breidenbach and some staff to reward him with false ammunition and negative information he wishes to take back to maligned me to what was remaining of the Ceesay Support Committee.

Richard Smith, though a newcomer to the committee want to run the show and got angry with me when he found me nut manipulability. He disliked the Diocese sponsoring me and fought it very subtle ways at time trying to illicit hot tempers from me. After meeting the staff at the American University of the Caribbean Richard Smith went on a tour of the Islands or what I apply duped "Island hopping."

We finally met at 7.45 pm in a very hostile encounter and animated indeed, which was punctuated with angry argumentative discussions between us. At the end I assured him that he was no God and did not leave my life and I do not wish him such an experience in his lifetime.

I made it clear that I was not going to worship him or any other human being for that matter in other to get to where I want. I left him fuming at his hotel and had a word with Breidenbach for untrue statement he spewed to Richard Smith.

David denied most of it but I know better for everything happened in my absence and I now did not care what Richard plans. I made up my mind to transfer to next-door medical school at Ross University if the AUC yielded to Richard Smith's dark plans.

He went back to Detroit, Michigan armed to destroy me. I wonder if he were not originally deep from the South? I learnt on the next day of his return he conveyed an emergency meeting of the Ceesay support Committee and gave them such scorching and negative report about me that the committee or what was left of it blindly swallowed his version wholeheartedly and felt obliged to cease raising money for my studies at American University of the Caribbean school of medicine.

He did his best and not being present to defend myself, he left my integrity standing on slippery grounds which lead to a surge of anger against me. He even told them that I do not attend classes where as the only class I missed was when I had asthma and had to go to hospital three days. Breidenbach took that as my not wanting to attend his classes.

All the remaining members, most of who were new members I never met, of then Ceesay support committee under Richard's wings, except Lois R. Leonard and those unable to attend that meeting felt that they no longer could solicited money for a cause that seemed to have some doubts or shadows in it being successful.

Mrs. Lois Leonard felt that or explained her reasons for dissenting with the decision of the committee as follows, "My reasons for voting against the rest of the committee was that I felt that we had made a promise and we were not keeping it.

We promised to send you enough for five semesters. And we stopped sending it before the time was completed." I finally heard from the committee current coordinator and one whom I have high regards, Rev. Hugh C. White. It said:

Diocese of Michigan
4800 Woodward Avenue
Detroit, Michigan 48201
December 28, 1988

Dear Alhasan

You are an important person to the many friends you made here in the Diocese area. The realization of this makes what I am about to say difficult. From our vantage point following Richard Smith's trip to see you in Montserrat, and following two meetings of the committee earlier this month we have concluded that we must suspend any further financial help for the reasons that we cannot continue to raise funds for your medical school education at AUC. By authorization of your support committee, and with the concurrence of Bishop McGehee, we have deposited to your account at Barclays Bank in Monttserrat, a check for $4121.00, which represented the balance of the funds.

You may use these funds towards your fourth semester at the school or you may use them for whatever purpose you see fit for your future interest. Please know that this decision was difficult for us to take. Also know that we have some understanding of the pressure and stress you have been under in attempting to make way through medical school.

If any additional funds are obtained for you in the immediate weeks ahead, we will forward them to you personally. Such additional funds are not likely to be in any significant amounts. The one dissenter on the committee to the action outlined in this letter was Lois Leonard.
She hoped that we would make an effort to raise the necessary funds for the balance of your studies.

It was the judgment of the committee that such an effort would not be credible or successful in the face of your situation and record. We hope you will let us know how you made out in the light of the action, which we have taken. We live in remembrance and respect of you.

Faithfully,

(The Rev) Hugh C. white

This note brought melancholy, darkness and grief to me and I grew more depressed and frustrated with life. I made several attempts to put forth my side of the story. It fell on deaf ears and failed to reunite me with the Ceesay Support committee.

Close sources told me that negative report given by Richard Smith made it very difficult to convince or convene a meeting even if Hugh White were willing to try to call one after his convention project was over. Under the circumstances I will not secure a visa to the USA to rally the committee into some sensible direction.

Richard Smith had fired the first short in this war and I shall return mine with having the doctor of medicine degree confirmed on me. I manage to talk to Bishop McGehee by telephone but found his head buried in sand like an Ostrich. He was eager to get to the Lambert Conference in England than deal with my case.

He did ask Hugh White to look into the affair and in reply to my inquiry Hugh White wrote but I never receive his letter. However, I received the following separate surprise not from the administrative assistance to the Bishop.

Diocese of Michigan

4800 Woodward Avenue

August 12, 1988

Dear Ceesay,

This will acknowledge receipt of your note dated July 27, 1988 to Bishop McGehee requesting more funding for your studies. The Bishop is vacationing in England and will return to the office September 6, 1988, at which time he will receive your correspondence.

In the meantime, I refer you to previous letters written this summer concerning your finances. The most recent of which is the letter dated July 28, 19888 from Hugh White informing you that the Episcopal Diocese of Michigan does not have the ability to raise any more funds for your continued support.

Hope you are able to re-think your situation and work towards another goal that will not only give you satisfaction, but also help others in need. You have come too far and your spirit is too great to give up completely. I urge you to find someone there who will be able to assist you in the getting on with your life. You do remain in the thoughts and prayers of the people of Diocese of Michigan. Peace.

Mrs. Sheila Gardner

Administrative Assistance

To the Bishop

The raw truth was that, for many of my friends interested in my struggles, their participation ended with my decision not to wait for the ruling of the INS Appeal Board.

I have always believed that God's ways were the best solutions. The waxing and waning of interest plus the fact that distance makes the heart fonder helped Richard Smith in landing his final knock out blows to my cause at this crucial moment in my life. I certainly forgive him and hope that the outcome, as it is today, will let him know he was no God and faith and hard work can indeed overcome the most difficult challenge one may be faced with in a given moment in time.

The core outcome of all these were that I found myself totally marooned, like Robinson Crusoe, in tiny Montserrat which only God and very few people or organizations to turn to for help. I again refused to allow this hillock God placed on my way to stop my journey. I had faith in God, hard work and the goodness of man.

I swallowed my pride and made a lasting ditch attempt, after offering prayers, for God to be on my side, to contact the committee. I knew a lot of them cared and that time might turn the tide to my favour. I could not nor would I accept that my good friends and foot soldiers at the Diocese of Michigan would throw me to the wolves as easily as they it occurred.

There were friends and good Christians who struggled and fought along my side all those trying years to help me realize my goal. What has Richard Smith, my Brutus told the Committee? Why would they not have patients knowing that we are not far from the end of the road? And the triumph of giving and receiving would have taken happen for the villagers. I dispatched the following.

School of Medicine
American University
Of the Caribbean
Plymouth, Montserrat
West Indies

Dear Support Committee,

The suspension of your aid for my studies at the above university was brought to my attention by your December 28, 1987 and July 28, 1988 letters, which were duly received. They are humbling notes by special friends of good will. Suffice it to say the loss of confidence of such special friends is indeed agonizing albeit challenging.

For me it was God's dictum and in humanistic terms a simple misfortune and coup de grace of a permanent festering sore. It marks another sad pivotal stage in my life and experience. I owe to all of you profound gratitude and highest regards for the noble deed.

The money sent has been paid to the school to fulfil the intention of the Church and Christ-like donors. Please tell your envoy, Richard Smith, that the shouts and inanimate discussions and anger de displayed when we met were all a burst of caring and his desire for me to get something good out of the venture.

I thank him but sadden that he took back wrong information and impression to the support Committee. Hence, the untimely decision has not only compromised and compounded my problems but made it very complicated. God's will has it that we are healed by our strive and made stronger by faith in Him and our sufferings will be painless.

I will believe that God love all of us and be assured that I will not let you down. All of you sought to be Christ like and have opened your arms and hearts to me. We are all God's children and I have no better friends than you. I will surely continue the struggle to the end. Thanks for letting me touch the core of your hearts.

May God continue to be our guide in today's light and tomorrow's darkness. Again all of you have my admiration and respect. My family is greatly indebted to you. I will do all I can to bring joy to my country and your hearts. I will look for solutions and do ask for your sincere prayers. Thanks a million and keep in touch. Goodbye for now.

Yours Sincerely

Alhasan S. Ceesay

This letter and many more fell on deaf ears. Some wrote to say how unduly influenced the committee was by Richard Smith's negative report and others expressed the feeling that the Church has disappointed me. Needless to say my goal suffered further delays under the circumstances as I worried more about my dwindling finances and the state of my family in the Gambia.

However, I never lost faith or direction towards my goal. I sent appeal letters to anyone, except the Diocese of Michigan, that I thought would reciprocate kindly upon hearing my plight. Among these was Dr. Nelson Herron, a friend and former colleague at Alpena Community College in Michigan.

He wasted no time in recruiting interested friends like Ms. Deirdre O'Leary, of Dublin, Ireland. They sent me $400 and contacted the Medical Missionaries of May in Drogfield, Ireland seeking assistance for me. The Mission responded favourably as can be seen in the following letter to Ms. O'Leary.

Dear Deirdre,

In reference to our telephone call of last evening, I am happy on behalf of Medical Missionaries of May (M.M.M.) to enclose a check for IR500.00 towards Alhasan Ceesay's final year medical fees.

I hope and pray that he will be successful in his exams. May his years as a doctor in his country of the Gambia be fruitful and rewarding for him and his people. Thanks for your concern for him and his many difficulties and wishing you all the very best. With kindness regards and with every good wish.

Yours Sincerely

Sr. Rosemarry Mohan, MMM

Central Business administration

God has His own ways of solving the impossible moments, which are incomprehensible to man. Help in small amounts continued to reach me from Mrs. Lois R. Leonard, Judge & Mrs. Viola S. Glennie, Dr. Charles T. Egli, Mr. Cloyd Ramsey, Mr. & Mrs. Bill Johnson of Birmingham, Michigan and many more who wish to remain anonymous donors. Despite all these inputs my financial obligation to the Medical School could not be met because of an increase in tuition fees.

The donations amounted to drop in the bucket with regards to what I owed the medical school, rent, and student permit fees to the government of Montserrat. I tittered upon the brink of starvation. I got my meals by picking fruit and berries from nearby hills. My over abundant pride made it impossible for me to beg for food from the street or from the students.

The weight of the burden became unbearable to make breakdown and lost my guard when I revealed my state one of the very reliable group of students. Rodney G. Carter, being one of them, was moved to tears and offered me whatever food was left over in his refrigerator and pantry.

We became great friends and he has since become one of my advocates and had spoken to lots of people in Alabama in an effort to raise more funds for my studies at the American University of the Caribbean Aside from this, he helped me type all my correspondence to various organizations, individuals, Embassies around the world and part of manuscript when he was not studying.

My deepest appreciation goes to this kind human being with great concern for needy people. My spirit never waned. Only my body started to shrivel and to give up for lack of rest and food. I lost tremendous weight and looked like a living ghost among the students.

I became a feather of less than forty kilograms that avoided strong winds and walked near walls during storms to avoid being swept away into the Ocean. Things got worse when money stopped trickling down. I no longer could pay for rent, light bills or buy gas to cook with.

William Ryan, my landlord turned out to be a kind and exceptional being, felt sorry that I had to undergo such brutal hardship away from home. He empathized with me know all that had transpired in my case since the suspension of my grant by my Detroit sponsors.

Willie Ryan assured me that I could stay as long as I needed and pay him whenever I have money or working at one of the hospital somewhere. In addition to this benevolent act he would once on a while bring food to me when it seemed to him that I have not had food for days.

Mr. Willie Ryan is my Montserrat just as Gayle Baumgartner was to me during hurricane Hugo. He has always been generous and kind to me. I look forward to the day I can reciprocate to him and his family for kindness rendered me. Not many in Montserrat bestrode such generosity to me.

In my experience, when it rains, that is when I get woes, it pours and does so with vengeance and incessantly. My life looked like an endless struck or string of bad news upon bad news. Coming to think about it; who would have expected the Ceesay Support Committee to be so easily bamboozled by someone seemingly from the South, who in the first place was not in support of my leaving the USA for the Caribbean.

With these roadblocks the Registrar, Mrs. Mary Rose Tuit (bless her heart) assisted me by releasing the following letter to potential contributors or donors to help alleviate my financial debts at the America University of the Caribbean.

America University of the Caribbean
School of Medicine
Plymouth, Montserrat
West Indies

TO WHOM IT MAY CONCERN

Mr. Alhasan S. Ceesay, student number 24026, is a student at the American university of the Caribbean School of Medicine, situated in Momtserrat West Indies. The school is listed in the Directory of the World Health Organizations (WHO). This student is in need of financial assistance to enable him complete his fourth and fifth semesters at the School. The tuition fees for a semester now is $4600.00 Any courtesies extended to him will be greatly appreciated by the administration of this Institution.

Respectfully
Mrs. Mary Rose Tuit
Registrar

The school failing to receive any payment in my behalf made the administration and Finance office pursue me with constant reminders that my tuition payment deadline had long passed. Finally, on October 12, 1988, I was asked to see the registrar no later than 4.00 P. M. that day. I went with full knowledge of what was about to befall me.

I was told that the school had waited patiently and long enough and that no substantial payments were made in my behalf. In view of this I was advised and instructed to take a leave of absence from the university and try to raise the money for the rest of my studies at the medical school.

With a leaden heart, I spoke to the Dean about my problems and other friendly faculty and I was advised no differently. I should have known that the Registrar was just an escape goat in the whole affair.

Anyhow, I thought it senseless to have to stop schooling in the middle of the semester. If allowed to complete the term I would only have to attend the next semester to complete my basic sciences. I went home and thought through about it and then concluded that perhaps explaining

my situation to Dr. Paul Tien, owner and president of the university, in a Desperate last minute ditch might lead to some type of reprieve if not a deferment of payments or new scheduling of payments. He hopelessness of the situation was such that wrote the following with my tears to Dr. Tien.

American University of the Caribbean

School of Medicine

Plymouth, Montserrat

West Indies

Dear Dr. Tien,

Most likely my situation has been brought to your attention. I will be most grateful if you would kindly grant me audience to explain the cause of the delay in my payments. Briefly, I lost my original sponsors in early part of the year but was able to recently get the Catholic Mission in New York to take over sponsorship the rest of my studies at the America University of the Caribbean.

This has just been recently approved and they promised to send an initial payment of $4500.00 within the next fortnight for me to pay some of my outstanding Bills at the school. Also, I have just received my application forms fromthe World Health Organization that has been completed and sent to Geneva.

The fellowship will cover the entire cost at this school and clinical rotations. Meanwhile, most of the embassies I contacted have promised to help me upon consultation with their home based offices. In view of these developments I am kindly pleading that you give me 45 days extension on my payments.

Again, I sincerely regret the delay and do promised to continue to make certain that such delays never happen again. Greetings and I am waiting anxiously waiting and looking forward to your kind considerations in this matter.

Sincerely

Alhasan S. Ceesay (4026)

Dr. Paul Tien was a forthright man and he granted me the audience I requested. We met and discussed my case thoroughly and I left that meeting with the impression that he would let me finish the current semester but may not be allowed to register for the next semester if no money appeared. Two weeks later the Catholic Mission's promise failed to materialize because someone told them of the difficulties I had with previous sponsors from Michigan. Whoever spoke to the Catholic Mission got to Dr. Tien for I shortly thereafter received the following thunderbolt memo from him in a memorandum directed to, copied to the registrar and the staff.

It simply said, "We inform you that you will have to leave the school if all outstanding payments to the American University School are not paid by November 18, 1988." By now I have weathered many thunder storms in my life but I have to admit this was the mother of them all and this bombshell did more than ruffle my feathers.

My plight magnified many fold. If I leave where would I head? I was not able to return to USA nor was it possible for me to return to the Gambia at the time. It was too close to my asylum fight that they would not be willing to look the other way. Montserrat was not a place to be stranded for help was certainly not going to come from a small poor island nation like it.

My having told school officials the risk I would be at if were not allowed to finish my education until the promises show up made them worry more for fear that I may after all not be able to get help with the payments needed to clear the outstanding bills. The school was not going to continue with the build up of unpaid bills surrounded by uncertainty that help may not surface sooner.

My fighting spirit was rekindled and I fought back with the only means at my disposal, my mind, pen and paper.
I wrote endless letters to America, Britain, France, Canada, Russia, Saudi Arabia, United Emirates, Japan and numerous other countries embassies appealing for assistance to

complete my medical training. I emphasized the need to help me out of my precarious state my standing was at AUC in Montserrat. The saying that, "A drowning man will hang onto any straw for dear life" Was very true in my case. I would write to any name or organization suggested to me. For some reason I was confident that Britain, Canada, France USA or Japan would come to my rescue.

Why? I guess it was just a hunch and out of admiration for these countries and their stand against injustice and currently having done a lot for people in Africa. Initial responses from the British, American, and Canadian Embassies suggested that I write to their counterpart embassies based in the Gambia for these administers assistance program available to the Gambian national. It dashed all my hope of getting help as long as it had to involve Gambia or emissaries located in the Gambia.

If the Gambia were able to influence the state department as the ambassador did in my asylum case, what would it not do with people next door and in the Gambia? Nonetheless, the embassies wished me good luck in my search for financial relief and continuance of my medical education. The replies were copied to their respective offices in the Gambia.

The Japanese embassy said it was unable to help at that moment. Meanwhile the medical school campus reeled with the news of my financial plight and the termination of my schooling until when I can pay up all outstanding bills to the American University of the Caribbean. The students rallied and collected donations in my behalf without my knowing for fear that I will feel obliged to them or feel pity for myself.

I will never ever forget their kindness especially Robert G. Carter, Luis Shone, Mohamed Saleh, and Nahil who spear headed the whole affair in my behalf with tact and respect. With the donation I bought food and reduced a portion of the outstanding bills. It neither dented the amount I owed the school nor gave me leeway to continue my schooling for that semester. I continued to be embattled by unforeseen events while time flies.

I kept on pleading for help worldwide. Finally I met the Dean and accepted to take a leave of absence effective from October 12, 1988 to January 1989 with hope that enough money would be raised to allow me to register for the upcoming semester. January 1989 has now become the new deadline but I cannot attend classes until then and only if all outstanding bills were paid by registration day.

Worse, I have to repeat the fourth semester all over as it was going to be erased from the record that I attended it. None of the exams I took during the said forth semester were acceptable for recording because of none payment of tuition fees. I left the Dean's office with tears welling uncontrollably down my cheeks.

What a life! I said to myself. I thank God for the challenge and asked for His guidance. The students felt very sorry and sad for me and feared the worst. There were those who seriously believed that I might end up taking my life because of the effect of series of disappointments from organization, churches and governments.

Hence the students made certain that someone was around me most of the time chatting or bringing notes for me to copy and read ahead of the coming semester. They reassured me that some have written to their parents requesting money earmarked for me to lighten my burden.

Yes, the human heart is good for all these acts of kindness were done without my knowing them taking place on my behalf. They certainly did their utmost in trying to enlighten and lighten my spirit.

The propensity to sudden roadblocks, somehow, seem to be the ordain way for me. Nonetheless friends like Mr. & Mrs. Bill Johnson of Birmingham, Michigan, Lois R. Leonard, Ferry Burns, Cloyd Ramsey and Nelson Herron among others became very special as they brought cheers to my life and accorded me all the moral and financial support they could give at the time.

Here are the synapses of the angels who made life bearable foe me the time. Jerry Burns and I met through a mutual friend and had since then built up a very unique friendship. He is a nurse and former Peace Corp who served in Niger during the John F. Kennedy era.

He fell in love with Niger and her people who inundated with kindness. He liked their culture and systems, their good nature and hard working of the Niger Fulas. He developed strong bond with the Niger people.

Never did two have similar philosophies, religious tolerance, and political views than he and I. We are just like twins living in distant lands both with nursing backgrounds and are committed to being our brother/sister's keeper.

Dudou Sisawo Ceesay holding grand daughter, 2017

Top L-R: Yata Ceesay, Fatou Koma-Ceesay, Famatanding Ceesay, Alagie Ceesay, and Binta Ceesay

Bottom: Famatanding Ceesay, Yata Ceesay and Binta Ceesay

We always had lively and cheerful meetings in which we discuss trends and shifts of values, global politics, governments, schools and at times about as flimsy as the decadence one sees at certain parts of Detroit' Cass corridor.

He helped relentlessly to lighten my plight and we remain in contact to today. Mr. & Mrs. William (Bill) J. Johnson came to my sphere through their son Bill Johnson, jr. who was at the time a class mate of mine at Wayne State University in Detroit.

There an unbelievable bond of friendship developed between Bill jr. and I. Biochemistry graduate level was not a forum where most make friends. But for Bill jr. and I it started here and never faded. My forty-third-birth day was just two weeks and because of it Bill calls me the grand daddy of the class.

I was the oldest and poorest in that class and very soon our classmates relaxed about my age. The Johnson's were very kind and friendly people and cared a lot about plight of others. Bill Jr. was intelligent, gentle, compassionate and alert to current affairs. Come my birthday he crowned the occasion with a special gift.

He met me at school and in his modest and gentle way quietly and simply said, "Please accept this little token to remember your day with." I was happy and grateful for we had only casually known each other less than a month and here was Bill sharing my day as he showers it with kindness.

The moment and graciousness of the act remained indelibly etched in my mind to today. Bill works part time for a mining company and anted school on part time bases. Our conversations ranged from the spiralling downward education, politics, the developing world of Africa, people's basic needs and how to meet these to bring relief to recipients. We believing improving the lives of others, in due course, improve our own. Upon learning about my difficulties at the American university of the Caribbean Bill Johnson, Jr rallied to assist me in my endeavours. His parents generously donated one thousand dollars in addition to the two advanced donations of five hundred dollars Bill jar sent me.

The Johnson's continued to touch my heart with tender hearts of generosity and sharing I will never forget. I visited the family few days before heading for Montserrat during which time they spoiled with gifts and dinner fit for a king. They tried to stuff me so as to put some pad of fat on my skeletal frame.

It goes without doubts that I engorged myself to the ears and yet remained the featherweight I came in with. Most of the discussion centred on my plight with the Gambia, my determination to overcome it and return as positive contributor to the Gambia. They told of having wonderful time and had lots of friends during their diplomatic tenure in Africa.

It is William J. Johnson's believe that the third world needed more aid from America then been forthcoming in recent times. I left them with full appreciation of the humane concerns for other and the wish to help the developing world. Bill Jr.'s father Mr. William J. Johnson was U.S. Ambassador to Kenya during the Kennedy presidency. He too fell in love with Africa.

He and lovely wife Majorette Johnson made many return trips to Kenya and other neighbouring African states. Hence, I was family from day one of our meeting to new.

Despite the fact that I have been away from the USA for years we still write to each other and they continued helping me find solutions to the seemingly endless financial woes that beset my life and educational pursuits. Hence, when AUC threatened to end my schooling, it was through kind contributions of the Johnsons' that helped pay an outstanding bill of three thousand dollars to the American University of the Caribbean school of Medicine.

This came in at the nick of time or at very critical moment for me in my adventure to gain medical education and return to serve the Gambia. AUC was taken by surprise in manner I cleared all outstanding bills in time to reregister for the forth semester I lost during the financial fiasco of 1988/89 academic year for the basic medical sciences courses.

Both AUC and I send a thank you note to the William Johnson and family for magnanimity and kindness shown by their helping out at the school. Praises be God's for letting such kind people come to my rescue at the nick of time when everything looked hopelessly bleak. Germane to my survival were insistence that failure be not the last chapter in the saga of my experience and that the Gambia be the benefactor in all these mesh, which will remain in my mind for some time.

The most rewarding element was the steadfastness with which my friends backed my seemingly never-ending stride towards the Doctor of Medicine degree (MD). Amongst these were long time friend and colleague at Alpena Community College (1967 – 69) in Michigan Nelson Herron, who became unique friend since we met at Alpena.

Upon hearing about decision of AUC regarding my medical training, Nelson Herron, out of kindness and concern for me, voluntarily lent me another $4600.00 to reduce the huge bill I then owe the school and to advance towards my registration fees.

Without these inputs from the Johnsons and Nelson Herron my medical education/training at AUC would have come to an abrupt nose dive for oblivion or a catastrophic end as envisioned by Richard Smith and his followers.

No matter how brilliant one is, going through uphill challenges the way I had was, to say the least, frustrating, challenging, and worse way to have to go through competitive medical school in such a fashion was never sure if my registration would be completed, cancelled or where the next penny was going to come from to help me finish my schooling.

By this time my pride gave way and I turned into a beggar as I had very little choice or control over events that kept unfolding in my path. Like a mule leaden with bags of salt, I struggled under the yoke of poverty being buoyed only by constant surge of inextinguishable ambition to forge ahead for the Gambia and my fellow men.

To this were the phenomenal encouragements I received from Americans. Channing Poiock said, "The only good luck many great men ever had was being born with the ability and determination to overcome bad luck." My life at this stage had blossomed to one percent inspiration and ninety-nine percent perspirations. Things were not relenting and I could not help my wife or parents back in the Gambia.

Remember, our cultural norms and obligations made it obvious that a forty plus male should be able to care not only for himself but also for his aged parent and others, rather than being stuck in class at a desolate impoverish island like Montserrat in the West Indies. Bellow is samples of requests and replies that trickled by after a lengthy wait and hope of getting help.

World Health Organization
CH1211, Geneve 27, Suise
March 29, 1088

Dear Mr. Ceesay,

In reply to your letter of March 8,1988, we would inform that WHO fellowships can only be awarded at the request of the candidates' national Health Authority. We would advise you, therefore, to write to the Gambia Ministry of Health asking to be nominated for such a fellowship. You will receive the relevant application forms from the Ministry if they are willing to sponsor your candidature.

Yours Sincerely

Mrs. B. J. Amara

Fellowship Division of

Health Manpower development

This was sent after I told them my predicament with the Gambia. The Canadian version ran thus

Bureau Des Conseillers Technique

De La Cooperation Canadiene

A. P. 3373, Dakar, Senegal
December 5, 1988

Dear Sir,

This is to acknowledge receipt of your letter of September 21, regarding a scholarship from the Canadian International Development Agency. The number of scholarships available is extremely limited and all applications are coordinated through the Ministry of Education of the Gambia, North American scholarships.

Thus we suggest that you contact the Ministry in Banjul for information on current scholarship programs. Thank you for your interest in studies in Canada.

Yours sincerely

Alime Touzim

Coordinator Des bourses ACDI

The only reply that shaded light of hope was from the British High Commission in Banjul, the Gambia of all places. Upon getting my letter the staff of the Commission got in touch with the Gambian authorities and after softening things, sent me the following response.

British High Commission
P.O. Box 507, Banjul
The Gambia, West Africa
November 29, 1988

Dear Mr. Ceesay,

The High commission has asked me to thank you for your letter of September 22, 1988, which did not arrive here until November 17, 1988. We were sorry to hear your financial predicaments. But unfortunately we are unable to help you as scholarships scheme is run as government to government basis only.

In other words, you would need to receive official backing from the government of the Gambia before we may consider sponsoring you. However we have spoken to the Ministry of Health. I do hope that you were able to find a sponsor in time.

Yours Sincerely

Paul Chart

These and many more like in kind from world embassies and countries left one thing clear to me that destiny is not a matter of chance it is a unique question of one's choice. And medicine is my committed choice for which I am willing to continue the struggle to the day I get the MD degree and eventual return to serve the Gambia as a dedicated physician.

I have always been convinced that all good things start in difficulty before becoming easy and rewarding. I again, in desperation, lunched another barrage of appeals and even contacted Mr. Paul Chart at the British High Commission in Banjul as if though his last letter of November 29, 1988 never reached me.

Paul replied reiterating reasons in this previous letter and made it clear that the High Commission will not sponsor me. He concluded by saying, "However, I have taken the liberty of mentioning your predicament to Dr. Hatib Njie, Director of Medical services at the Department of Health in

Banjul, in hope that he may be able to suggest a solution to your problems." Here you have it.

The Pandora's box opened by Paul Chart's discussion of the matter with the Director was the following:

Medical and Health Department

Medical Headquarters
Banjul, The Gambia

February 21, 1989

Reference MED/109

RE: application for sponsorship

Dear Mr. Ceesay

I write to inform you that Permanent Secretary Management Office is the person in charge of training at home and abroad. You may therefore apply directly to him for sponsorship. Send your application to him as quickly as possible.

Yours Sincerely,

Signed for Director

Medical services

The Gambia

At this juncture small opportunities like this one were not left alone or unexplored. I at the back of my mind was expecting nothing to come out from the Gambia. However I wasted no time and prepared an application with the following letters of support from various staff and current

Dean of Medicine at the American University of the Caribbean School of Medicine in Montserrat, West Indies. Here are a few of the letters sent along with my application.

American University of the Caribbean
P.O. Box 400
Plymouth, Montserrat
West Indies
March 23, 1989

TO WHOM IT MAY CONCERN

Mr. Alhasan Ceesay has requested that I write a letter in support of his request for financial aid in completing his medical training. I have known Mr. Ceesay for several years as his professor in Physiology and as the Dean of the Medical sciences.

Mr. Ceesay is a very personable and articulate man who interacts well with both the faculty and his classmates. He is a hard working student who is totally dedicated to becoming a physician and practicing medicine in the Gambia.

Thus far Mr. Ceesay has had to endure major financial problems in his pursuit of a medical degree. I feel Mr. Ceesay is very deserving of financial support for the remainder of his training and will become a compassionate, competent and caring physician for his people.

Sincerely
Miss Mary White

American University
P. O. Box 400
Plymouth, Montserrat
West Indies
March 25, 1989

Sincerely
Robert J. Chetok, PhD
Prof. Of Physiology

Dean of Medical Sciences

Another letter was from. Dr. D. E. Vonwomer, my professor of Pathology and retired former Dean of the College of Medicine, AUC.

American University of the Caribbean; Sch. Of Medicine

TO WHOM IT MAY CONCERN

Mr. Alhasan Ceesay has asked me for a letter supporting his application for financial support for the remainder of his medical schooling. Mr. Ceesay is a hard working student and who spends many hours preparing him to become a physician. He is highly motivated and spends most of the hours of his day studying so be might become a physician to serve the people of the Gambia.

Mr. Ceesay is extremely conscientious, very diligent in his work, and is also very pleasant cooperative young man. He is well liked by his fellow students and his professors and gets along well with all.

This young man has a very critical financial problem. And he needs financial support to continue the last half of his medical school curriculum. I hope it is possible for someone to assist this dedicated man so he will be able to return to his country and practice medicine.

Advisor Sincerely

D. E. Vanwormer, MD

Professor of Pathology

The final addendum from the American University of the Caribbean to be sent to the Gambia was a note from the Registrar of the university, Mrs. Mary R. Tuit, Who sent the following.

American University of the Caribbean

School of Medicine

Plymouth, Montserrat

West Indies

RE: Application for financial Assistance

Mr. Ceesay is 5th semester student at the American university of the Caribbean School of Medicine. He will finish basic sciences in August 1989.

Mr. Ceesay is expected to take up clinical assignments at the East borne District General Hospital, England coming September 1989.

The administration of the school will be grateful if you will facilitate financially his continuance of his studies. Any further courtesies extended to him will be greatly appreciated. Clinical in England will cost another $6450 per semester.

See enclosed breakdown of payments.

Respectfully

Mary R. Tuit

Registrar

These and lot more from my professors at the university were packaged and sent registered mail to the Permanent Secretary, Personnel Management, Banjul, the Gambia, as advised by the Director of Health's letter of February 12, 1989.

The school staffs were relieved and confident the financial burden would soon become history and be off my shoulders since to their expectation the letters of support were going to be the barometer of my progress and for the scholarship committee in the Gambia to look at in making final decision on my appeal.

Knowing what I knew and have gone through from the hands of the Gambia government, I just prayed for the reversal of tides in my favour so that I can move forward with my objective of serving the Gambians.

My fears and expectations were brought to light three months later when I received the following reply from an official in behalf of the Permanent Secretary, Personnel Management Office. Here is the full text of that heart-wrenching missive in reply to my request for financial assistance at a crucial stage of my medical training.

Personnel Management Office

The Quadrangle, Banjul

The Gambia

West Africa

June 13, 1989

EST/X811E/TEMP/C82

REQUEST FOR SPONSORSHIP TO UNDERTAKE A MEDICAL DEGREE: MR. ALHASAN S. CEESAY

I wish to acknowledge receipt of your letter dated March 28, 1989, in which you requested this office to seek assistance on your behalf from the British government in the form of scholarship award, so as to enable you to complete your medical degree at the American University of the Caribbean School of Medicine.

In this regard I am directed to inform you that our 1989/90 overseas Development Training Program has been finalized and it is therefore too late to make any provisions for you in the aforementioned program. Sorry for our inability to be of much help to you in this circumstance.

Sincerely,

L.T. Jorbateh

For Permanent Secretary

If I had not applied prior to writing then doubts wound continue to linger between the Gambia Ministry of Health and I. I had prior to applying for financial assistance asked the Director if the said Oversea Development Program was then still available.

I was told by the Director to send my application quickly for he had had a word with the Permanent Secretary of the Personnel Management Office. Anyhow, if adversity reveals genius now was the time for something to happen for me.

I had already been assigned to a hospital for my clinical training and now the last straw of hope and source of financial relief I expected slipped by in thin air. Like before, I accepted my fate and said, "God I know you care and love me and you will help me solve this difficult hillock. No one can stand the assault of sustained challenges. I will endure as ordained by your wish."

Louisa May Alcott said, "Far away there in the sunshine are my highest aspirations. I may not reach them, but I can look up and see their beauty, believe in them and try to follow where they lead."

Is it not true that obstacles are those frightful things we see when we take our eyes off our goals? No hillock or crisis like this development will ruffle my feathers. I continued to swim towards my ship, instead of waiting for it to come to me.

I braced up again and wrote several letters and asked friends to write in my behalf to any organization or government they think would come to my assistance for the medical degree meant a lot not only for me but the villager whom I intend to provide modern affordable medicines.

In this desperate state of my life, Jacob Riis' statement said it best for me. He said, "When nothing seem to help, I go and look at the stonecutter hammering away at his rock perchance a hundred times without as much a crack showing in it.

Yet, at the hundred and first blow it will split into two, and I know it was not that blow that did it, but all that had gone before." I am another stonecutter, mine comprises of humans, the most harden element on earth, so to speak, that I will be relentless with my unyielding rock, the MD degree, for my people, until I receive the right to practice in Gambia and Africa.

Each day is a specific thrill that leads to that exhilarating moment of victory for Gambia and mankind. It is a hard march toward the day I will be able to serve the Gambia as a physician. I feel favoured, if not blessed, having Mrs. Lois R. Leonard on my side.

I became her potage when she came to discover my strength, perseverance, and endurance to face very difficult challenges. She was the only member of the remaining Ceesay Support Committee that did not throw the towel at my face, present at the backstabbing meeting held while my friends Richard castigated me.

Lois Leonard shared my agonies and ecstasy as events unfolded during my stay in Montserrat, West Indies. She and a few others were source of relief and blessings to me. Lois Leonard would once on a while send me fifty dollars to put food into my dying body held by skeletal frame that refuses to be dismembered by starvation.

Upon hearing about my assignment do clinical rotation at Eat Borne she rallied friends and collected seven thousand dollars to help me start my clinical clerkship. Unfortunately the money had to be applied to clear unpaid past bills I owe the school. The university would not let me move without the remaining financial bill being cleared.

This development adversely affected my classes for that semester. However, I remained obliged to Lois Leonard even though she was no longer able to help since she had exhausted all resources and contacts available to her, which she lamented.

On hindsight had the Gambia not fought back my clinical clerkship would not have been delayed or postponed to September 1990 the very least cost went higher as tuition was increase to $4600 a semester.

Henry Forth said, "Failure is the opportunity to begin again more intelligently." So like Abraham Lincoln who said, "I will do the best I know how, the very best I can, and I mean to keep on doing it to the end. If the end brings me out all right, what is said against me will not amount to anything. If the end brings me out wrong, then ten angels swearing I was right would make no difference."

Mrs. Fatou Koma Ceesay and Keith Robinson, Gambia

Chapter 10
Welcome to the United States Texas

Let our narration detour in time to bring other events I passed through before the above developments. The kaleidoscope, which followed hurricane Hugo, only multiplied the whirlwinds of worries that were running through my head.

I had just finished three courses and had taken the last of nine exams I was assigned and needed $18,000 us dollars to enable me start the clinical phase after my last semester at the Texas Campus.

A void followed despite a series of telephone call to would be sympathetic persons in the USA and Canada. I waited for days and weeks and nothing seem to materialize to allow me start the clinical clerkship after Texas.

On December 19, 1989, Rudolf Kurt and his wife Sophie Kurt invited me for a chat and lunch with them. This day was another pivotal one in the saga of my life. After lunch and a detailed history of my case, these aged German couple, turned events around for a good start in my career.

As reneged will have it, one thing lead to another until when, to my delightful surprise, Rudolf and Wife Sophie Kurt, revealed that they have agreed to lend me $6000.00 (six thousand dollars!) to help me start my clinical studies in England.

Rudolf went cross and brought a checkbook and made two separate checks of three thousand dollars each to the American University of the Caribbean. One was to be applied toward completing the outstanding tuition bills and the other to be used directly towards my clinical training in the United Kingdom.

I, in utter disbelieve shrouded with gratitude, hugged and thanked them several times and promised them that they will never regret helping me. I was released to go and I ran from the condominium to the American University of the Caribbean financial officer, Mr. Soong, supervising the renovation of the campus.

I made the payments to the University's account at the Barclays Bank down town Plymouth and he issued receipts to that effect and cleared my outstanding bills with the university.

Mr. Sung then called Texas to AUC allow me join the students at Wayland Baptist University where AUC is piggy bagging the after effect of hurricane Hugo, in Plainview. The following letter and events after them signaled some relief in my blighted life.

Some earlier appeals for sponsorship yielded enough to allow me start arranging for a visa to travel to the United States to complete my basic medical sciences. Two days after I made those payments and for some reason the owner and president of the American University, Dr. Paul Tien, showed up on campus with engineers to estimate the cost of rebuilding the university.

I wasted no time bringing my newfound luck to light and went to meet him as soon as friends told me of his being in the Island. I requested that he add his weight to my attempt to secure a visa from the American Consulate at Antigua for me to travel to Texas and join the rest of the students at the campus of Wayland Baptist University in Plainview.

He was very happy to oblige. When he finished he paid part of my clinics school fees and said, "Ceesay, you are a good fighter. You have my respect and good luck in your clinical training." This was what he told the US emissary:

American University of the Caribbean
School of Medicine
P.O. Box 400
Plymouth, Montserrat
December 20, 1989

Consulate
Visa Section
U. S. Embassy
Antigua, West Indies

Dear Sir,

This is to inform you that I support the request for a visa application made by Alhasan S. Ceesay. Mr. Ceesay is a student of the American University of the Caribbean. He wishes to enter the United States in other to take the last classes of the basic sciences before proceeding to England for his clinical experience.

Upon completing his residency program, he will return to practice medicine in the Gambia. All assistance to him to enable him complete his studies would be most welcomed. Thank you for your help in this matter.

Sincerely

Dr. Paul Tien

American Univ. of the Caribbean

The following day I bravely held onto my letters and flew to Antigua and reported at the visa section of the U. S. Embassy 8.00 A.M the next morning. I was among first to be interviewed and I imaged smiling gleefully for a visa had been granted and affixed on my passport.

I can now join my colleagues four months after hurricane Hugo and very laborious work at the condominiums. I boarded TWA and headed once more for the United States of America. This time I landed in Miami International Airport in Florida and took a shuttle flight to Lubbock airport in Texas.

I was expecting to meet Dr. Steve Deschner at this Airport but he failed to turn up because of changes in his scheduled lectures and that of my flight. This posed no difficulty for me, having been in America as long as I did. I just went to the bus stand and took the one marked Plainview.

I arrived at the Wayland Baptist University in Plainview, where the American university of the Caribbean had temporally relocated after hurricane Hugo. I lodged with a student until the next day when I completed the formalities of registering for my last basic medical science courses. The office used money lent to me by the Kurts of Montserrat to cover areas I thought had been taken care off.

The officer insisted that the previous semester was not fully covered even though I showed that three thousand us dollars was paid in Montserrat. This stalemate put me back into square one and only worst I had no one to turn to in Texas except the Almighty God. I still feel cheated by AUC for having to find that my payments were not regularized to erase the outstanding bill on record.

The financial nightmare of my life surfaced at a very difficult transition time for me.

Again, I accepted that one must whittle today for a rewarding tomorrow. All that mattered was for work and struggle to go on, the curse endured, hope still lives and that my dream shall never die. I am part of all that I have endured and met.

I will strive to seek, to find and never yield to challenge. I made a concerted effort to visit churches and tell whomever I meet on the way what my plight was and that I desperately needed a loan to help me finish my medical education. It was during one of these trips that I came across an angel from the blue, in the body of Rev. Mark D. Meyer.

He was then in charge of St. Mark's Episcopal Church on 710 Joliet Street, Plainview, Texas. I found him at the entrance of St. Mark's Church just about to leave to minister to an old man, a member of the Parish who was under the weather.

One look at my faced made him decide to listen to my narrative and about the urgency of it. He expressed dismay at the fact that I was left stranded for four months in tiny Montserrat hopelessly destroyed by hurricane Hugo. He could not believe the heartlessness of not being evacuated along with the American students.

The American University of the Caribbean just abandoned me to find my way out of Montserrat while the American Consulate flew American and Canadian students back to America. The end result of the short conversation was an extensive interview about my goal and utilization of my training was an invitation with his Sunday service group on the following Sunday.

He revealed, during our meeting, that he too was a medical aspirant but changed his vocation to the Priesthood before getting too far into the art of Medicine.

He also said his father was a doctor and a member of the board of the American Medical association. My eyes opened widely hearing that I now have someone interested in me whose father's recommendation to any medical school would give weight for consideration by admission committees.

I therein and then prayed silently for God's help so that this angel of His would heed my plight. Rev. Mark D. Meyer turned a God sent relief to my challenge. He spoke to his congregation and came to Wayland Baptist University and made a down payment of $4200 (four thousand two hundred us dollars) in my name as a loan.

He contributed one thousand and the rest came from Church funds. Another member of the church, Mr. John Morse gave $500 as a personal gift to me. Rev. Mark D. Meyer's efforts did not end here for as the year waned and my financial blight remained unbearable, he asked me to stay with him at his residence on 1409 Garland Street, Plainview, Texas.

I stayed there with him until it was time for me to proceed to do my clinical clerkship in England. Through him I made a lot of friends in Plainview among who were Dr. Thomas Allen of Grace Presbyterian Church, Dr. Hoyt Huff of First Christian Church, Dr. & Mrs. Douglas E. Kopp and (The Rt. Rev) Bishop Sam B. Hulsey, Bishop of the Episcopal Diocese of North West Texas at Lubbock, just to name a few of Christ's modern day disciples who came to my aid while I was in dire financial state in the last leg of my basic medical sciences.

In response to the overwhelming generosity and Christian stand these people took in my affairs I wrote the following note of appreciation for the uniqueness of their gesture towards me and for enabling me move forward in my aspiration to serve the Gambia as a physician. In the mean time various small gifts kept pouring in to keep me happy. Many invited me to their homes to meet with their families or have some meal with them whenever convenient.

Plainview was my Texas and rev. Meyer my redeemer from earthly hell. We refer to each other as brother in Christ and humanity. He solicited help for me from groups like the Domestic and Foreign missionary Society of the Protestant Episcopal Church in the United States and numerous other church organizations in the USA and England.

Between us we used to write more than twenty-five letters a day appealing for help to enable me meet my goal for the Gambian villagers. Rev. Mark D. Meyer and I have same objective in life, i.e. to seek piety, by having strong faith in God, to gain knowledge to better serve our fellow human being by providing hope and relief to those we may come across in this life and finally to live a simple human trail of love and commitment to peace and good will to all on earth.

It entailed a life of sacrifice, devotion to our faith and commitment to move forward despite deterring challenges and roadblocks we may come across. Rev. Mark used to jokingly say to me, "Ceesay, if all Muslims were like you then the whole world would be one big Christian brotherhood."

This told more about our sense of oneness that a dictionary could define in a billion words closeness of two earthly creatures of God. Here is the letter I mentioned earlier on.

American University
C/O Wayland Baptist University
Plainview, Texas, USA

Dear Editor and Friends,

Sometimes god has a way of stepping into our lives when we least expected it. Such was the state which Rev. Mark D. Meyer and I. He stepped forward at a critical time of my plights and was kind and generous also helpful to my mission to serve the Gambia as a physician.

Without further adieu, I humbly and most gratefully acknowledge the loan he got for me from his kind congregation and other interested persons in Plainview. Your kindness has touched me deeply and made me more determined to succeed and return to my country, the Gambia, in due course.

Rev. Mark D. Meyer and I have become good friends and brothers in Christ. I am most grateful to all of you for this continued contribution to the Gambian people. Please convey our profound gratitude for this unique assistance to not only members of your church but to all those who one way or the other, in various gestures of generous acts, have helped to make my path a little bit easier to walk on.

You are very special to me and in the hearts of my villagers. I will certainly return to provide much needed modern medical service to the villages in the Gambia. We are indebted to all of you. Please come visit us.

The villagers are itching to meet you and serenade you for kindness and your willingness to share generously with us so as to bring hope and relief to people in rural Gambia. Finally, God bless you and be rest assured that I will keep you informed of my progress wherever I am. Please continue to pray for my success and eventual return to serve my people in the smiling cost of the Gambia, West Africa. Cheers and regards to all.

Your friend

Alhasan Ceesay

Gambian AUC student

This letter ushered in more friends from far and wide of Texas. I had people asking me to meet with them as far away as Huston, Dallas and other heartland cities in Texas. It was also while at Garland Street that our discussions vied onto my idea of a village clinic in the future with which to fulfill my dream of bringing modern medicine to the forgotten and neglected villager's health care needs.

Again, we went into full gear and wrote to hundreds of charity groups asking for ideas and assistance on how to get started on what would later be the present Manding Medical Centre at Njawara village, The Gambia, West Africa.

Most of the replies stress that only local organizations were eligible for possible funding and that most were already too committed to take on any other aspirants like my clinic. These negative replies had a little dampening effect on our drive but we pushed on as hard as can be to raise funds for the future Manding Medical Centre.

We did developed friendship with architectural group, L. James Robinson and Associates, located at 205 West 4th Street, Plainview, Texas, 790723, headed by Mr. L. James Robinson. This friendly rapport led to the first architectural plan of Manding Medical Centre. We only altered few parts to suit the Gambian environment and the board and any who saw it had unanimously adopted the plan.

The above made a unique hospital plan that would when completed will stand the test of time and will serve its intended purpose. Time flew fast and soon came the most difficult event between two that have become one in spirit.

My basic medical courses ended in July 1990 and arrangements were afoot for me to proceed to either Kinston Hospital, Kingston upon -Thames, or Essex County Hospital, Colchester, England by September 1990 to do my clinical clerkship.

The last week was very intense for both of us. Leaving for good or for a long time was unbearable. Rev. Mark D. Meyer had, like Mr. L.A. Bouvier, become the ideal friend and an honest person to turn to. We are totally devoted folks to our belief and causes and we care a lot about plight of the downtrodden of life.

Meanwhile, the American University of the Caribbean sent the following letter to Mrs. Mickey, Program Coordinator, Kingston Hospital informing her about my plans to do my clinical clerkship at their hospital.

American University of the Caribbean
School of Medicine
P. O. Box 400
Plymouth, Montserrat
West Indies July 14, 1990

Mrs. Mickey,
Program Coordinator
Kingston Hospital
Gals worthy Road

Kingston upon Thames
Surry KT2 7BE
England, UK

Dear Mrs. Mickey,

This letter is being sent on behalf of Alhasan Ceesay, a student of the American university of the Caribbean School of Medicine. Mr. Ceesay is a citizen of the Gambia and in other to obtain his visa to come to England the British Consulate requested a letter be sent from you stating that he has been accepted into your clinical program.

I have spoken with Dr. Youel in this regards and he has informed me that he will be assigning Mr. Ceesay to your program to begin on September 3, 1990. I have sent the student a letter to this effect to take to the consulate's office. However, they also require a letter directly from the hospital.

As the US visa will be expiring in July, at which time he will need to relocate to England, will you please send a letter as soon as possible to the British Consulate-General, Suit 2250, Dresser Tower, 601 Jefferson, Huston, Texas 77002, attention, Mrs. H. M. Tanks, British vice Consul. We appreciate your assistance in this matter. May I also request that you send a copy of the letter for me to place it in Mr. Ceesay's file. Thank you.

Sincerely

Jackie R. Allen

Secretary to Liaison Official

Another letter dated September 1990 was sent to Essex County after an unforeseen delay in hearing from the British High Commission in Huston, Texas. It read,

American University of the Caribbean
School of Medicine, P. O. Box 400
Plymouth, Montserrat
September 6th 1990

Dear Dr. Peter R. Wilson,

Alhasan Ceesay has been assigned to begin clinical clerkship at Essex County Hospital, Colchester on October 8, 1990. This is to certify that Mr. Ceesay is academically qualified and administratively approved to begin the clinical clerkship program at the American university of the Caribbean School of Medicine as a third year medical student in September 1990. Signed: David Bruce Youel, MD: Dean Clinical Sc. Robert Chertok, PhD: Dean of Medicine Sciences

 I took this last with me to Huston and after a lengthy interview disproving allegation I choused England to emigrate instead of just doing my clinical.

I made it very clear that had that been my intention I will not select UK being already on American soil. The officer after few minutes of reflection concord and offered me student visa to attend Essex County Hospital's clinical program in Colchester, Essex, England in October 1990.

Miss Binta Ceesay, daughter

Chapter 11
England at last clinical Training, 1990

I flew to the British Consulate at Huston, Texas to be interviewed for a visa to enter the United Kingdom to do my clinical clerkship at the Essex County Hospital in Colchester by October 8, 1990. No, my financial curse never left me. It was a dragon that would show its head again and again while I was in England.

Rev. Mark D. Meyer went with me up to Lubbock airport on the day of my travels to the UK. At Lubbock airport, we prayed and hugged each other, with eyes full of tears, several times before we could say our final goodbyes. I left Huston with a student visa and boarded BA flight 0224 on the September 12, 1990 heading for Heathrow International Airport, London, England.

I landed at Heathrow on Wednesday September 12, 1990. My impression of England and her people never disappointed me. The people were friendly but much more business like. The immigration Officer received my document and placed a call to Essex County hospital to verify status as student with them.

This done a leave to remain in the U.K was stamped onto my passport and allowed to proceed to my final destination, Colchester. Arrangements were made for me to stay at a hotel call the George located at the High street down town Colchester, Essex County.

The hotel staffs were very kind and helpful as they brought food from nearby restaurant because the hotel kitchen had closed for the night when I arrived at o1.35 a.m. The following day at about 8.30 am I reported to Dr. Peter R. Wilson's office, clinical program director for the American university of the Caribbean, at Essex county Hospital in

Colchester. I later on that day met Mrs. Penny West, a very kind lady, the program administrator for further briefing of our program and what was expected of us while in England. There I met two other Americans ladies and two gentlemen students from previous classes at the American university of the Caribbean School of Medicine, who also came to do their clinical clerkship at Essex county Hospital.

I was moved from the hotel to flat 2 Kensington Court, 47 Roman Road, Colchester administered by the Pullars estate agents. We went through one week of orientation and familiarizing ourselves where about the shops and postal services, bus stations for the National Express services and many other things of interest in the city. We were then issued schedules and units and department/ assignment to begin our clinical training.

I was only able to pay for the first semester of the training because promises to help me finish failed to materialize. This led Rev. Mark D. Meyer to lend me another $2000 (two thousand us dollars) on March 6, 1990 and again another personal loan of $900 (nine hundred us dollars) later.

These monies were deposited to the university in my name but the cost per semester was $4600 leaving me $1700 short of meeting my financial obligation to the school for the second semester at the clinics. It was during those frustrating moments that I decided to bite the bullet and called a long time Gambian friend of mine, Dr. Ebrahima M Samba, to come to my rescue.

This he did by promptly calling his bank in London and authorizing them to send me three thousand seven hundred pounds sterling loan to help me complete the semester. I received it with gratitude and humility. Praises be God's for only through Him have miracles been happening for me.

Two weeks later the same bank sent another equal amount allotment from Dr. Samba. In my acknowledgement letter I thanked Dr. Samba for the two disbursements and told him that the University had already debited them to my accounts to clear the outstanding bills.Later that week the bank called and wrote to say they made a mistake by sending me the second allotment from Dr. Samba's account and that I should return the money forthwith.

At the time all monies sent to me had already been applied toward my fees at the American university of the Caribbean. Dr. Ebrahima M Samba kindly intervened and blamed the bank for the mistake and let me now owe him Four thousand four hundred pounds sterling instead of the original approved three thousand seven hundred pound sterling. No other Gambian would have acquiescence other than this angel friend of mine. He proved to be true and true real friend in need and in good times.

I will reimburse him all monies I owe him whenever my earnings improve. This saga allowed me to sail on through until November 11, 1991.The bubble busted again. AUC threatened to throw me out of the program upon my failure to meet payment of the balance of my areas with the school. This treat lead Dr. Peter R. Wilson, Program Director for AUC at Essex County Hospital to intervene with the following letter to Dr. Bruce Youel, Dean of Clinical sciences for the American university of the Caribbean.

Colchester and North Essex
Postgraduate Center
Essex County Hospital
Colchester, Essex CO3 3NB

Dr. Bruce Yuoel
Dean of Clinical Sciences
American University of the Caribbean
April 24, 1991

Dear Dr. Youel
RE: Alhasan Ceesay
As Director of the AUC students in Colchester I take exceptions to the highhanded and unreasonable attitude in regards to this trainee doctor who has hitherto given you no cause for anxiety in respect of his funding and through no fault of his own has found himself in dire financial distress because his government has in some way delayed funding. I am making every effort on his behalf to find someone to help him financially by contacting the Gambia High Commission etc and I expect you to allow him adequate time to sort out his finances.

I shall continue to provide him with clinical training here and I expect you to honour that and I shall be in touch with you before the end of May to see if we can reach suitable compromise. I would like you to decide whether you can offer any financial help yourself and when and what scholarship you are prepared to offer him.

Yours Sincerely
Dr. Peter R. Wilson
AUC Program Director
Colchester General Hospital

Dr. Peter Wilson not only looked for more sources of help to alleviate my situation but he generously donated one thousand pounds sterling from his bank for me to pay AUC and the rent at 47 Roman Road in Colchester. Among other letters seeking financial help for me was one sent to the student adviser, Mr. Peter Bird, of the African Education Trust on 38 King Street, London on March 20, 1991.

Dr. Peter R. Wilson
Program Director for AUC
Essex County Hospital
Colchester, Essex CO3 3NB

Mr. Peter Bird
Advisor
African Education Trust
38 King Street
London
March 20, 1991

Dear Sir,

RE: Alhasan S. Ceesay

I enclosed confidential letter of recommendation for the above student for your consideration. Please do not hesitate to contact me if you feel I can be of any further assistance.

Yours faithfully
Dr. Peter R. Wilson
AUC Program Director

CONFIDENCIAL LETTER OF RECOMMENDATION FOR MR. ALHASAN S. CEESAY

Alhasan is an extremely conscientious and competent man, determined against all odds to complete a Doctorate course in medicine, so that he can return to use his knowledge to serve his people. I have no doubts about his sincerity of his purpose nor of his dedication and hard work and various scholarships he had earned en route.

He managed to be one of few rural students without financial backing from his family or government to receive secondary education and gained one of the extremely rare university entrances and took a master's of Science degree before embarking on his medical studies.

Enrolled after years of hard work in the USA trying to save enough money during his undergraduate career in science in the states, he joined the American University of the Caribbean as a matured student for his clinical training and funded himself through the first five semesters of this course.

He applied to come to England as do many students from this university in order to gain his clinical experience in an English hospital and was assured by the Gambia high Commission that he had been awarded a Commonwealth Foundation training scholarship for the remainder of his clinical training.

Only after beginning his training in the UK did he discovered that the Commonwealth foundation Training body were unable to fulfill their apparent promise to the Gambia High Commission and since then he has been desperately borrowing money from those who sponsored him during his training hitherto and has written many letters since then begging for help from the Gambia Ministry of Health and Education Department. He has been unable to any more than token financial help. Anything you can do to help now will enable this very conscientious man to complete his course. It would be tragedy if he were not able do so. He has, to my knowledge, many letters of support to back mine, which he will also be submitting to you. I have no doubt.

Peter R. Wilson

Program Director

Severals' Hospital

Colchester, Essex

On February 22, 1991 the Bishop of Colchester, The Rt. Rev Michael E. Vikers, sent the following appeal in my behalf to Hon. Bakary Darboe, Vice president and Minister of Education, Banjul, The Gambia, West Africa. It read:

Dear Vice President

Minister of Education

RE: Mr. Alhasan S. Ceesay

I understand from Mr. Ceesay, with whom I have been speaking this morning, that he was on the telephone to you either yesterday or the day before, about the financial crisis, which threatens to place the completion of his studies in jeopardy and end the possibility of his returning as a trained physician to the Gambia.

I have been drawn into Mr. Ceesay's situation over the last four months, partly through a colleague in the United States who was able to give some assistance and encouragement during an earlier stage of his studies. I can vouch for the critical nature of his present situation and I am sure that you will wish to do anything that you can to assist him.

His university has recently told him that, unless he is able to pay the tuition fees due, $5200 (five thousand two hundred us dollars) by the 5th of April, 1991 he will be placed on a financial leave of absence during which time he will not be permitted to continue classes. With best wishes

Yours sincerely

Bishop Michael E. Vickers

Some help surfaced but not from the Gambia government. A Liza Gilbert replied to one of several appeals both Dr. Peter R. Wilson and I sent to The Africa Education Grant Advisory Service in London and gave the following good news for decades.

Assistant student Advisor

African Education Grant

38 king street

London

May 23, 1991

Mr. A. S. Ceesay

Flat 2, Kensington Court

47 Roman Road

Colchester, Essex CO1 1UR

Our ref: EG91/0123

Dear Mr. Ceesay,

Further to your case I am pleased to inform you that the Education Committee of the family welfare association has kindly agreed to make you an award to assist you in your present difficulties.

A cheque in enclosed made payable to your place of study as previously explained. I would be grateful if you could acknowledge receipt of this check. It you take the enclosed cheque to the finance office of your college they will be able to administer it for you and will either draw up a further cheque or pay the grant in cash.

Enclosed is two thousand six hundred pounds sterling for fees. The committee has asked that if the ministry in Gambia do eventually pay the fees, they could be re-embossed but do not expect repayment otherwise. With best wishes for the future

Yours Sincerely

Liza Gilbert

Assistant student Advisor

Prior to the above letter I had applied to dr. Peter r. Wilson to contact the Postgraduate Committee in my behalf for possible assistance with an emergency loan of six thousand five hundred pounds sterling to enable me pay the rest of the remaining two and half semesters of my clinical training.

Rev. Mark Meyer and Mrs. Lois R. Leonard also made efforts to collect money for me. Mark sent $500 on 28/10/91 followed by another $2600 on 25/11/91 and finally $900 on the 27/3/92.

All these monies went into payment of tuition fees and rent. To add fuel to fire, the university increased its tuition fees up 6% throwing students like me into more financial crisis than can be imagined. Dr. Peter R. Wilson was also successful with his appeal from the Postgraduate Committee to which amount he added his own one thousand pounds sterling as a loan to me. He informed me of the grant from the Postgraduate Committee thus;

Colchester and North East Essex
Postgraduate Medical Center
Essex County Hospital
Colchester, CO3 3NB
May 10, 1991

Ref: PRW/PAH

Mr. Alhasan Ceesay
Flat 2, Kensington Court
47 Roman Road
Colchester, Essex

Dear Alhasan,

I am able to give you good news. The Medical advisory Committee of the hospital agreed to my recommendation that you should be offered immediately a loan, interest free, of six thousand five hundred pounds sterling to enable you to complete your studies in medicine and take your degree as you had hoped to do.

The M.A. C. recognize that you have studied conscientiously and I do not believe you would have receive this offer unless several of the tutors with whom you have had contacts had not spoken up enthusiastically in your support on knowledge of your conduct. The M. A. C. recognize that you are in no position to guarantee repayment of this loan and in any case do not expect you to begin repayment until June 1994 when they hope you will be in a position to do so.

I would strongly recommend that you advise your friends that you would have completed your studies and then give them priority in repayment.

At least two of the consultants in this district know the Gambia intimately and are aware of the effort you have made in your efforts so far to get in your course and training and all wish you well in fulfilling your ambition to become a doctor and serve your people as I am sure you will be able to do.

We shall expect you to complete your clinical training including the electives in the near future. Please come and see me.

Yours Sincerely

Dr. Peter R. Wilson

AUC Program director

This was a historic relief anointed by the Gods on mount Olympus. It marked a pivotal point in my quest for the elusive medical degree for the Gambia. Needless to say I was flabbergasted, more than delighted and terribly relieved that the tuition fee problem has now been laid to rest forever. Wife and I prayed for all, especially for Dr. Peter R. Wilson and M.A.C.

We felt eternally indebted and profoundly grateful for their generosity, understanding and stand to see me get the medical training I want to serve my people with in the future. I sent the following note of thanks and appreciation for the good will to the Postgraduate Committee at Essex County Hospital in Colchester.

Flat 2, Kensington Court
47 Roman Road
Colchester, Essex CO1 1UR
May 20, 1991

Mr. Kitchen, chairman
Medical Advisory Committee
Postgraduate Medical Center
Essex county Hospital
Colchester, Essex CO3 3NB

Dear Committee,

RE: In Appreciation/grant

This is to acknowledge receipt of the six thousand five hundred pounds sterling loan you approved to help me complete my clinical training here at Essex County hospital in Colchester. Thank you is awfully inadequate and words cannot aptly convey to you the gratitude and appreciation Gambia and I have for the help you so kindly rendered us. We are profoundly grateful got this kindness and generous contribution in our behalf.

Rest assured that the fruits of this benevolence would be fully shared with the sick and needy villagers. This humane gesture now makes that venue more certain. Finally the six thousand five hundred pounds sterling loan will be repaid in full and in time. I will return to serve the Gambia, especially villagers. I will keep in touch with most of you, especially the M.A.C.

Again, God bless and a million thanks for being so helpful to us. I remain ever so grateful to all of you. Cheers and regards.

Yours Sincerely

Alhasan S. Ceesay

Gambian Medical Student

I met Dr. Peter R. Wilson the next morning and we had a cordial and memorable chat that day. He was very relieved that I could now work toward serving my nation and fulfilling my dream for my people who are desperately in need of medical care.

I gave him a note of thanks for him and his staff who worked acidulously to help me resolve my financial woes. I felt happy with Mrs. Penny West, Mrs. Hornby and all those who assisted to bring hope to my venture. It simply said:

Flat 2, Kensington Court

47 Roman Road

Colchester, Essex CO1 1UR

May 20, 1991

Dear Dr. Wilson,

Thank you for your May 10, 1991 letter informing me of the six thousand five hundred pounds sterling loan the Medical Advisory Committee approved in my behalf through your relentless kind initiative efforts. I am most grateful to you and the committee for this humane gesture as such critical state of my medical education. It is very kind and generous and the Gambia and I remain touched by it. You have again extended your healing hands to touch us in the Gambia. Wife and I remain profoundly grateful and feel privileged having you on our side and as a friend.

Secondly, we thank you the trip to Hartfield House and the dinner with the Rotary Club. It was our first time out of Colchester and we really fully appreciated the gesture. Hartsfield House is an appreciable history of English Monarchy. The loan will be fully repaid within the stated time.

Finally, kindly convey sincere thanks to the Committee, Mrs. Penny West and Mrs. Horny and all the staff for their love and kindness showed us. It was an admirable ceaseless effort from all of you that brought light at the end of the tunnel for the Gambia and I.

Wife and I are deeply touched. I will be at your office for us to plan the rest of my medical training. Cheers and regards. God bless you, my friend.

Yours Sincerely

Alhasan S. Ceesay

Gambian Medical Student

This phase of my life in Colchester will be incomplete without mentioning of few other angels wife and I met. Our first friendly contact, aside hospital staff, was an unusually easy going old lady, Mrs. Maureen P. Smith, who lived across our building on Roman Road.

She was the first neighbour who came to visit with us and we hitherto formed the warmest long lasting bond of friendship with her. We tease her as UK's deputy ambassador for Africa and Japan. Why?

She had friends from all over the world but more so of Japanese and she spends nearly all her holidays in Japan. We loved her for breaking the social ice for us and through her we met lots of other good people in Roman Road. I first met Nurse Lorna V. Robinson while at my surgical rotation at the Colchester General Hospital.

She had just returned from vacationing in the smiling coast, the Gambia. She came to see me at the surgical ward the moment she was told of a Gambian student doing his clinical training at the hospital. The meeting was brief but I found her friendly and we decided to meet my wife at the end of the day.

The meeting will not be until the birth of our first daughter, Famatanding Ceesay, on the 17/9/91 that Lorna and husband turned up at the Colchester Maternity Hospital to congratulate us. Lorna Robinson took the most important photograph; baby Famatanding Ceesay, in the history of my family. Meanwhile she and wife got on as if they had known each other for centuries. They became sisters since that meeting.

The two visited each other frequently and we maintained links with Lorna Robinson. Last but the least was friendship we built with the Gassons of the Causeway, Boxford in Colchester. We met this lovely family through my contact with one of their sons, Daryl Gasson, who was then working at the Colchester General Hospital. He was interested in the Gambia and hence invited to meet with the rest of the Gassons.

At Boxford the Gassons were more than delighted to meet wife and I. Everyone wanted to pick baby Famatanding and we had exhilarating and memorable two days with this family before returning to down town Colchester.

We really cherished friendships we built with countless families in the Colchester area and did try to keep up with all after leaving friendly Colchester in 1992. As time passed we lost contacts with some friends but Lorna Robinson became our extended family in the UK. She visits us while in the Gambia during her summer holidays.

My daughter, Famatanding Ceesay, calls her "Auntie Lorna." We always look forward to her next visit to the Gambia. Her personal contribution to my family is immense and we remain grateful to her untold number of kind gestures to the family.

Being interested in helping others and having observed my work with the villagers, this lady took interest in it and agreed to help me get drugs, equipment, and to sensitize would be interested sponsors of a village health organization, when she returns to Colchester. She did as promised and had for years sent numerous packages of materials donated to Manding Medical Centre at Njawara village.

She visited Njawara, my home village, in 1995 and saw how much need there was for the contribution to help provide much needed medical service to the villages. She was swamped at the village by throngs of villagers wishing to thank her for being kind to them and for helping in their medical care needs.

Moved by this show of gratitude from villagers Lorna Robinson braced to do even more and today there is the usual, "Gambit Night" or Gambia Bazaar fund raising activity every weekend at Colchester.

Through her efforts we today have the Colchester friends of Manding Charitable Trust, which is and extended arm of Manding Medical Centre and serves as our liaison for the

UK and the European Community countries. The Charity was formed through her relentless efforts help of a solicitor the Charity Commission has registered the friends of Manding as a charity in England and Wales since August 21, 2001 to further the objectives of Manding Medical Centre at Njawara in the Gambia, West Africa. As far back as June 6, 1993 Lorna Robinson released the following flyer on behalf of Manding Medical Centre.

The appeal read thus:

82 Finchingfield Way
Black Heath
Colchester, Essex CO2 OOAU
England
6/06/93

Dear Friends,

I am writing on behalf of Dr. Alhasan Ceesay of the Manding Medical Centre at Njawara village in the North Bank Division of the Gambia, West Africa. My husband and I are helping Dr. Ceesay and the villagers establish a hospital that is surely needed as the nearest hospital is some 70 miles away strewed with bad roads, and no ambulances or proper transport for the ill villagers.

It will provide valuable medical, surgical, obstetrics, gynaecology, Paediatrics and other ancillary medical services. We hence write to you to join us as a partner in this humanitarian venture. Fifty pounds will buy a tone of cement and we need about 480 tones to build the center.

Any help in the form of money, equipment, contacts etc will be more than welcomed. We want to contribute in a positive way by providing medical aid and facilities to the villages, which will generate interest with greater participation, form a healthy agricultural society that may lead to improved nutritional and economic gain.

Finally, your help in bringing this gift to the villagers will be more than welcomed and deeply appreciated. Please help us catch dream for the villager. Also feel free to contact me should you or any need further information on the above project at Njawara in the Gambia. Regards

Yours Sincerely

Lorna V. Robinson

These and many more Colchester human angels were picked on the way as the years unfold. It has been my home away from home and a support line, if not lifeline for Manding Medical Centre at Njawara village, the Gambia, West Africa. God bless all.

L-R: Dr. Alhasan Ceesay, Prof. Sulayman Nyang, Mr. Cloyd Ramsey and Professor Francis Conti

Chapter 12
The MD Degree, 1992 and Home sweet Home

If there remain any out there who happens to be skeptic or cynical disbeliever in the existence of a curse or anything like it, be warned not to become a convert by the following events that are about to unfold right before you in these pages. These events herein cannot just happen or come out of the blue by themselves after all my life had gone through these twenty-five years.

Every major step of my life had met with stiff resistance compounded by painful, wretched, ill fated, contemptible, if not unsatisfactory, bitter experiences. It is unbelievably hard to contemplate the challenges and inhuman roadblocks I had to face in my life.

Hence dear reader, I suggest that you take a seat and prepare to be mesmerized. My life seem to follow the path of a sailor who, no, not that of the ancient Mariner and his Albatross, nor would Barron Murchison's adventure match it or be more thrilling in nature, finds himself sailing uncharted waters of life without a compass.

Yes, I am sailing through this life as if though no other hell surpasses this very one I am traveling. Let me tell you what happened few years ago, in 1989, when I was in Montserrat. While there hurricane Hugo decided to sweep by the Island nation hitting it with such ferrous vengeance that the roofs of buildings, including one we took shelter at, were blown away to the Caribbean sea leaving only the sky our mantle.

It poured torrential waves of rain bringing water up to our necks. The razor sharp wind blowing at 175 to almost 300 miles per hour speeds nearly took me to sea like a kite.

Wife and I held onto a pillar all night with micelles flying from all directions pass us. Each of those heavy poles, corrugated sheets or doors hitting us would spell our doom. Wife and I prayed and readied us for our survival and all those on the path of this devil hurricane with such ferocity and evil wind cum rain-washing away life.

We were lucky to survive that night but lost most of our belongings, including house we took shelter at. Why I survive if I were not to face another holocaust of a greater magnitude? Do not worry this was just the top of the iceberg. I hope I have whetted your appetite and that you are braced or ready for what good old Montserrat would spew at me after graduation ceremonies.

Like any aspirant completing medical school, I was excited and looked forward to a rewarding life of devotion to helping likewise bringing hope and relief to the sick and needy for the Gambia. I had looked forward to the good life and leaving behind most of, if not all my woes and financial troubles and follow a new path of devotion to God and service to my fellow man. Life is full of choices and I made mine to do medicine.

All I ever yearned for was the simple contribution of what my skills and strength can for others. My heart yeaned for relief, but do you think the elements would let me have a little peace with which to appreciate family and the beauty of life? Having completed my clinical training at Colchester General Hospital and having met all the requirements for graduation, I bid farewell to my Colchester friends and headed for Montserrat on March 21, 1992.

 Check-in time was scheduled for 7.40 a.m. at Gatwick North Terminal, London. You guess it right, the car we were traveling with lost a wheel six miles to Gatwick and the spare had busted in two places the night before.

Luckily an observant traffic police officer noticed us and decided to come and find out what was going on or what we were up to and how he could help us. Being an unusually kind and nice Bobbie he decided to call a repair crew to come to our rescue. What an omen for traveler! I made it to Gatwick North Terminal at the last announcement for boarding British Airways to Antigua, West Indies.

The departure for the flight was 9.45 a.m. Everyone at the BA checking-in counter rushed to help me get on board the plane, delaying the take off time another twenty minutes. Some of the passengers thought I was some diplomat or VIP, to cause the pilot to want to wait for my joining the flight. This brought me publicity and attention I did not bargain for on board.

Finally, BA flight for Antigua managed to take off and away we went into soon blue skies with jet engines purring like a tamed cat sleeping on a couch. The initial first four hours of flight were perfectly calm but not for long afterwards. The plane started to experience all of sudden bad weather and steeply went into turbulent weather.

Luckily the captain was an exceptionally good, good experienced and adept enough pilot to get us through very serious thunderstorm and lightening. It was a frightening fifteen minutes before we were clear above most of the heavy clouds and on course to Antigua.

We were relieved for no one sustained any injuries and the rest of the flight was bearably comfortable. We finally landed in Antigua around 3.45 P.M. an hour late but safe and sound. I had no problem at Antigua International arrival terminal. I even recognized some of the old hand at the terminal. Hence after hour's airport formalities we boarded Liat 596 flight heading for Montserrat, now my favourate island nation in the West Indies.

The flight took only fifteen minutes over the Caribbean Sea and we were at Montserrat Airport. I took a taxi to Plymouth, capital city of the island and very soon was reunited with my former landlord, Willy Ryan and other friends. This was March 25, 1992 three solid years after hurricane Hugo and one could still see the scars of the then mighty Hugo. My landlord's house and many others were still in disrepair and only few strong buildings were worth to dwell.

Hotels and Condominiums were in full gear and I was to stay at the residence of Miss Gayle Baumgartner until after the graduation ceremonies scheduled for the 28th of March 1992. This was an unbelievable big day I had worked very hard for and nothing was going to spoil it for me. I planned to savour every minute of it as historical for the Gambia and my family. Sadly neither my wife nor any friend of notary could make it to my graduation because of the cost of transportation and lodging them in broken down Montserrat.

I was to secure a visa and head for the US to do my internship and residency programs after receiving the MD degree from the American University of the Caribbean at Montserrat, West Indies. What happened or followed next is worse than my other recent bad experiences.

It was like a dream, but let us for the meantime continue on about graduating. Every graduating student was happy when March 28, 1992 dawned. It was a day we all had dreamt of in our ambitious push to better our lives and those whom we touch on our path. As for me, I was ecstatic and more than thankful that God had let me see the day I will finally receive the Doctor of Medicine degree.

However mixed feelings emanated because not one of my friends showed up, despite having promised to do so, and worse of all my return to America was uncertain.

Miss Roheyata Ceesay, daughter

Being on the Island brought back all those bleak and difficult day seven months of starvation and solitude I had to endure in Montserrat before being able to join the students at Wayland Baptist University, Plainview, Texas. We were on the graduation procession three days after my landing in Montserrat.

There was a big fanfare and neon signs congratulating and wishing every graduate well and a mélange of blooming verities of roses in full glory and splendor. There were blooming verities of roses everywhere the eye can see on campus. Like all graduations, whether in Plymouth, Montserrat or any institute of learning, long speeches mark the occasion.

In Montserrat, it always shows the Governor at his best political cum academic jargon. This was normally followed by advises of a few other dignitaries in attendance. We took the Hippocratic Oath with all its solemnity and I again thanked God for the favor He has done by allowing me see the day of my graduation from medical school and I renewed my covenant to return to serve the Gambia no matter how difficult it might be getting to my objective of providing modern medical aid for the rural Gambian villagers.

Very soon we dispersed and parents and friends of graduates wished us well and retired to their hotels. We had a graduation party that lasted through the wee hours of the night for some but I had to leave around 11:00 Pm because I missed my wife and family back in the Gambia.

Gayle Baumgartner was away in America and the room I currently occupy was already booked but another guest arriving on the March 29, 1992. It meant that I had to find a place as quickly as I can before the arrival of the people whose room I was at.

I needed few more days to seek a visa from the US Consulate in Barbados before I can proceed to do my internship and residency program in medicine in America, or so I thought until when I got to Barbados, West Indies. My former Landlord, Willy Ryan, tried to buoy me up by being overly kind and even helped me look for vacancy for me to stay until I sort things out from Barbados and could fly to the USA to start my medical program as hoped or worse head for the Gambia.

I left my luggage with Willie Ryan and flew to Barbados the next day to seek for a visa to enter the United States for the sole purposes of doing my internship and residency program in medicine before returning to the Gambia. At Barbados I met an almost impossible visa consular officer who insisted that I return to the Gambia and seek a visa from the American Embassy in Banjul, the Gambia.

I pleaded with her that I had at the time spent all my money and by so doing it would cost more to travel to the Gambia and I would loose my chance for doing the promised internship and residency program and other consideration that were taking place at teaching hospitals in America. She called one of these hospitals in the US and was told that unless I am able to visit with the institute no further action in my behalf would be considered.

Despite the fact that it was now made clear to her that my going to Africa would mean losing the chance of further training in medicine in a US setting earmarked for me. The officer rejected my visa application request to travel to America.

Unless I am able visit with the teaching hospital in America my dream of being an American trained physician is abruptly brought to rest. No, her reason for rejecting my request to travel to the USA was not based on my having previously asked for political asylum in America. My voluntary departure from America in December 1987, removed that record from the books and immigration data, and hand had nothing to do with subsequent entries.

On hindsight, I was even able to renter in 1982 and 1989 after hurricane Hugo to join the AUC students at the Wayland Baptist University campus in Plainview, Texas. Previous visa counselors would have not let me in had the asylum request been a deterrent. I thanked her after several attempts to reason things with her and thanked God before returning with a laden heart to Montserrat. At which place I contacted Rev. Mark D. Meyer in Nebraska.

He and other American friends along with Congressman Doug Berreuter of Nebraska agreed to intervene in my behalf by writing to the Ambassador, G. Philip Hughes requesting favourable review and reconsideration of my visa application.

All my friends agreed with me that traveling to the Gambia to seek a US visa was an unnecessary expense and time consuming drill or venture in my own history with the Gambia I could afford at the time. My brother and friend in Christ, Rev. Mark D. Meyer sent the following communiqué to the Immigration officer at Barbados.

St. Mark's Episcopal Church

1714 Grant Street

P. O. Box 72

Blair, Nebraska, USA
April 22, 1992
To: The United States Immigration Officer
From: Rev. Mark D. Meyer

Dear Sir/Madam,

I write on behalf of Dr. Alhasan S. Ceesay and appeal to you to please award him a visa to enter the United States in order to finish his internship. Alhasan came to my office in January of 1990, when I was a priest at St. Mark's Episcopal Church in Plainview, Texas.

The campus of the American University of the Caribbean had been offered some vacant classroom and dormitory space at Wayland Baptist University in Plainview. Alhasan had then used up all his funds in coming to Plainview from Montserrat, and I was able to help him with room and board to finish his classroom training.

At the end of that time he was able to get the United Nations Scholarship for clinical training in England. He was forced to spend to spend four months in Plainview trying to get a visa into England to do that clinical training. During that time, he stayed with me in a spare bedroom and I get to know him very well. He is a devoted man and passionately believed he has a mission and duty to serve his people in the Gambia.

I am so convinced of that fact that I have spent over $10,000 (ten thousand dollars) of my own money to help with tuition, plane fares, and telephone calls to the Gambia government and the like. My father congregation in Plainview added their own funds, as did the Roman Catholic Archdiocese of Lubbock, Texas.

I understand your concern. I know how many foreign medical students end up staying in the United States. My father is a former president of the Illinois State Medical Society and was at one time on the AMA Education Committee, and I heard a great deal about foreign medical graduates, believe me I also read the recent Newsweek article on the subject.

I know the problem. Alhasan Ceesay is not part of that problem. As a priest, I believe I have some degree of discernment of a person's devotion and I have rarely seen devotion and conviction to a cause as to his commitment to serve the villagers in the Gambia who are so medically under-served.

He has suffered a lot for that end and I stake much of my life savings on it, and countless prayers gone to his way in these past years. Please believe Alhasan Ceesay when he says that his desire is to return to the Gambia and serve his villagers. He is telling the truth.

His time is short to take the necessary licensing exams in the United States. He needs a visa if he is to do internship here. I have little money of my own to send him for plane fares to Barbados or the United States and he has absolutely none of his own and is living from hand to mouth. His future is very much in your hands. Please do not hesitate to call: home 403-553-2412, Church 403-462-2057. Thank you

Sincerely

The Rev. Mark D. Meyer

Mark further wrote to his congressman, Honourable Doug Berreuter, who in turn sent the following appeal on my behalf to the US Ambassador G. Philip Hughes in Barbados, West Indies. It read,

Congress of the United States
House of Representatives
Washington, D.C. 20515
April 2, 1992

The Honorable G. Philip Hughes
Ambassador
U.S. embassy
Barbados, (PPT. Miami, Florida 34054)

Dear Mr. Ambassador,

This is a request for your service in behalf of my constituent, the reverend Mar. D. Meyer who has befriended Alhasan Ceesay, a young man from the Gambia. Alhasan Ceesay is a graduate of the American university of the Caribbean in Montserrat, West Indies.

He is training to be a doctor and has completed his clinical work at Colchester General Hospital in England. Alhasan must now do a year's internship here in the United States to complete his licensing training before returning to the work in the Gambia villages.

I have been advised that his request for a visa was denied. Therefore, I am now asking that his request be given reconsideration. What he needs at the time is visitor's visa with prospective student designation so that the internship can be completed. He will return to his country to practice medicine with his own people.

We need to be able to assist him in this direction. Should you need to contact this young man he is Alhasan S. Ceesay, C/O Gayle Baumgartner, P. O. Box. 27,

Plymouth, Montserrat, West Indies. I call your kind attention to this request for its most sincere and any help accorded him will be sincerely appreciated. Best wishes.

Doug Berreuter

Member of Congress

Along with this were letters from Lois Leonard, and numerous others, which I packaged with the following, appeal, requesting to be allowed to enter the United States of America.

P.O. Box 27

Plymouth

Montserrat

West Indies

The Counselor

Visa Section

U. S. embassy

Barbados

West Indies

Dear Sir/Madam,

I am a Gambian self-sponsored student from Njawara village. I initially did my undergraduate and graduate studies in the U.S. A. 1967 –1973 before attending the American university of the Caribbean school of Medicine in Montsetrrat, West Indies.

All my previous schooling and recently earned M.D. degree came through the kindness and help of American friends and hard work on my part. I am committed to my people in the villages and do seek your kind considerations to issue me a B2 prospective student visa for me to go and complete my training, i.e. do my internship and residency program in medicine, so that I can be proficient physician serving the Gambia.

Please take my word of honour that I will return to the villages as soon as I complete my residency program in internal medicine. This is my objective in life and I will not fail my people for there is an overwhelming need of proper modern medical service in rural Gambia. I will contribute towards that end in due course.

In brief, the villagers and I appeal for your understanding of our situation and real need for this assistance. We thank you for taking time to reconsider our request and do look forward to seeing you in the Gambia some day.

Again, my obligation to the Gambia is supreme and I will return to serve people as soon as I finish the next phase of my medical training. Go bless and thanks a million for your considerations in this matter.

Yours Sincerely

Dr. Alhasan S. Ceesay

AUC/Gambian Student

It would not be until April 22, 1992 before a sinister reply came from the U. S. ambassador in Barbados addressed to Congressman Doug Berreuter of Nebraska, USA. The fight to and from Barbados had already dented the little money I had left with me. And the silence was like lead over my shoulders for every passing moment spells a tragic loss and waste of time.

Most inhabitants of the island were foraging for food and might or would not just be able to add mine atop of theirs. That stab at the back letter in a memoranda form reads:

Office of the Ambassador

U. S. embassy

Barbados, West Indies

April 22, 1992

To: the Hounorable Doug Berreuter

House of Representatives

2348 Rayburn House

Office building

Washington, D. C.

Dear Mr. Berreuter,

Thank you for your letter of April 2, 1992, concerning the non-immigrant visa application of Dr. Alhasan S. Ceesay, your constituent Rev. Mark Meyer contacted you on behalf of his friend. Dr. Ceesay applied for a non-immigrant visa on March 31, 1992 and was found ineligible for the visa under section 214 (B) of the Immigration and Nationality Act.

This section of the law requires that all applicants for non-immigrant visa be able to determine to the satisfaction of the consular officer that they have social, economic or family ties that would compel them to return to their home after a temporary stay in the United States.

The officer who interviewed Dr. Ceesay was not convinced that Dr. Ceesay has sufficiently strong ties to the Gambia to compel him to return there after a medical internship in the

United States. Dr. Ceesay has just finished two years of clinical training in England and was refused a non-immigrant visa in London under the same section of the law when he applied there before applying to Bridge town.

Dr. Ceesay may reapply for the visa and a different officer will review his case. His application will be given every consideration under United States Immigration law. Please do not hesitate to contact me again if I can be of further assistance in this or any matter.

Sincerely

G. Philip Hughes

Ambassador

This reply to congressman Berreuter reached me very late and as such left me dumfounded and angry at the unnecessary cost the strictness and red tape placed on my visa request by the Immigration officer at Barbados.

It would not be until August 1992 before the way was cleared for me to fly back to the UK and eventually the Gambia. Before then I lived on one can of sardine, which lasts three days before I dare open another.

And I stayed at a partly destroyed house with no running water or good toilet. Half of the building was without roofing, as it was among the casualties of hurricane Hugo in 1989. I plaid hide and sick with rats, which wanted some of food and crumbs, I managed to bring from town. I have to stay awake almost all night for fear of being swept away into the Atlantic Ocean.

My former landlord once on a while would bring some fruits or yams for me to boil for food to keep me bone and skin together. Simply, I lived by the skin of my teeth with no hope of help coming from any angle for me.

My U. S. friends were discouraged and I became embarrassed to ask more than I have already done. Mrs. Lois Leonard and Rev. Mark D. Meyer kept plugging in as much as they could humanly afford.

It reached a point I could not walk to town because of lack of energy. I would stop every fifty meters to rest and did the same on my return from town, a distance of three miles from my shanty.

In fact I duped this half-roofed and blown windowless house, as Hotel Gambia and entered in my diary the snakes, various lizards and Iguanas that crises cross my bed room at night or come to take shade during the day. That I did not loose my mind or get bitten by some unknown wild rodent was pure luck.

The nightmare ended abruptly when Rudolf and Sophie Kurt, stepped in the second time and help me with an airfare back to the Gambia. I could not believe it when I boarded Liat flight 596 heading for Antigua and later BA flight to Heathrow International Airport, London.

These few words or phrases sounded musical to my ears. They spell freedom from being marooned and from the inhuman conditions I found myself after graduating from medical school. In the back of my mind was the Gambia political chasm but life I endured had made me inert to fear of dying any longer.

Normally, elation follows events like graduation, wedding or the arrival of the first and subsequent babies, but in my own case hell lost its head and metered the worst punishment it could throw onto a living being. I never at any moment wished for death and had strong believe that God, who had this test for me, will pull me out safely when His time comes.

I was vigilant in my prayers and seek that the Almighty come to my salvation sooner. I hope you have seen why it was necessary for me to prepare you for the curse I faced in Montserrat. It looked unreal but I had endured worse than I am able to say to you.

So faith, or devotion to God and kind people got me out of that mesh, just as happened when I was at the Mariner's Inn in Detroit, Michigan, USA. There too it was very challenging if not difficult and crazy living among former drug addicts, alcoholics, felons, gun turting teenagers and the downtrodden of Cass Corridor in Detroit.

At Heathrow I met a very kind Immigration Officer who was very sympathetic to me. The haggard sight and story he heard almost moved him to tears. He verified my passport and allowed me to proceed and actually my skeletal state and euphoria was so high that it was bound to carry anyone one I came across.

I did not at this time cared whether or what the Gambia might say or do to me. All I wanted to close that history and chapter of my life by either resting eternally with my maker or serving the Gambia. The officer and I joked and laughed through the time I was before him.

It was big and stark difference between my experiences with my good U.S. visa officer at Bridge Town, Barbados, West Indies. I contacted the Gambia Embassy and had the voice of a long time friend, Mr. Bai Ousman Secka, and he came to my rescue and lodged me for forty-eight hours I had before my next flight to the Gambia via Paris, France. Secka took me to stay with him at 35 The Avenue, Kilburn, London NW6 7NR.

Here all my hidden fears were wiped out for I met with lots of Gambians who assured me that tranquility and civility had returned to my beloved home, the Gambia. There were no more witch hunting and that the Senegalese troops have disband and gone home for good. With my confidence rejuvenated about the Gambia,

I was happy lad that boarded Air Sabina flight from Heathrow, via Brussels and to one of the best homes on earth, the smiling coast of the Gambia. Flying over Senegal gave me so much lift and euphoria that made me very eager to meet my family. By the way my father died while I was in Montserrat. I had lost one of the dearest and best of all fathers. Mother on the other was very poorly health wise.

My arrival's dramatic effect on her gained extensive recovery even though her failing heart would not bounce to health. She was in her nineties and very frail. Legend and luck had it that I landed in the Gambia August 9, 1992 not the least scared of anything going wrong.

I was shocked by the dry state of affairs, especially the weather and dust that seem to envelope everything it comes across.

I later learnt it was the Desert that is causing such havoc.

I encountered no problems at the Airport or with the security and two of best friends Latif Sanyand and Kering Marenah were there to pick me up from the Airport. This gave me confidence that the political problems were then over for my friends and perhaps me.

All said and done my return surprised many except my sister Binta Ceesay who was expecting me more than a month ago. She joke saying, "I dreamt of meeting you at Njawara. I was certain of your return in one piece."

That is my lovely sister Binta Ceesay for you. She loves to lighten people's hearts. Everyone was eager to find out what happened to me and how everyone copped during the challenges. The next day it was agreed that that I stay at uncle Sherif A. Sey's place at Fagi Kunda until we know the direction and development that may follow my return. I stayed at uncle Sey's for six months.

While at Fagi Kunda alhaj Kebba Sanneh and his wife, Matida Sanneh, surpassed all friends in making sure that my resettlement was bearable. I met the rest of my family, relatives and friends at different villages in the Badibous. I visited relatives at Njaba Kunda, mother's home village, Saba and finally Njawara, my home village. I found Njawara turned into a ghost town.

All the familiar shops and businesses were either closed or moved to either Banjul or Farafenye village, and other new trading centers which surfaced after independence. The village was dead and in need of a socio-economic spark to rejuvenate it back to her golden good old days. I felt at lost and sad being in Njawara without my father and to see my home village as dead as I found her.

Most of the youth moved to where they can get jobs or hoped to pick up one. Some became teachers while others tried their luck at other vocations. The population of a once thriving three thousand or more inhabitants has now dwindled to no more than 800 residents. The cattle and sheep looked hungrier than I ever known and again the dust seems relentless.

Even the old colonial roads were abandoned for new dirty potholed once leading to dying hamlets. Despite these horrors, I was very pleased being home once more in my life. Foe once there were familiar cheers and laughter I can relate to and not feel alienated.

My elder brother, Dudou Ceesay and I had a long chat about everything ranging from the last days of dad to current state of affairs of the family and our younger siblings who relocated to the Kombo area by the Gambia's Atlantic coast.

I was taken back and pretty ashamed of the way our compound had ran down through the years. It shadows our pride and for what resources existed if everyone cooperated. I was relived about how much he knew about my sufferings persistent determination to bring joy not only to the family but also to all those we can charitably touch.

My poverty stricken life made me very depressed but I bounced back quickly and started implementing one my promises I made to myself and for my people. I returned to Banjul to recuperate and plan my future in the Gambia. My wife was at her home in Kindia, Guinea Conakry, at this juncture and was aware of my return but we had agreed to test the waters first before calling her to the Gambia and having to let her loose again.

It would be December before I ventured to the villages. This time, I went there with a mission in mind for them. I started at my village and later many others. My message was simply to start doing something that will not only unite us but would be beneficial to generations to come.

I made it very clear that the going would be worst than climbing a slippery mountain with bare hands and very little food to take along, but the summit holds a great reward for all concerned. I suggested need to create some form of self-help village health organization to cater for our sick and needy.

Even though I made sure it was known that projects like these take time and hard work and perseverance from all of us and worse some of us may not live long to reap its fruits. Even where that happens or turns out to be our fate we should be happy that we stood and did something for the next generation Gambians.

The villagers were more than enthused and right away Torro Bahen village donated land between Torro and Njawara for the prospective medical center project. This then was christened as Manding Medical Centre, to be located at Njawara, Lower Badibou, North Bank Division, the Gambia, West Africa.

I followed this with monthly health field trips at which nearly 1500 sick villages attend the secessions. We had our meeting at health centers were with help of volunteer doctors we treat the sick, give health education, talk about sexually transmitted diseases,

Aids and guidance for family planning along with antenatal and postnatal advises to would be mother and mothers. I did this until September 1993 before taking up a job as a house officer at the Royal Victoria hospital (RVII) Banjul, the only referral hospital in the Gambia at the time.

The RVH currently caters for 350 patients. I was delighted resuming duty at the RVH as one of the physicians serving my motherland. Ninety percent of the nursing staff was new to me as most of my classmate and those that followed had either gone to higher paying jobs or retired and opened their own mini-pharmacies.

Colonial discipline I left in our nursing day had gone with its master and now the changes make one wonder whether that noble commitment we had in becoming nurses had not melted away because of salary interests and the political era. Time has certainly changed. My wife and daughter rejoined me in the Gambia by May 1993 for the first time since they left me in London.

We moved to a new rental apartment in Bundung Mauritania, a suburb of Sere Kunda. I had to change my monthly trips to the villages to a bimonthly field trips because of my job commitment at the Royal Victoria Hospital and because the cost to me.

My salary at the RVH was an insulting meager D1567 (One thousand five hundred and sixty seven dalasis) on integrated grade 8 scales. Whatever that meant, it was not sufficient to keep a dog alive more over the extended family that doctors encounter in the Gambia.

I enjoyed my work at the RVH despite the ranges and insults that followed. I plan my travels to these field trips for the benefit of al Gambians. Meanwhile, I was able to register the organization Manding Medical Centre and called attention of the International charities to the establishment of the center at Njawara village, the Gambia and our need for assistance to fulfill our dream of providing modern medical aid to the villagers.

Manding Medical Centre is now a registered charity in England and Wales at Colchester, Essex County, UK under the name of "Friends of Manding Charitable Trust" with charity number 1088136 effective since August 21, 2001. Also Alpena City in Michigan, USA, under leadership of Dr. Avery Aten have spearheaded and established the Alpena Friends of Manding Charitable

Trust, Michigan, USA; since May 2005 after the Alpena Community College's leadership class' visit of the center in same year.

Mrs. Fatou Koma-Ceesay, Oldham, Manchester UK 2017

Mrs. Mariam Bah, Hassan Bah and their children, London

Chapter 13
Medical Officer RVH, The Gambia

There was no fanfare welcoming me back to the Royal Victoria Hospital (RVH) were I started putting into gear my medical dreams and ambition of providing much needed quality medical service to the villager. I resigned from the Medical and Health Services, while a Dresser Dispenser, in 1967 to travel to the United States and study for a medical degree with which to serve the Gambia and man.

My re-entry to the Medical and Health Services, per say RVH, coincided with turbulence at the helm of the RVH. Dr. Hassan Jange had just tendered his resignation as chief executive of the hospital and the new tsar was one Dr. Ogbaselasse, a WHO technical assistance to the Gambia for many years. My employment was left to him and like all new brooms Dr. Ogba Selaisse swept well and clean. He left no stones untouched regarding my qualifications and background.

Dr. Ogba Selaisse contacted my university and requested my transcripts sent directly to him. It took two months of investigation before he called me in for an interview. At the interview he made it clear that he could only start me as a House Officer for one year and that I most do a three months rotation in Pediatrics, surgery, medicine and Obstetrics and Gynecology under consultant supervision. My monthly salary was fixed at grade 8 level with a starting point of an insulting meager, if not measly D1567 per month on the integrated scale.

This amounts to $156.70 us dollars or poultry seventy-five pounds sterling a month. My colleagues started at grade 9 upward but Chief Executive Ogba Selaissse deemed it proper to set mine at grade 8 integrated scaling. Family and loyal friends begged me to take the offer for the time being and so this salary disparity continued on from September 1993 to October 1998. I agreed to the rotation schedule but had to point out the fact that there existed a limited number of consultants at the RVH units that I am supposed to do my internship.

Ogba was not happy with my observations. All doctors of my level were sent to teaching hospital in Ghana, Nigeria or Sera Leone but I was made to do my internship at the RVH with scant consultants to supervise me. Ogba left my file pending because of I knew I was not treated right to start with.

I had to take the bull by the horns when my starting date dragged on and on beyond two calendar months by appealing the case directly to the Permanent Secretary and Minister of Health for a ruling on the matter. In the interim the America University of the Caribbean faxed the following to Dr. Ogba Selaisse, Chef Executive of the Royal Victoria Hospital.

Dr. G. Ogbaselasse

Chief Executive, RVH

Banjul, The Gambia

Dr. Alhasan S. Ceesay is a graduate of the American university of the Caribbean School of Medicine. Most of our graduates practice medicine in the United States. Our graduates must earn the Education Commission for Foreign

Medical Graduates (ECFMG) certification. To earn ECFMG certification the graduate must pass step 1 and 2 of the United States Medical Licensing examination (USMLE) and an English language proficiency test. Most states in addition would require additional postgraduate training in specific area (residency) for an unrestricted License. I hope this information is beneficial to you.

Sincerely

Robert J. Chertok, PhD

Dean of Medical Sciences

Mrs. Fatou Koma-Ceesay, Brusubi, Gambia 2014

This information help to speed up the processing for it was also copied to the Ministry of Health. Hence an angry chief executive called me the following Monday and asked start rotations under watchful eyes of Dr. Ayo Palmer, head of the Pediatrics unit. Ogba added a stern warning to me while I was just on my way out of his office. He in an angry tone said, "You most not forget the protocol in the medical field.

I am the head of this hospital and not some politician beyond the RVH fence." With my letter in hand, I smiled at it all and asked if he dare make such remarks before the very politicians who have been his umbrella in the Gambia. We eventually developed mutual respect for each other but never turned to be, as the saying goes, one's beer drinking friends.Ogba never liked his authority challenged and was one that had very little trust for power zealous folks.

Hence my presence some time ruffles his feathers because of question I asked and seeking intervention where I felt some foot-dragging was going on in the matter. Another branch assisting the chief executive was the Medical Advisory Committee (MAC).

This comprised of heads of units of the hospital and it helped in the maintaining of proficiency, ethics, and standard of medical practice in the units. I met with the MAC after chief executive Ogbaselaissse sent the following letter to me.

Hospital Management Board
Royal Victoria Hospital
Banjul, The Gambia
May 11, 1993

Ref: RVH/21/vol.v

Dr. A. S. Ceesay
5B Ingram Street
Banjul, The Gambia

I am pleased to inform you that the Hospital Management Board has, in principle, approved your appointment as House Officer in the Royal Victoria Hospital. Please note that your appointment is subject to successful internship with the Hospital Advisory Committee (MAC) and the appointment Committee. You are advised to report to Dr. Oldfield, Chairman of MAC for further information and action.

Sincerely

Dr. C. Ogbaselaisse
Chief Executive, RVH
Cc: Permanent Secretary, MOH
Chairman: HMB, Chairman: MAC
File & R/file

Dr. Oldfield, Chairman of MAC sent this follow up after the committee reviewed my file forwarded to it by the CEO of the hospital.

Hospital Management Board
Royal Victoria Hospital
Banjul, The Gambia
June 15, 1993

Ref: RVH21/vol.v

Dr. A. S. Ceesay
5B Ingram Street
Banjul, The Gambia

Dear Dr. Ceesay,

RE: Provisional Registration with the Medical and Dental Council

Further to my letter Ref: RVH21/vol.v May 10, 1993 the Medical Advisory Committee has scrutinized your application for internship. You are required to be provisionally registered with the Medical and Dental Council. Your internship will commence as soon as you present a certificate of provisional registration.

Sincerely

Dr. F. S. J. Oldfield
Ag. Chief executive

Cc: file & R/file
Chairman: MAC

A memo was released to the various heads of units, Registrars Gambia Medical and Dental Council (GMDC) and copied to me.

Hospital Management Board
RVH, Banjul
The Gambia
September 9, 1993

Ref: RVH21/vol.v

Registrar
GMDC
PMB 137
Banjul, The Gambia

Sir,

The above doctor will do a supervised rotating house job three months each in Pediatrics, surgery, medicine, Obstetrics, and Gynaecology.

Grateful if Council can consider him for provisional registration.

Yours Faithfully

Dr. G. Ogbaselaisse, FROG

Chief Executive
Cc: Permanent Secretary, MOH
Chairman, HMB
Dr. Alhasan Ceesay, File & R/file

The Gambia Medical and Dental Council is an autonomous body of doctors who by act of Parliament is authorized to verify qualifications of new doctors wishing to practice in the Gambia. The Accreditation Committee of the GMDC interviewed me and the following was sent in response to the chief executive's September 9, 1993 request.

The Gambia Medical and Dental Council
Kanifing
P. O. Box 137
Banjul, The Gambia
October 5, 1993

The Chief Executive
Hospital Management Board
Royal Victoria hospital
Banjul, The Gambia

Dear Sir,

Ref: Provisional registration for Dr. Alhasan Ceesay

Reference is invited to your letter RVH21/vol.v on the above subject.

The provisional registration is granted on the terms of your letter. Dr. Alhasan Ceesay had been requested to formally apply for provisional registration. This does not preclude his commencing the rotation house jobs.

Yours Faithfully

Mr. Mbye Faal (MBBS FROG, FWACS)

Registrar

My official appointment to the Medical and Health services of the Gambia would not surface until October 26, 1993, almost five months from the first day I applied for a job at the RVH. It takes less than a week to process application from other doctors but for me it dragged on endlessly for five solid months.

Here is the full text of my reunification with the Royal Victoria Hospital visa avis the Medical and Health Services of the Gambia. It is dream come true indeed.

Hospital Management Board

Royal Victoria Hospital

Banjul, The Gambia

October 26, 1993

Ref: RVH/Board/3/vol.11

Dr. Alhasan S. Ceesay

Bundung, Serekunda

The Gambia, West Africa

Dear Dr. Ceesay,

APPOINTMENT

I am pleased to offer temporal appointment as House Officer with effect from the first of September 1993 for a period of one (1) year.

Your Salary will be at the rate of D18, 768.00 (Eighteen thousand seven hundred and sixty-eight dalasis) per annum (i.e. D1564 per month) of the integrated pay scale.

You will be required to conform to the General orders regulations, Financial Instructions and Public Service Commission regulations in so far as they are applicable to you. You will be entitled to 22 working days leave for every completed twelve months of service.

Please indicate in writing whether you will accept this appointment on the above terms. This appointment is terminable either by the Hospital Management Board or you upon giving a written notice of one month or payment of a month's salary in lieu of written notice.

Yours Sincerely

Dr. G. Ogbaselailesse

Chief Executive, RVH

Cc: Permanent Secretary MOH
  Permanent Secretary PMO
  Chairman: HMB
  Accountant General
  Auditor General
  Principal Accountant
  Personal file & R/file

As indicated earlier on in the chapter I reluctantly accepted the above insult duped as appointment because of pressure from family, close friends and my love for the Gambia.

The salary would not feed a rat much more help me get a compound to raise a family.

Having made up my mind to serve my people I worked long and hard hours. I persevered more than any of my colleagues at the RVH; this earned me coveted respect within the administration and the staff. if nothing else. The MAC continued managing my Internship and sent the following:

Medical advisory Committee
Royal Victoria Hospital
Banjul, The Gambia

Ref: HLS/MAC/1.94

Dr. Alhasan Ceesay

RE: Posting to Surgical Unit

As part of your rotation of duties in fulfillment of registration for full professional registration, you are being posted to the surgical unit for six months with effect from August 1, 1994. You will of course be assessed in the usual manner.

Sincerely

Dr. F. S. J. Oldfield

Chairman: MAC

Cc: Consultant Surgeon I/C
Consultant Obstetrics & Gynecology
Chief Executive, File

The Chief Executive wrote:
Hospital Management Board
Royal Victoria Hospital
Banjul, The Gambia
August 1, 1993

Dear Sir,

Re: Dr. Alhasan S. Ceesay

Further to our discussion (Ogba/AgbakwuruI on the above this is to confirm that Dr. A. Ceesay would be deployed to the surgical unit under your supervision for his house job with effect from 1/8/94 for a period of six months. You are kindly requested to submit progress report to this office at the end of three months.

Yours Sincerely
Dr. G. Ogbaselaisse, FROG
Chief Executive, RVH
Cc: Dr. Azadeh, OBS & Gyne unit
Dr. Alhasan Ceesay, File & R/file

Dr. Agbakwuru left for Nigeria and was replaced by Dr. U. Jones who at the end of my surgical rotation sent the following report about my performance in the unit.

Hospital Management Board
Department of Surgery
Royal Victoria Hospital
Banjul, The Gambia

The Chairman
Medical Advisory Committee
Royal Victoria Hospital
Banjul, The Gambia
June 14, 1995

RE: Surgical Internship

Dr. Alhasan S. Ceesay

I write to affirm that Dr. Ceesay completed an internship in the General surgery between August 19994 and February 1995.

He was punctual to duty and his performance was satisfactory. He was a good colleague to have in this unit, with good relations with the staff and patients alike. His standard was satisfactory.

Sincerely

Dr. U. O. E. Jones

Head of Unit
Cc: Chief Executive, RVH
File, & R/file

Dr. G. Ogbaselasse resigned his CEO post early 1996 and was replaced by Ansuman Dampha, as Chief Executive of the RVH. Mr. Dampha got on my case immediately in an attempt or effort to restore the long and dragging affair about my being fully registered with the GMDC. He contacted the registrar Mr. Mbye Faal as follows.

Hospital Management Board
Royal Victoria Hospital
Banjul, The Gambia
May 3, 1996

Ref: HMB/PF

Dr. Mbye Faal, Registrar
Gambia Medical and Dental Council
2 Radio Gambia Road
PMB 137
Banjul, The Gambia

Dear Sir,

RE: Application for full Registration

I forward herewith for your consideration application from Dr. Alhasan Ceesay for full registration with the Gambia Medical and Dental Council (GMDC).

Supporting documents are also attached.

Yours Faithfully

Ousman Dampha

Chief Executive, RVH

Cc: Dr. Alhasan Ceesay

File & R/file

Dr. Mbye Faal, Registrar for the GMDC insisted on having more appraisal report sent before he would proceed. He did not like the format of the ones presented in my behalf.

In a nutshell this was one of many ways this Registrar would forestall my registration for years to come. Nonetheless we persevered and sent him different forms designed by his office.

Hospital Management Board

RVH, Banjul

The Gambia

June 11, 1996

Ref: RVH/21/vol.v

The Registrar Gambia Medical and Dental Council

RE: Submission of application report on Dr. Alhasan Ceesay's rotation

Please you will find copies of appraisal report from various heads of units of the Royal Victoria Hospital about Dr. Alhasan ceesay's performance during his rotation at these units.

We forward these for consideration by you for full registration with the GMDC.

Yours Faithfully

Ousman Dampha

Chief Executive, RVH

Cc: Dr. Alhasan Ceesay

File & R/file

The delays went on until September 1996 when I decided that enough was enough and I wrote the following reminder to Dr. Mbye Faal alias Jack Faal and copied it to various officials including the Director of Health Services.

Royal Victoria Hospital
Banjul, The Gambia
September 5, 1996

Dr. Mbye Faal, Registrar
GMDC, PMB 137
Kanifing, The Gambia

RE: reminder regarding my application for professional registration with the GMDC

Dear Dr. Mbye Faal,

This is to remind and call attention that my application remains pending despite my having completed the assigned rotations and having submitted all relevant documentation for you to kindly consider a year ago.

I would be most grateful if you would kindly deliberate on my application for professional registration. I am anxiously awaiting your kind considerations. I now have waited for more than a year. Thanks

Yours Sincerely

Dr. Alhasan S. Ceesay, MD

Cc: Chief Executive RVH

Director of Health Services

Two weeks later Mr. Ousman Dampha, CEO of the RVH following reminder to the GMDC's registrar with his own.

Mr. Mbye Faal's refusal to act on my application was frustrating both the administration and me.

The Chief Executive of RVH again sent the Council a reminder but instead he was replied by a Mrs. M.C. Jallow on behalf of the Director of Medical and Health Services.

Republic of the Gambia
Ministry of Health
The quadrangle
Banjul, The Gambia
September 16, 1996

HP/89/01/(77)
The Chief Executive
RVH, Banjul
The Gambia

RE: Reminder regarding my application for Professional Registration

Please find attached a photocopy reminder of an application for professional registration from Dr. Alhasan S. Ceesay, MD for your attention.

Kindly take appropriate action on this application as soon as possible.

Your Faithfully

Mrs. M. C. Jallow

For Director of Health Services

Again the CEO of hospital sent another reminder to Mr. Mbye Faal, alias Jack Faal, in other to seek appropriate action from Council on my behalf.

Hospital management Board

RVH, Independence Drive,

Banjul, The Gambia

September 8, 1996

Ref: RVH/21/vol.1

The Registrar

GMDC, Kanifing

PMB 137

The Gambia

RE: Reminder for the professional Registration of Dr. Alhasan Ceesay

I wrote series of letters with regards to the registration of DR. Alhasan Ceesay with photocopies of all relevant documents and appraisals reports from the various units in the Royal Victoria Hospital (RVH) but still no action has been taken.

The Hospital Management Board would like your office to kindly take the appropriate action as soon as possible.

Yours Faithfully

Ousman Dampha

Chief Executive, RVH

Cc: Director of Medical Services

Management Advisory committee

Dr. Alhasan Sisawo Ceesay, MD

Hospital Administration

Chairman, HMB

Dr. Alhasan Ceesay

The CEO received, as usual, no response from Mr. Mbye Fall, alias Jack Faal, Registrar. It was now clear to me that my case was being bandied and deliberately left pending by none other than Mr. Mbye Faal, alias Jack Faal.

The delay and refusal to give any tangible reasons for the GMDC's indecision about my case left no doubts in my mind that Mr. Mbye Faal, alias Jack Faal would play God with me until when it suits him or until he discovers that he was far from being a deity and that he cannot break my spirit, will, and determination to serve the Gambia.

Nonetheless he was reminded about the need to act urgently on my request by Ousman Dampha, CEO at the Royal Victoria Hospital, Banjul.

RVH, Banjul
The Gambia
October 17, 1996

The Registrar
GMDC, PMB 137
Kanifing, The Gambia
RE: Registration of Dr. Alhasan Ceesay

I am sending a reminder for the registration of Dr. Alhasan Ceesay. If you can remember some time ago the Hospital Management Board had written to your office with copies of internship appraisal from unit heads to back up Dr. Ceesay's registration, which were submitted to your office. Thank you for your usual cooperation.

Yours Faithfully

Ousmab Dampha

Chief Executive, RVH

cc: Management Adviser

Hospital Administrator

Chairman: HMB

Dr. Alhasan Ceesay

File & R/file

Dr. Faal, alias Jack Faal, disregarded his previous appraisal forms and made new ones himself and asked that evaluations be submitted again on my behalf. This was done, with everyone wondering if I had wronged the Registrar inadvertently. I told all concerned that I have no personal knowledge of having offended or said anything that should ruffle his feathers or turn him so callus towards me.

I made it very clear that I shall continue to pursue what were my due, if not my rights, to whatever reasonable ends it may lead. There were lots of sympathizers and people who believed that the Registrar was wrong in dragging my registration for as long as he did. The new forms, I duped Mbye Faal registration forms, were dully signed and sent to Dr. Mbye faal along with a letter from Chief Executive Ousman Dampha:

Ref: RVH/21/vol.v, dated November 8, 1996 in which he categorically stated, "Here are enclosed copies of comments for the full registration of Dr. Alhasan Ceesay. I do support the recommendation from the heads of units." Well dear reader, I hope you can make sense out of the above nightmarish jigsaw or puzzle.

Mr. Mbye Faal continued to wield his seal of power over poor fledgling medical doctor Alhasan Ceesay. He refusal to act while hiding behind elusive authority is laid bare by the above sequence of event and exchange or the one way traffic of support correspondence from the Royal Victoria staff and its Chief Executive.

It was slap on the face of the system and very discouraging as I later found out that all Banjul born returning doctors from Russia were sent to teaching hospital in Nigeria or Ghana and even Sera Leone while I was be subjected to the whims and caprices of the registrar of the GMDC.

Mr. Mbye may become the tsar of doctoring in the Gambia but with such exercise of power as he has taken in my case it was certain he would not be in the post forever and not for longer than he has. He will either retire or be forced out by lawful means in due course. If I were in his shoe, I would write a letter of support for him and plead with the visa consular to reconsider issuing B2 prospective student status to allow my doing the internship and residency program as was scheduled.

No instead I was used to be pond for power tug of war that I had nothing to do. I doubt if he ever saw it that I was a Gambian like him needing his guidance. Why on earth was this man putting me through the grill and unnecessary roadblocks on my way?

Did he fail to realize that God is the only ultimate and everlasting power in this life and after it? My measly salary of D1564, in other words an equivalence of seventy-five pounds sterling per month, was woefully inadequate and not able to sustain my family's need.

I have three daughters in school and poverty is depriving them the normal things and privileges their peer children are enjoying. Hence, I decided to try the big guns to bring relief to my situation and my family to allow me provides better footing for my children, if not my sanity. Here is a drowning man trying to cling onto straw floating towards him.

Bundung Mauritania
Serekunda
The Gambia
December 16, 1996

The Chief Executive
Royal Victoria Hospital
Banjul, The Gambia

Dear Chief Executive,

I would like to call attention that my House Officer Job started September 9, 1993 and end September 1994. However, I have since the completion of my house rotations been left on grade 8, receiving D1564 per month of the integrated pay scale.

The only other emoluments include transport fee or allowance of D150 per month and D100 per month call allowance.

On the other hand my colleagues are paid a total of D5246.67 per month as follows.

Salary	D1979.00 per month
Responsibility allowance	D1250.00 per month
On call allowance	D100.00 per month
Car allowance	D400.00 per month
Residential allowance	D200.00 per month
None Practice allowance	D416.00 per month

Total payment per month to my colleagues equals D5246.76 (five thousand two hundred and forty-six Dalasis and 67 Butus per month) While I earned a mare D2750.00 per month.

I am hereby submitting this claim covering a period of two years, i.e. from 1994 t0 1996 inclusive at which time I have been kept at grade 8 scale of D1564 per month. Hence the difference in wages and allowances is D2492.67 per month which multiplied by 24 months will amount to D59, 624.04 C fifty-nine thousand six hundred and twenty-four Dalasis and 4 Butus) due me to date.

Again, banking on your good judgment and sense of fair play I look forward to a speedy, likewise a positive resolution of the above request. Thank you for being kind and for reviewing the above matter. I anxiously await your response.

Yours Sincerely

Dr. Alhasan S. Ceesay, MD

Cc: permanent secretary, MOH

Director of Health Services

Chairman, HMB

Accountant General

Auditor General

Secretary Public Service Commission

Management adviser

I was not sure what got to Chief Executive Mr. Ousman dampha of the RVH but his letter to me was no longer someone I had hoped would stand his grounds and do what was dully right for the Gambia. Here, in his cold feet, is what he thought was appropriate to get my case off his back. I duped it my 1996 Christmas card.

Hospital Management Board

Royal Victoria Hospital
Banjul, The Gambia
December 24, 1996

Ref: HMB/PF/091

Dr. Alhasan S. Ceesay
House Officer
Thro, Head of Medical Unit
RVH, Banjul, The Gambia

Dear Dr. Ceesay,

I refer to your letter dated December 16, 1996 relating to the above-mentioned subject and to inform you with regret, that the Hospital Management Board cannot entertain your claim in view of the fact that you are still a House Officer on grade 8.

I am to inform you further that until such time that you obtained full registration with the Gambia Medical and Dental Council and promoted to the post of Medical Officer Grade 9, you will continue to receive your present salary and allowances.

Yours Faithfully
Ousman Dampha
Cc: Permanent Secretary, MOH
Permanent Secretary, PMO

Director of Health Services
Accountant General
Auditor General
Secretary, PSC
Management Adviser, HMB
Hospital Administrator
Personal file & R/file

Here is another in the saga to laugh, cry or wonder about. I would be until March 1997 when the Registrar of the GMDC, Mr. Mbye Faal, ventured to break his traditional silence in my case by finally breaking the lull from his end and throwing out the following insult, as usual of his attitude towards my registration request. It is a shame that such cruel raw power would be exercised for no earthly dignified reasons. So here if is letter and vomit he sent to the chief executive, RVH.

The Gambia Medical and Dental Council
PMB 137
Banjul, The Gambia
March 4, 1997

Mr. Ousman Dampha
Chief Executive
Royal Victoria Hospital
Banjul, The Gambia
Dear Sir,

RE: Registration of Dr. Alhasan Ceesay

Reference is invited to your letter Ref. RVH/21/vol.v of November 8, 1996 on the above subject. I am to draw your attention that the recommendations from the Heads of Units that have your support were incomplete in all cases as indicated on the certificate that are now being returned.

The certificates from Obstetrics & gynecology units, please note that there is no entry in the Registry of the Medical and Dental Practitioners in the name of Dr. B.S. Camara, consequently this individual cannot sign a pre-registration certificate. Enclosed are new forms of certificate completion of apprenticeship, which you can now use in place of the old ones, which are no longer valid.

Yours faithfully

Kinay Drammeh

Administrative Secretary

As you by now noticed nothing new comes from Mbye Faal, alias Jack Faal. He is not the leader who encourages his juniors nor does he really care how much my innocent children and Gambia were affected by his foot dragging callous act.

Let me magnify this statement by just saying that a happy doctor is great asset to his patients as he or she would be able to give more of their time to the practice of medicine than groping for crumbs to keep their families fed. No wonder, most of our professionals, especially doctors are staying abroad. At times one tends to believe that self-interest kept them away from the downtrodden poor of their countries.

I now can see why some choose to stay rather than go through this shameless and doggy dog treatment day after day, In August 1997 we received another joke from the Administrative Secretary, GMDC; adding insult to injury. **Notice that this one-man show tends to show its toothless dragonhead with definite loss of** memory. The Secretary's last letter was four months ago to a matter as urgent as had been my case.

Again, I vowed to keep fighting for my rights no matter how long or how much foot dragging Mr. Faal may choose to do regarding my registration. Let me remind him that the darkest tunnel has light at the end of it. I just wished him well and he can continue enjoying his folly. I will serve God and work for the Gambia. My family and country are my concern, not personalities.

The Gambia Medical Dental Council
PMB 137, Banjul, The Gambia
August 25, 1997

The acting Chief Executive
Royal Victoria Hospital
Banjul, The Gambia

Dear Sir,

RE: Registration of Dr. Alhasan Ceesay

Thank you for your letter Ref: HMB/PF/091

Dated June 1997

Please note that section 2b of the certificate of Apprenticeship in Internal medicine reads, Save with the limits herein specified work under supervision." The Accreditation and Registration Committee (ARC) accordingly recommend that Dr. Alhasan Ceesay do extra four (4) calendar months at the RVH department of Internal Medicine with the current head of the said department.

Following the satisfactory completion of the full registration status may be granted to Dr. Ceesay. Kindly let us know the name of the current head of Internal Medicine, so as to address a letter directly to him.

Yours faithfully

Kinay Drammeh

Administrative Secretary

This sort of reply not only delayed my registration but tantamount to a stab on the backs of the head of units at the RVH, the MAC and the administration of the hospital. Hence, the current head of unit at the Internal Medicine department RVH was urged by well-intentioned members of the staff, to write letting the Registrar reconsider this unnecessary request imposed on me.

It would now be complete three years since completing my apprenticeship and he still continues to spew out poison and disgust onto my face. Anyhow, here is the letter from then head of Internal Medicine at the RVH.

Department of Internal Medicine

Royal Victoria hospital

Banjul, the Gambia

September 22, 1997

The Registrar

Gambia Medical and Dental council

Kanifding, The Gambia

Dear Registrar,

We are in receipt of your letter dated August 25, 1997 concerning Dr. Alhasan S. Ceesay's need to do another extra 4 months internship at the Department of internal medicine. Having worked with Dr. Ceesay since May 1996 to the present time September 22, 1997 I came to know him and his abilities as a doctor. He is capable and a very confident doctor.

I find him proficient and a hard worker. I hence, recommend him to you for your kind consideration and for full registration. I here by enclosed a completed form from May 1996, the time I met him at the Medical unit to September 22, 1997. Thank you very much for any assistance given in behalf of this dedicated and capable Gambian doctor. Regards

Yours Sincerely

Dr. Jimenez Osvaldo/ Consultant

Head of Medical Unit
Cc; Chief Executive, RVH
Chairman HMB
File & R/file

Again, this was met with the usual silence or refusal to respond to letters concerning me. At this juncture of my Another Chief Executive, Dr. Mariatou Jallow, came to the helm of the Royal Victoria Hospital.

I was urged to do the 4 extra months on internship at the department of internal medicine as recommended by the registrar to get him off my back and bring this ugly chapter of my life to close. We all held our breath and plied through the bitter four months of anguish and callous injustice to my children and family.

So I did the rotation with malice but with much more zeal to work harder for the good of my patients and the Gambia. I worked long hours and at times volunteered to take emergency night calls for a sick colleague or to make life easier for one that had an unexpected urgent need to take care of important family business in the interior or as far as in neighboring Senegal. The four months Apprenticeship that were supposed to be trying flew past so quickly by the time anyone noticed.

We again filled evaluation appraisal form or certificate of completion of Apprenticeship form, as the registrar Mbye Faal calls his new invention. I stopped anyone urging me or volunteering to have a face-to-face chat with the registrar in other to soften him.

I felt that no human being of good intent would treat a beast or a dog in manner I already endured from the hands of this person that calls himself a Gambian. No, no! I will not demean myself for such a person. He does not deserve the blessing of anyone trying to reason with him. Let him keep at his high pedestal and I will be with the common man who appreciates being human.

Let me assure him that he has only waxwings and they do melt at unexpected heights and temperature making the fall very sudden and devastating if the person survives the encounter. I am certain he will come down to us earthlings one fine day. I use to tell my wife and family when their spirits seemed to be broken because of this senseless saga, to humbly submit to the Almighty God's will for me.

The new Chief Executive, Dr. Mariatou Jallow, passed the completed appraisal forms from the heads of unit at the department Internal Medicine RVH, to the Registrar, as requested, on January 6, 1998. You bet your bottom dollar the registrar did not care to reply up to today. Dr. Jallow sent the appraisal with the following covering letter.

Hospital Management Board
Royal Victoria Hospital
Banjul, The Gambia
January 6, 1998

Ref: HMB/PF/(091)

Att: kinnay Drammeh, Administrative secretary

The Registrar
Gambia Medical and Dental Council
2 Radio Gambia Road
Mile 7, Bakau, The Gambia

RE: registration of Dr. Alhasan Ceesay

Thank you for your letter dated August 25, 1997 in connection with the above caption. Please find attached certificate of completion of apprenticeship in the medical unit covering period August to December (4 months). Dr. Ceesay is currently still in the Medical Unit. The head of Medical unit is Dr. Jimenez Osvaldo.

Yours Sincerely

Dr. Mariatou Jallow

Chief Executive

It was not until November, 1999, five grueling years after completing my Internship, that a newly appointed revamped and dynamic Hospital Management board, lead by Mr. Kenneth Njie, that light started to shine at the end of the tunnel for me.

These Gambian angels, being convinced that I was not properly treated during the past five years, decided to put their feet down and did the correct thing by promoting me to the post of Medical Officer to stop the starvation and pain inflicted upon my family by this long drawn inhumane saga Mbye Faal's refusal to register me imposed.

Words are aptly inadequate with which to thank and register profound gratitude to them for brining this phase of the saga to an end. Deep appreciation and sincere thanks to the new Hospital Management Board members and especially the Chairman, Mr. Kenneth Njie, the Director of Health Services, the Chief Executive, RVH, and last but not the least Dr. Alieu Gaye, an admirable and respectable man with whom I have worked with at the medical unit on and off for three years.

Though younger than me he had always shown courtesy, willingness to encourage his colleagues and is pleasant to team up with. Alieu, a million thanks for the interest you have in the Gambia and service you are so diligently rendering the Gambian people.

I wished I were endowed with youthful energy you devote to the Gambia. Yes, Alieu, any time you appear in the wards, it brings a spark of joy to my heart for I know you will give the day all you know and to the best of your abilities with due respect and concern for the patients.

Thank you for weathering so much for our people. Be happy that many noticed and are very grateful for your relentless service to our people.

My dear reader, the coveted letter from the management board is thus reproduced for your perusal. I hope, like me, you will be able to let a sigh of relief at the pinnacle of hell the above experience dragged my life.

Hospital Management Board
Royal Victoria Hospital
Banjul, The Gambia
November 22, 1999

Ref: HMB/PF/091/(41)

Dr. Alhasan Ceesay
Medical Officer
Thro Head of Medical Unit
Royal Victoria Hospital
The Gambia

Dear Sir,

RE: Appointment as MEDICAL OFFICER

I am directed by the Hospital Management Board to inform you that approval has affirm in appointing you as Medical Officer, grade 9.1, with effect from October 1, 1999.

You will be paid allowances commensurate to your grade in addition to your salary as Medical Officer accordingly.

By copy of this letter, I am informing the Principal accountant accordingly. Congratulations.

Yours Sincerely

Mrs. Corea: For Chief Executive

Cc: Permanent Secretary, MOH

Permanent Secretary, PMO

Accontant general
Accountant General

Auditor General

Chairman, HMB

Principal Accountant, RVH

File & R/file

It was a courageous act for which history will crown them as one of the highest dedicated board that ever served the RVH. Their stand to right wrong is an admirable yearning in many hearts and it dwarfs the high pedestal our registrar assumes his post.

Needless to say everyone concerned was happy about this outcome and asked me to extend personal gratitude to the board and the entire administration at RVH for having the foresight, decency and moral courage to stand up and do justice to the Gambia and me in the face of the past ceaseless wrong that the refusal to register me inflicted upon me since the completion of my Internship five years ago at the RVH.

The appointment letter did not address the sticky point or business of compensating me for the five years in which I worked underpaid compared to my colleagues. I will pursue that avenue but for meantime let the elation ride its course until when things are sorted out.

I thanked God many times more than I ever did and now worked even hard for my people. My new income went into clearing old debts incurred over the years to pay for school fees and other necessities to allow my daughters attend school.

I was not able to buy a compound or a car to take my children to school. God has His mysterious ways of solving seemingly incomprehensible problems to human minds. At this juncture matters had gone too long and it would be foolish of me if I did not get my redress. Now I decided to take the bull by horns by taking my case to the nation's second highest authority, vice president and Secretary of State for Health, Social welfare and Women affairs, H.E.

Isatou Njie-Saidy. Doctors do not like being involved with politics but there comes a time and experience in one's life one must take a stand for what is just and rightfully ours. I went before these officials because of sincere conviction that only they can move the registrar into recognizing that he has dragged my case unnecessarily for too long a time. Having gone through all the expected authorities of the RVH, I sent the following appeal requesting arbitration to resolve my Professional registration saga with the GMDC. Some friends were hesitant about the move believing that drawing politicians into the scenery might just be another cause to make the registrar feel big and further prolong my agony by stifling intervention any kind in the case.

I told them that it was Parliament that enacted such power as the registrar wheel and it may just be their onus to step into the arena to make sure that coming Gambian doctors would not have to undergo such experiences as I endured from the registrar's delaying tactics. Armed with confidence of being on the right I told my wife and friends to believe in one God and His name was not "Almighty GMDC Registrar" Here is one of several appeals I made to higher ups.

Department of Medicine
Royal Victoria Hospital
Banjul, The Gambia

February 23, 1998

H. E. Isatou Njie-Saidy
Secretary of State for

Health, Social Welfare
& Women Affairs
The quadrangle
Banjul, The Gambia

Dear Vice President and Secretary of State,

RE: Request consideration of resolving Professional registration raw.

I write calling attention to a dilemma regarding my professional registration with the Gambia Medical and Dental Council that has been unsolved for the past four years. I took up service with the Royal Victoria Hospital in September 1993 as House Officer and was asked to do three months Internship rotation in Pediatrics, Medicine, Surgery, gynecology and Obstetrics as stipulated by the enclosures in this letter.

My registration has been, since hitherto hindered by sequence of unnecessary delays and foot-dragging by the registrar Mbye Faal. My colleagues receive a salary of D5246.67 while I remained on a salary of D2750 since 1994, under grade 8 integrated Scale. Various chief executives of the RVH sent a series of reminders to the Gambia Medical and Dental Council (GMDC) registrar but I am yet to be registered despite having completed my rotation and dully recommended by heads of units at the Royal Victoria hospital since 1994.

The last reminder was sent the GMDC registrar on January 8, 1998. To that reminder the administrative Secretary told us that I would not be registered unless a head of unit at the gynecology department, who signed one of the certificates, registers with the **Gambia Medical and Dental Council.** Now Dr. Jimenez Osvaldo is the current head of unit at the department of Medicine and the only one authorized to sign such evaluations. He has done so as per enclosed. Let me reiterate that both the chairman of the board and chief executives have done all they could within their jurisdiction to resolve my case.

Hence, banking on your good judgment and sense of fair play and as a Gambian, I am appealing for redress of my case to allow me to be registered and as well be compensated for the four years I have been left on grade 8 at not fault of mine. Thank you very much for your kindness as well as for taking time to resolve my case. I am anxiously awaiting your reply.

Yours Sincerely

Dr. Alhasan Sisawo Ceesay, MD

Cc: Permanent Secretary, MOH

Permanent Secretary, PMO

Director of Health Services

Secretary General. PSC

Chairman, HMB

Chief Executive, RVH

Chairman, MAC

Registrar, GMDC

A meeting with Vice President H.E. Isatou Njie-Saidy was arranged for me to discuss my problems her for she double as the Secretary of Health of the Nation. Sure enough she was the right authority to turn to for arbitrate the case when everyone else was unable to move Mbye Fall to unravel the dilemma. The Vice President listened to my woes for a good ten minutes and then told me that although she empathized with my unfortunate case, she was not familiar with the Medical and Dental Council's yard stick for registering doctors. This discovery came to me as a surprise I expect persons appointed to head the health of the nation should be verse in how people are allowed or disallowed from practicing medicine in the Gambia.

She did promise me to have a staff look into the affair She suggested my petitioning the president's Office to help since the Council was under that sector. This to me seemed like throw the buck to another person to do one's dirty job. I thanked her for giving me audience and with laden heart I promised to press forward with the idea of meeting with H. E. President Jammeh to have my case solved.

I wrote to the president but protocol has it that as a civil servant, I need to bring my case before the Secretary General, president's office. I passed through the Secretary of State for presidential affairs who redirected me to the Secretary General's Office were the matter should be handled. There I met, Mr. Tamsir Mbye, a colleague when we were students in America.

Seeing him calmed me down and gave me confidence that perhaps the matter will soon be resolve. Tamsir and got to business after a short reminiscence of the good old days in Washington, D.C. with this light or welcome atmosphere I thought things might not be as horrible as I had braced myself. I gave him a complete rundown or trend of the case and he, in the normal politician's way, promised to do all he could to solve it to satisfaction of all concerned with the case.

Being an in-law to the registrar Tamsir Mbye assured me that there was no need to speak with the president about my case or fiasco he just heard and that he would do all he could to resolve sooner than later. I left his office naively happy because I believed Tamsir Mbye does know how much I struggled in America to get my schooling done. He used to visit with me at my flat.

So there was doubt in my mind that someone like him would take my cause with alacrity and seriousness to bring it amicable resolution. That much confidence and relaxation about him knowing was a costly mistake because Tamsir Mbye was about to go to China or some place with the president and the juniors he delegated my case only cared to talk to the registrar and communicated what they got from that office back to me.

I have no doubts that H. E. president Jammeh never heard a word about my plight with the GMDC. A letter was written to me purporting to represent the president's views as stated in the following below. Mr. Tamsir Mbye came back and took a retirement leave and so I was not able to meet with him because he traveled out of the Gambia. First let me give you the reply that came from the state house. Brace yourselves.

Republic of the Gambia
Department of State for
Health, Social welfare &
Women Affairs
State House, Banjul
The Gambia
May 3, 1998

Ref: AD 543/01/(172)

Dear Sir,

RE: request for consideration of resolving Professional Registration raw

I am directed to acknowledge on behalf of Her Excellency the Vice President and Secretary of State for health, Social welfare and women's Affairs receipt of your letter of February 23, 1998 relating to the above mention subject.

Such matters fall under the purview of the Gambia Medical and Dental Council.

However, this office will approach the registrar of that body with a view to resolving this long drawn issue. Thank you.

Yours sincerely

Sukai Bojang

For Permanent Secretary

Two weeks later I heard from the Secretary General's Office as indicated below. Both letters threw mud at my face for they strengthened the noose the registrar had around my neck. Both offices totally relied on wrong information supplied by the registrar instead of even checking with people on the ground and in the know about my case at the RVH.

To put it mildly they agreed with everything the registrar spewed. Whatever dossier the registrar may have on me was nothing other than his inventions or inventive creation.

I would like to make it clear that this was just round one in a boxing bout between the GMDC registrar and I.

In the next round I will meet with H.E. President Jammeh and lay my complaints before him. I will demand for just resolution and compensation for the four years I was under paid because of the aforesaid saga.

The appropriate person(s) will make the compensation when God's time comes. I was certain that someone out there cares and knows about my pains and deprivation this registration nightmare has done to my family and Children.

The Republic of the Gambia
Office of the President
State House, The Gambia

May 17, 1999

Ref:OP277/14/01/1V(8-JP1)

Dr. Alhasan S. Ceesay
Department of Medicine
Royal Victoria Hospital
Independence Drive
Banjul, The Gambia

RE: Request for consideration and arbitration to resolve Professional Registration raw. I am directed to acknowledge receipt on behalf of His Excellency The president of the Republic, your letter of July 8, 1998 in which you sought intervention and redress with regards to your bid to registrar with the General Medical and dental council.

Regrettably, this office is constrained by its inability, in the fact of the council's decisive position, to interfere in the registration process.

Yours Faithfully

Joseph P. Jassey, Capt. (RTD)

For Secretary General

These two heart wrenching letters left me much more ready to fight my case to the courts. The weak gives up easily but determined one does continue and become heroes. I am not giving up because of this first volley of blows in the fight. This fight will go on to the final minutes no mater how long it takes to resolve.

The truth will make up for the pain my life endured and mistakes made in dealing with it. God will have me have the last laugh in this kaleidoscope. I am by the above poised to struggle against injustice and misuse of power in office. Both friend and foe warned me to accept that this was a fate accomplish for me from God and that any further act will only continue the agony my life has endured since my return to the Gambia.

Dr.Alhasan Ceesay graduating from the America University of the Caribbean School of Medicine 1992

Hassan Bah and his children, London, UK 2015

Hassan Bah with friends at Eid 2014

I laughed at such suggestions and asked the person if he or she were present when God was planning my life or would they have stopped knowing that they right? I made it clear that this rift had to be dealt with squarely and there will be no cowardly surrender by me.

Letting matters end now would only set a very bad precedence for future doctors or civil servants as it will allow monsters to gnaw innocent souls like me that may come their way. No, no chance for that to happen in this case and this will be the last time a registrar of the Gambia Medical and Dental Council would toy with a Gambian doctor's bid for registration at will as if the registrar were dealing with powerless little children.

Some prayed for my success while others left bewildered at my determination. Of course my integrity and professional right were at stake plus my children's future relied heavily on the outcome of the stalemate. I am not in any going to give up my entire life's investment lying down for all the wrong reason of the registrar.

I know the truth is on my side and in the long run it will be so apparent that even Mbye Faal or some God fearing person will bring this Alice in wonderland Gambia tale to an abrupt and amicable end. Meanwhile, I continued my daily work schedule at the Royal Victoria Hospital and the bimonthly health education activities I started in the provinces.

This and my family became the only relief to me. All my plans of buying a compound and a car to take the children to school went over the window because my measly salary hardly feeds us to the end of the month.

My wife, who deserves the highest commendation throughout the saga, never for one moment broke down. She had been fully supportive throughout this ordeal and has helped me a lot with the children by selling tie-dye materials.

My friend, the going is rough if not very turbulent at present but it's true that "laughs best he who laughs last." The struggle continues until the dawn of justice for all future doctors wishing to register with the Gambia Medical and Dental Council.

Roadblocks, roadblocks everywhere when will these treacherous immoral obstacles be removed out of my way? I will hop, skip and jump over every one of them if need be to bring medical service to villagers. Till then, meet you at the next appeal round of this elusive jerkily and Hyde saga of an entrant doctor.

By now you have heard me mentioned monthly health field trips to the provinces and I hinted at some point the formation of a village health organization at Njawara called Manding Medical Centre. The next few pages will be devoted to the interesting part of my life instead of boring saga with the Gambia Medical and Dental Council (GMDC). First let us take a break and contemplate on how I chased elusive time since birth to now.

Chapter 14

The way forward and How I fit into the Picture

Being one not willing to point fingers at other for work to be done I tell my African folks that none is our Salvatore other than us. The ills and shortcomings of Africa are no greater than any other but the difference is that others never rested on their laurels nor adopted indiscipline as yard stick for governance.

The burning embers of a wish and hope for my people became a prison wall that kept caving onto me any time I relaxed my effort. Ambition to bring the Golden Flees, in the form of medical qualification and aid, to the villager constantly hunts me and reminds me of my covenant for the Gambia.

There were no doubts in my mind that I was rightfully engaged in bringing much needed medical service to the regions served by Manding Medical Centre in the Gambia. I literally became the fugue of the family as I push to bring my desire to provide proper medical aid into fruition for the villager in the North Bank of the Gambia.

This quest for a better medical service to neglected villagers led to my disappearing from the family horizon to America as early as 1967.

There I started the challenge of my life in a drive to become a doctor of medicine serving the Gambia. The path of this adventure is well documented in my first book, "The legend against all odds" published by Publish America, Baltimore, Maryland, USA in August 2002. The strength of my conviction along with a mindset to do something concrete for my people made me give up today's pleasures for a better tomorrow for the Gambia.

An Armchair psychologist, Dr. Kube Lonna (nick named Dr. Hamham), once told me. "Dreamers are a pain in the neck." I asked why? And he replied, "They wake up with one of the most ridiculous ideas and try not only to live in that nonsense but implement them for the rest of their lives.

Us pragmatics and wise become sceptical and weary of the dreamer and brand him either a total loony or one living in a planet by himself or herself." I replied quoting Lawrence of Arabia. Who said "All men dream but not equally.

Those who dream by the night in the dusty recesses of their minds wake in the day to find that it was vanity; but the dreamers of the day are dangerous men, for they act their dream with open eyes to make it possible." I further made it clear that nonetheless many dreamers have converts.

I asked what converted the sage to the dreamer's path. To this he gave the most amazing reply in favour of dreamers and people with strong convictions like mine. My armchair psychologist, Dr. Kube Lonna, told me "We only become flabbergasted as the dream unfolds to bits of reality opening up wide realms unknown to us before that day."

He continued by illustrating what he meant. "Take for example the case of the Rights Brothers and their attempt to fly. Boy oh boy! Some critics who strongly believed that only birds, goblins, and angels had the privilege of flight ridiculed the Rights Brothers as Witches.

Today you and I know better for we now use the Rights Brother's dream to fly round the world at ease and by it we have catapulted to the moon and beyond." I hope this has cleared the air for the reader as to why some of us are considered as whacks and a challenge to my friend the sage armchair psychologist Dr. Kube Lonna.

Very early in my high school days friends labelled me as a reclusive person not knowing that my whole psyche was based on going aboard and becoming one of the future doctors of the Gambia. I am fully aware of all work and no play not only turns us into monsters but also indeed a very dull one at that.

I just moderated my life and made certain that I never lost track of my direction in life and my ambition for the Gambian villager. After ten years in America my family considered me being lost in zealous desire to gain book knowledge or Western Education.

I learnt that my father, while on his deathbed urged that prayers be offered so that I, the family fugue would return home. Like Maco polo or Sinbad's adventures mine had seen me fly on several times to America, Liberia, the West Indies and the United Kingdom seeking more skills with which to serve my people.

It is said that life is lonely at the top but I found it even lonelier when struggling from ground zero with no hope of financial assistance at sight. Every hour of my life had to be organized in a way to minimize loss of income and to maintain progress in my academic pursuits.

Hence I worked on three jobs during the summer breaks and at school libraries to raise funds for my education or repayment of loans which enable me continue schooling. To me every ounce of energy and Centre spent on my aspiration to become a doctor in the Gambia was as exhilarating as becoming an overnight multimillionaire.

It is a joy I wish I could share with you. Graduating from medical school and my first patient in the Gambia are indelible blessed moments I hold dear to my heart. The rewards will forever be for my people and humanity.

Hence having been first hand witness to the shortages of health personnel which aggravates point of delivery of a needed service I decided in 1967 to plunge head over heels into the unknown seeking the Golden Flees for my people of the smiling coast of West Africa. At first many thought I was getting out my head thinking of going on my own to overseas to train to become one of doctors serving in rural Gambia.

Dr. Alhasan Ceesay taking break from writing, 2016

Chapter 15

PRISONER OF MY AMBITION FOR THE VILLAGER

The burning embers of a wish and hope for my people became a prison wall that kept caving onto me any time I relaxed my effort. Ambition to bring the golden Flees, in the form of medical aid, to the villager constantly hunts me and reminds me of my covenant for the Gambia. There were no doubts in my mind that I was rightfully engaged in bringing much needed medical service to the region served by Manding Medical Centre in the Gambia.

I literally became the fugue of the family as I pushed to bring my desire to provide proper medical aid into fruition for the villager in the North Bank of the Gambia. This quest for a better medical service to neglected villagers led to my disappearing from the family horizon to America as early as 1967.

There I started the challenge of my life in a drive to become a doctor of medicine serving the Gambia. The path of this adventure is well documented in my first book, "The legend against all odds" published by Publish America, Baltimore, Maryland, USA in August 2002. The strength of my conviction along with a mindset to do something concrete for my people made me give up today's pleasures for a better tomorrow for the Gambia.

An Armchair psychologist, Dr. Kube Lonna (nick named Dr. Hamham), once told me. "Dreamers are a pain in the neck". I asked why? And he replied, "They wake up with one of the most ridiculous ideas and try not only to live in that nonsense but implement them for the rest of their lives. Us pragmatics and wise become sceptical and weary of the dreamer and brand him either a total loony or living in a planet by himself or herself".

I replied quoting Lawrence of Arabia. Who said "All men dream: but not equally. Those who dream by the night in the dusty recesses of their minds wake in the day to find that it was vanity; but the dreamers of the day are dangerous men, for they act their dream with open eyes to make it possible."

I further made it clear that none the less many dreamers have converts. I asked what converts the sage to the dreamer' path? To this he gave the most amazing reply in favour of the dreamers and people with strong convictions like mine. My armchair psychologist told me, "We only become flabbergasted as the dream unfolds to bits of reality opening up wide realms unknown to us before that day".

He continued by illustrating what he meant. "Take for example the case of the Rights brothers and their attempt to fly. Boy oh boy! Some critics who strongly believed that only birds, goblins, and angels had the privilege of flight ridiculed the Rights brothers as witches. Today you and I know better for we now use the Rights brother's dream to fly round the world at ease and by it we have catapulted to the moon and beyond".

I hope this has cleared the air for the reader as to why some of us are considered as whacks and a challenge to my friend the sage armchair psychologist Dr. Kube Lonna. Very early in my high school days friends labelled me as a reclusive person not knowing that my whole psyche was based on going aboard and becoming one of the future doctors of the Gambia.

I am fully aware of all work and no play not only turns us into monsters but also indeed a very dull one at that. I just moderated my life and made certain that I never lost track of my direction in life and my ambition for the Gambian villager. After ten years in America my family considered me being lost in zealous desire to gain book knowledge or Western education. I learnt that my father, while on his deathbed urged that prayers be offered so that I, the family fugue would return home.

Like Macopolo or Simbad's adventures mine had seen me fly on several times to America, Liberia, the West Indies and the United Kingdom seeking more skills with which to serve my people. It is said that life is lonely at the top but I found it even lonelier when struggling from ground zero with no hope of financial assistance at sight.

Every hour of my life had to be organized in a way to minimize loss of income and to maintain progress in my academic pursuits. Hence I worked on three jobs during the summer breaks and at school libraries to raise funds for my education or repayment of loans which enable me continue schooling. To me every ounce of energy and Cent spent on my aspiration to become a doctor in the Gambia was as exhilarating as becoming an overnight multimillionaire.

It is a joy I wish I could share with you. Graduating from medical school and my first patient in the Gambia are indelible blessed moments I hold dear to my heart. The rewards will forever be for my people and humanity.

Dr. Alhasan Ceesay, Oldham, Manchester, UK 2017

Chapter 16

DISTIGUISHED 2005 GRADUATE AWARD TO DR. Alhasan S. CEESAY

I attended Alpena Community College (ACC) in Michigan, USA, from September 1967 to December 1979. My contact with friends at Alpena never waned. Hence the wheels of profound recognition by the institute started rolling when Mathew Dunckel called me to let me know he read my book, "The Legend against All Odds".

He was very impressed and intrigued by my experience and fortitude since my leaving Alpena Community College in 1979. I met Mathew when he was twelve years old. His father Dr. Elbridge Dunckle was my academic advisor while I was at Alpena community College. I will without any reservation still recommend Dr. Dunckel for academic advisor to any foreign student attending the college.

It was during one of our telephone conversation (02/01/05) that Mathew told me of the possibility of ACC recommending me for the Distinguished 2005 Graduate award offered annually by Alpena Community College to its outstanding Alumni.

Alpena Community College foundation recognizes its graduates annually for their academic and their career accomplishment for their communities. It simply recognizes the aspirations of Alumni for their people. The Pandora's Box was opened by innocuous telephone conversation in recognizing my aspiration and goal for providing medical aid to Gambian villagers. Mathew asked me to fax him any and all possible documentation about me and work I do in the Gambia.

He would then speak to the relevant authorities regarding my being nominated for the Distinguished 2005 graduate of Alpena Community College coming May 5th 2005 spring/summer commencement. Mathew did just as promised. In a nutshell, here is the letter from Mrs. Penny Boldrey, Executive Director Alpena Community College Foundation. It read:-

Alpena Community College

666 Johnson Street

Alpena, MI 49707

January 6, 2005

Alhasan S. Ceesay, MD

245 Great Western Street

Manchester M14 4LQ

England

Dear Dr. Ceesay,

Mathew Dunckel shared the information that you recently provided to him regarding your professional achievements since your early years at Alpena Community College. I'm extremely pleased to share with you that your many outstanding accomplishments have earned you the distinction of Distinguished Graduate of Alpena Community College (ACC) for 2005.

We commend you for your humanitarian efforts in founding and developing the Manding Medical Centre in Gambia, West Africa. I'm anxious to read your book. "The legend against all odds" once Matt has finished with it. Without a doubt, you serve as an example of how a solid educational foundation from Alpena Community College can launch a lifetime of achievements.

You will be honoured at our spring commencement exercises on Thursday, May 5, which begins at 7 pm, in the Park Arena at ACC.

We invite you to join us on that evening. However, we certainly understand that making a trip to the United States, on so short a notice, may not be feasible. During the commencement program, I will share a synopsis of your extraordinary career that has earned you the honour of Distinguished Graduate.

If you are able to join us, you will be invited to join me at the podium to receive your award and to address the audience if you wish. Would you be willing to provide us with the following: 1) a copy of your professional resume; 2) a paragraph on your memories of ACC and how your experience helped you achieve your goals; 3) a professional photo for use in our alumni newsletter as well as in an ad that will appear in Alpena news. Please feel free to call me or e-mail me with any additional questions you may have. Again, congratulations! We look forward to hearing from you in the future.

Sincerely

Penny Boldrey

Executive Director

My response to this honour and invitation to my second home America was swift and obvious as penned bellow. I e-mailed Penny forth with as my heart was overwhelmed by joy for being recognised by my Alma Mata ACC. It simply stated:-

13/01/05,

Manchester, UK.

Dear Penny Boldrey,

I am overwhelmed and do not know where to begin this note of thanks to Alpena Community College. In my mind it's the American people who deserve such honour and distinction for I am only recipient of the goodness of the Americans. I am humbled and further rejuvenated by the thought and recognition of my goals and work for the Gambia.

I remember in the 60s when people used to tell me, "You will end up just like all foreign students who came to America. They end up getting trapped by the greener pasture syndrome of America." To such challenges my response had always been; I for one will disappoint a lot of you for I will never rest until I bring to my people the American know how and willingness to share with others.

This stance has never changed and will not ever change because the only way I can, in a small measure compared to what you did for us poor ones, pay back is to be able to show what the USA is all about and her stand for the little guy anywhere on this planet. I will look into my schedule to see if I can afford to be in Alpena May 2005.

I will let you know by the end of February 2005. Mean while I'm faxing a resume and will try to send my photos by e-mail. Where it is not possible for me to attend in May, would it be okay for my first Alpena family friend, Mrs. Rita Riggs to represent me at the ACC' spring Commencement Ceremony.

She was the first people in Alpena that opened their homes to me. She and her family will certainly appreciate recognition of their help to this simple Gambian. None the less rest assured that I have not yet slammed the door to my seeing Alpena once more. Timing and visa problems might make it unattainable. Again, please accept profound gratitude to all of you and to Alpena Community College. God blesses you and rain peace on earth in 2005. Cheers and regards.

My lovely daughter: Binta Ceesay

Sincerely

Dr. Alhasan S. Ceesay, MD

Mrs. Boldrey replied thus:

ACC, Michigan 49707

13/01/05

Hi Dr. Ceesay,

Yes, I did receive your curriculum vitae and thank you for forwarding that to me! We are extremely proud of you and your accomplishments! Once I get my hand on your book, I will pay special notice to the ACC chapter. The best part of my job is the opportunity to meet former alumni and learn of the impact ACC had in their lives.

Please believe me that we understand if you are unable to join us at commencement on May 5. Indeed we would be pleased to have Rita Riggs accept this honour on your behalf. Rita is remarkable and kind woman. My husband speaks fondly of her and has stayed in close contact with her.

I look forward to getting to know you better through our correspondence! And meet you in person someday. Regards

Its

Mrs. Penny Boldrey

Executive Director

At the end it was not possible for me to attend the ceremony in person. So Rita Riggs and her family stepped in for me. Her elder son Robert Riggs was designated to receive the award in my behalf as representative of Rita who was in her 80s at the time. I emailed the follow short remarks to be read by Robert Riggs at the time the award is given. It is titled:-

A FUTURE FOR ALL

Mr. President, staff, Graduates, Ladies and Gentlemen; I am deeply moved and humbled being chosen Alpena Community College's Distinguished Alumni for 2005.This recognition belongs to America. Without the good will and foresight of the staff, students and the community of Alpena in 1967, I might never have had the chance to earn education with which to help my people move forward in life.

Hence, allow me reiterate profound gratitude to Alpena Community College, my fellow students, people of Alpena and America at large. My life after Alpena has been full of trials and tribulations detailed in my first book, "The legend against all odds". One relief in it is the robust blessing and peace of mind I have knowing that I am right in what I am doing for my people.

There are those who claim Heaven in being rich but for me it is reaching out to help others that matters in life. Upon graduating from medical school, I returned to the Gambia and setup a self-help village Health organization (Manding Medical Centre) at Njawara village in an effort to provide a much needed medical service to the rural sector. I am happy to report that membership has grown beyond twenty thousand villagers.

Please join me to catch a dream for my villagers. Manding medical centre will help portray the America we all dream of and yearn to be part. We are on the verge of building the children's unit and do need monetary, equipment and medicines assistance in our drive to provide this unique service to villagers.

To the graduates, I would like to remind you that, the great tide of history flows and as it flows it carries to the shores of reality what binds us as one human race. Be aware of the extent, depth and gravity of the challenges ahead as you set out to transform, reconstruct and integrate America into a global icon. Sincere congratulations for your march towards success and fulfilment. Alpena Community College has given you the first footprints. Walk your way with head held high and determination to succeed in the world. Confucius said, "Our greatest glory is never failing, but in rising every time we fail."

Stockpiles of atomic bombs or weapons of mass destruction and dictators do not measure greatness. I believe strongly and sincerely that with deep-rooted wisdom and dignity, innate respect for human right and lives, the intense humanity will make us more cherished and better leaders. This will make us able to contribute towards the future and progress of mankind. I am happy for you and hope that you will fly the American flag for it is the great American constitution.

Finally, I would like to pay tribute to pass and present staff, students of ACC and Alpena community for having given me the opportunity to forge for my people. Allow me make special mention and express thanks to the remarkable and noble friends I met in Alpena.

Sincere thanks from my family, villagers and I to Howard & Rita Rigg, Judge Philip & Viola S. Glennie, Mr. Henry V. Valli, Dr. Elbridge Dunckel, Dr. Strom, Bill & Magritte Cruise, Dr. Charles T. Egli and the Alpena medical association, Mr. Cloyd Ramsey & the Medical Arts Clinic and all who helped make my sojourn to Alpena a remarkable success. If I have a million friends, I would like many more to be like you. I hope you will believe in, as well as join me, in my dream of providing modern medical aid to the Gambian villagers. Thanks a million and God bless America!

BY: DR. ALHASAN SISAWO CEESAY, MD

Mrs. Penny Boldrey called to let me know she confirmed the details with Robert Rigg, who was selected by the family to deliver the speech. She assured me that Bob was all set with my remarks and had been practicing many times. Rita and Donna will also be attending with other friends. To make it official she sent this note to Robert Rigg (Bob).

April 21, 2005

Robert Rigg

312 Liberty Street

Alpena, MI 49707

Dear Bob,

Dr. Alhasan Ceesay has informed that you will be representing him at our commencement ceremony and accepting the Distinguished Graduate Award on his behalf. Our spring commencement exercises will be held on Thursday, May 5, at 7 pm.

There will be VIP seating near the front left section of the Park Arena for and your family. During the commencement program, I will share a brief synopsis of Dr. Ceesay's career.

I will invite you to join me at the podium to receive Dr. Ceesay's Distinguished Graduate Award. Following the presentation, you will have the opportunity to share Dr. Ceesay's remarks. I shared with Dr. Ceesay that his comments must be kept brief (2-3 minutes) because our program consist of many individuals who will also be addressing the graduating class.

After the ceremony we would like to take some photographs, so if you could remain near your seats, I will come to you. A reception at the Jeese Besser Museum follows commencement and you are also invited to join. Enclosed you will find a copy of Dr. Ceesay's remarks. I look forward to hearing from you. Please call me to confirm your participation.

Sincerely

Penny Boldrey

Executive Director

Two weeks prior to the ceremony I received an e-mail letting me know that Karen Eller, administrative assistant in the president's (ACC) office of Public information will be writing about me in the Lumberjack Link spring /summer alumni newsletter publication. Penny also told me that Kerrie Miller (also alumni) and news writer for The Alpena News would like to feature me in the local paper.

I immediate e-mailed the following to Kerrie Miller at the Alpena News. Hi Kerrie, I just received Penny's email with the good news that you want to feature me in the Alpena News. For me this would be a dream come true. Yes! By all means go ahead and feel free to contact me should you want more information about me or the work I'm doing in the Gambia.

I am a simple person that loves to help others get on with life the best way they can during their short sojourn on mother earth. I strongly believe that hose of us who had the privilege to learn from America have responsibility to share American goodwill with our people. That is the only way they, our people, can experience the real America that stands for the down trodden and the innovative. I still feel very happy when come across an American.

If your paper is able to help me get Manding Medical Centre at Njawara out of its current limbo, then you would have participated in the most noble and worthy course that will outlive us and will be a spring board of hope and medical service for generations we can ever dream of.

It is my Binta Ceesay

We are still on fund raising stage to build the first phase, the children's unit, which according to estimates will cost around £250,000 or about $500,000 dollars. I committed all proceeds of my book, "The legend against all odds", to the centre but it is not selling enough to get things in fast gear. I need help to bring relief to my villagers. Well, this is enough introductions until I hear from you. God bless you and thanks a million for being kind towards us.

Sincerely

Dr. Alhasan S. Ceesay

Kerrie Miller replied and asked that I send her a synopsis of how I found out Alpena in the 60s. So I sent her the following summary. "I came to be in Alpena by simply going to the then American Consulate in Banjul, the Gambia and asked for a catalogue with information on American colleges.

As a beggar normally has no choice, I started from the top alphabets. Well, Alpena Community college was there and was the first that accepted my application among the schools that replied to my desire to pursue further education in America. This part is well expanded in chapter in my book "The legend against all odds" highlighting my experience at ACC from 1967 - 1969.

I was born and bred in abject poverty and I'm only fighting for my villagers to have a chance to proper medical care etc, etc nothing more and nothing -less. I hope you will help get your readers interested in Manding Medical Centre and its objective for the villagers.

Thank you for taking upon the task of writing about me and my work in the Gambia. Manding Medical Centre is in limbo and we year for a boost or a short in the arm to get things moving faster. Please visit our website: www.Friends of Manding gambimed.com

It's

Dr. A. Ceesay

I will later reproduce both articles written by Karen Eller for the Lumberjack Link and Kerrie Miller's in the Alpena News respectively. For now let us head to the spring commencement podium and listen to what Mrs. Penny Boldrey has in mind about this simple village doctor. Bob and his family attended in time and it was now time for Penny's remarks about my achievements from the days of Alpena Community College to now. It is simple and movingly started thus:-

"Good evening and congratulations graduates!

The Alpena Community College Foundation created the Distinguished Graduate award not only to recognize, but to honour our graduates who have gone on to contribute to society through successful careers. Our recipient tonight serves as an example of how a solid education foundation from ACC can launch a lifetime of achievements.

I'm pleased to share with you that our 2005 Distinguished Graduate is Dr. Alhasan Ceesay from the Gambia, West Africa. Dr Ceesay received his Associates of Arts Degree in 1969, exactly two years after leaving the Gambia. He credits many individuals, and the generosity of others, as the driving force behind his success.

Following his graduation from ACC, Dr. Ceesay transferred to Olivet College, on a full-tuition scholarship provided to him by the Besser Foundation. In 1971, he earned a Bachelor of Arts Degree in Biology from Olivet, and in 1973 completed his Master of Science degree from Michigan Technological University at Houghton Michigan, USA.

Dr. Ceesay taught biology for several years in the Gambia before entering into medical school in 1992, he was awarded his Doctor of Medicine Degree from the American University of the Caribbean. Dr. Ceesay again returned to the Gambia, and provided free medical assistance to the villagers for an entire year before he took a position as House Officer at the Royal Victoria

Hospital, Banjul, the Gambia, and was eventually promoted to the post of Medical Officer in 1999. He is the proud founder of the Manding Medical Centre, a self-help village Health organisation located in the Gambia, which has provided much needed medical care to over 8000 villagers.

In his autobiography, "The legend Against All Odds", Dr. Ceesay shares his struggle to survive in his quest for an education. All the proceeds from his book go to supporting the Manding Medical Centre. Dr. Ceesay and his wife have three daughters, ages 14, 11 and 7. In my correspondence with Dr. Ceesay over the past few months, he shared his profound gratitude for his American education.

He said, "In my mind, it is the American who deserved such honour and distinction, for I'm the recipient of the goodness of the Americans." Due to travel difficulties, Dr. Ceesay is unable to be here tonight to accept this award. However he has asked his first American family, the Howard Rigg family to represent him. At this time I'll ask Bob Rigg to join me at the podium to accept the award for Dr. Ceesay. Indeed, it is truly an honour to recognize Dr. Ceesay for his many accomplishments and humanitarian efforts.

We congratulate him on earning the Distinction of Distinguished Graduate of Alpena Community College. – Penny Boldrey- Robert Rigg eloquently delivered my remarks aimed at the graduates and residents of Alpena city. It was welcomed as I was later told by those who were able to e-mail me. Alpena city and ACC were very happy. This Distinguished Graduate award came thirty 36 odd years since I last visited Alpena, Michigan.

Mathew Dunckel sent me the following comments about the evening of the award. "Alhasan, your address was given at commencement. It was the portion of the evening that was enjoyed by most. Partly because it was delivered well and partly because of my father was mentioned. I think what you said was inspirational for our students and brought home the need for them to think internationally.

Tom Ray is making final preparation to depart for Gambia early next week. What a great adventure for the students. I am looking forward to hearing about it on their return. Thank you for helping make it happen.

Your friend

Matt.

I sent Penny Boldrey the following; "I received both the award and enclosures. Accept my deepest appreciation for the kind words spoken about me in your presentation speech during the spring graduation ceremony. Thank you very much for your kindness." I suggested we pursue the possibility of twining Alpena with two villages in the Gambia. Dear reader, I hope your patience is not running out as you eagerly look forward to the publication for alumni and friends of Alpena Community College.

Karen Eller wrote to let me know that she was assigned to write a news article for the local paper announcing my receiving the Distinguished Graduate award. She read my book, "The legend against all odds," to garner more information about me to help her on the matter at hand. She continued by letting me know that she found my story very interesting and she intend to do a good job at the article.

Here without further ado is Karen Eller's article about me. This idea unfolded to reality in the chapter on sister city proclamation.

THE LUMBERJACK LINK: ALPENA MICHIGAN

DR. CEESAY NAMED DISTINGUISHED GRADUATE

Dr. Alhasan Sisawo Ceesay of the Gambia, West Africa, was recognized with the Distinguished Graduate award at the ACC spring commencement ceremony in May 5th, 2005.

On hand to receive the award for Dr. Ceesay was members of the Howard Rigg family, his first host family when he came to Alpena in 1967. According to Dr. Ceesay, "The Riggs were the ideal American, an average working class who readily shared the little bit God gave them with others less fortunate."

Dr. Ceesay earned his Associate of Arts degree from ACC in 1969 and went on to Olivet College to earn his Bachelor's degree in biology with the help of a full-tuition scholarship from the Besser Foundation. He earned his Master's degree in biological sciences from Michigan Technological University in 1973.

In 1979, Dr. Ceesay returned to Africa and entered the University of Liberia Medical School in Monrovia. Because of political unrest in the Gambia in 1981, Dr. Ceesay escaped to the United States in hopes of completing his lifelong dream; "to provide medical relief to the villager who is forced to walk miles on end to seek medical aid for his already dying child, wife or friend."

During the time he was seeking political asylum in the United States, Dr. Ceesay never gave up his quest for education, and he continued to take classes at Michigan State University and Wayne State University. He was finally accepted at the American University of the Caribbean in the West Indies, and he began the final segment of his journey to becoming a doctor. In 1992, after 25 years of educational struggles, Dr. Ceesay was awarded his Doctor of Medicine degree from the American University of the Caribbean. He returned to the Gambia where he provided free medical assistance to the villagers for an entire year before taking a position at the Royal Victoria Hospital, Banjul, The Gambia.

Dr. Ceesay founded Manding Medical Centre in 1993. This is a self-help village health organisation which provides much needed medical aid to the villagers of the Gambia, West Africa. His autobiography, "The legend against all odds," chronicles his struggle to survive in his quest for Western education.

Proceeds of his book go to support Manding Medical Centre at Njawara village and provide scholarships in medicine and agriculture for indigent rural candidates in the Gambia. To learn more about Dr. Ceesay's ambitions, you can e-mail him at alhasanceesay@hotmail.com.

Dr. Ceesay was honoured to receive this distinction from ACC and would like to "express thanks to the remarkable and noble friends" he met in Alpena. He credits the goodwill and foresight of the staff and students at ACC for giving him the chance to earn an education and help move his people forward in life.

-Karen Eller-

I thank Karen Eller for this revealing commendable article. Here now is that featured by the Alpena News written by news staff Kerrie L. Miller. This is Miller's version about me and my goals.

ALPENA NEWS, MICHIGAN, USA 2005

A LONG ROAD FROM GAMBIA TO ALPENA

When he was about 14, Dr. Alhasan S. Ceesay saw a family tragedy unfold that would change his life forever. As he was walking to school, he saw a woman, pregnancy full-term, who was obviously ill. Her husband was carrying their young son who was nearly comatose from illness. Ceesay later found out the pregnant woman's baby died in uterus and she died from the toxins built up in her body as a result.

The young boy also died three quarters of a mile before his family was able to reach the health centre at Kerewan village. "That day I said, "If God will help me, no one will ever have to go through that again. That picture is what made up my mind for me," Ceesay said. Ceesay, a native of Njawara, Gambia, is a graduate of Alpena Community College, class of 1969. He earned his Associate's of Arts degree from ACC before attending Olivet College, Michigan Tech and Howard University, earning his doctor of medicine degree from the America University of the Caribbean in 1992.

But how does a young man from a village in Gambia get to Alpena to attend its community college? In an e-mail message, he stated that after reaching the American Consulate, and asking for a listing of American colleges, Alpena Community College was at the top of the alphabetical list. And Acc was the first to respond to his application. Once here, life was not without challenges. In a telephone conversation, he said it was the first time he had left his country, and when he got here no one spoke his language. "But I don't give up," he said.

Another goal Ceesay never gave up on was making it possible for village families, such as those like the one who affected him as deeply as a young man, to have access to health care services. With the creation of the Manding Medical Centre, which has helped over 8000 patients free of charge, he is doing that.

Though progress has been very slow in coming to the centre; Ceesay said officially he is employed by the central government and is only on the weekends is he able to man the centre, along with three or four other doctors who volunteer their time. Ceeesay say the centre sees no fewer than 500 patients and as many as 1,500 patients in a weekend. He said currently the centre is in limbo and is a little more than a shed.

He has been working on fund-raising to get the first phase, a children's unit, built. It is expected to cost approximately $500,000. Members of the ACC Leadership Class are currently conducting fund-raising to go to Gambia and help with the children and volunteering at the centre. The trip will last two weeks. Ceesay is the author of a book chronicling his life's experiences called "The legend against all odds" (available at Amazon .com) and he has committed all proceeds of its sale to the centre.

He said he's never regretted the decision he made to become a doctor. "Sometimes I feel like I have oil on my feet and I'm climbing a very steep hill." Ceesay said. "I have always believed I'll reach my goal... you have to be crazy like me and you have to ignore lots of things that take you away from your goals."

A typical day in Ceesay's life begins at 5 am with prayer, before boarding public transportation to the hospital where he works, 7 miles from his home. From 7 – 11 am he does morning rounds, followed by clinics, then evening rounds. Days can last up to 10 or 11 pm before he heads back home. "In between, I try to please my wife and children. It's a very simple life really," he said. He and his wife have three daughters, the oldest of which has dreams of attending Alpena High School and ACC before going onto medical school like her father.

Ceesay's long-term goals revolve around the medical centre, which he hopes will continue to grow for generations, helping thousands more patients. "I plan to stay at the centre until the day they bury me. That and have my children educated. That's it," he said.

-Kerrie Miller-

Kerrie sent me a copy of the Alpena news. And I sent the following in appreciation of the good work in the article. Kerrie, I just received a copy of the Alpena news featuring me. It was a job well done. I hope it help move my dream of providing medical aid to villagers a notch higher for Manding Medical centre and the Gambian villagers. The Gambia and I are most grateful for enlightening your readers about us and our need for a medical facility.

Extend our thanks and deep appreciation to the staff and Alpena-news. We shall definitely be in Gambia in due course. We look forward to your crew attending the ground breaking ceremonies in Gambia soon. I have started a collection of documentations about me to be placed in Dr. Alhasan S. Ceesay's achieves. Kerrie Miller replied saying that they missed me for the ceremony but she look forward to attending the grand opening of the centre.

Penny Boldrey simply said, "I will certainly make sure you receive a copy of our alumni newsletter once it's completed. Indeed, we are very proud of your accomplishments and humanitarian efforts."

Dr. Ceesay and Father: Sisawo Ceesay, Banjul 1960

Chapter 17

AMERICAN GUESTS VISIT MANDING MEDICAL CENTR, NJAWARA, THE GAMBIA, IN MAY 2005.

The telephone call on 5/01/05 from Mr. Mathew Dunckel as well as that from Mr. Thomas Ray (TOM) four days later opened the Pandora's box and became harbingers to a remarkable trip to Manding Medical Centre, Njawara village, Gambia by the Alpena Community College's Leadership class headed by none other than their instructor Mr. Thomas P. Ray.

I contacted Mr. Thomas Ray as soon as it was brought to my attention that some ACC students were contemplating visiting my centre at Njawara in May 2005. My message on the 6/01/05 to Mr. Ray ran thus:- "An old friend, Mr. Mathew, staff of ACC, had a long chat with me last night and he brought to my attention of a possibility that a class wanting to travel to the Gambia as guest of Manding Medical Centre at Njaswara.

I am more than willing and happy to pave the way for those that would venture the trip. I do need an e-mail or fax from you indicating desire to go to the Gambia on a mission for Manding Medical Centre. I will speak to both the schools and the district authority about your most welcomed trip to the Gambia.

Manding Medical Centre is a self-help village health organisation I setup in upon returning to the Gambia in1992. We provide medical service to villagers and land has been donated for the location of the centre and its ancillaries. We only have a corrugated shed as clinic. We are now on the verge of building the first phase, being the children's unit of the centre and need monetary assistance. I am delighted to know of your intentions. Please contact me as soon as you speak with the class."

Thomas Ray replied on 7/01/05, "I was thrilled when Mathew discussed the possibility of a trip to Gambia for our leadership students. I will meet with the whole class next week to discuss the possibility. As I am sure you are aware the cost of airfares from Alpena to Gambia is high, so I will need to be certain the students are committed to raising the money needed before we begin making plans.

I have travelled to many locations, but never to Africa, so I am also very excited about the prospects for myself. After I meet with the students on Tuesday of next week, I will e-mail you with further information. I wish to also commend you for your personal achievements; I plan to purchase a copy of your recent book to share with my students and for my personal reading. Thank you for your help and enthusiasm."

I emailed Tom advising that to bargain for insured group tickets. Tom further contacted me on 12/01/05 stating that he has spoken to the students and they have agreed to take on a service trip as part of the course. He told me that they would only be able to travel in a group for 10 – 14 days in May 2005. Tom wanted to know if there was an existing program at Njawara that would be able to accommodate the students.

He assured me that the students would be comfortable in a dormitory housing or make shift dormitories. In addition I let him know on the 14/01/05 that I have spoken to the commissioner, North Bank Division and the local authority in Lower Badibou district regarding their pending trip to Njawara as guest of Manding Medical Centre and the region.

I assured him that these authorities would be more than happy to have his class visit with them. I requested an e-mail from him stating that they are visiting in behalf of Manding Medical Centre at Njawara and specify what they would want to do while in the Gambia. I suggested that they can help teach in some of the schools. I assured them that even though business and some residents have moved out there is still some activity at the village.

Tom in reply sent the following on the 15/01/05. "Thank you for the great news. I am very excited about the prospect and have begun searching for group airfares with special student rates. I will inform the students on Tuesday and contact you immediately afterward via email. I have a few questions. What costs do we need to expect in Gambia and in your village? How will we travel from Banjul to the village?

We need to be certain we have a clear idea what expenses we will have to help us set specific fundraising goals both for ourselves and for the foundation from which we hope to receive grants. When I write the other e-mail, are there tasks other than tutoring that I should include? Are there other ways we can help while we are there? I am more excited about the prospect of this service trip everyday and the students are quite enthused."

In another e-mail dated 15/02/05, Tom wrote, "The students in the leadership class are so committed to this project that they voted to contribute their own money toward the travel if they cannot raise enough. This means that the number of students who actually travel will likely be fewer, but that we will be able to travel to Njawara in May. I have begun drafting the letter to the commissioner many times, but I have some questions.

Am I asking the commissioner to help organise local housing for us? Do I want his permission to visit Njawara? Should I tell him what we would like to do there? What subject might they tutor? Are there any construction projects for the centre or the village with which we could help?

I would also like to know if there are any material supplies we could bring with us to donate to the centre or the village. One possible way for us to save money would be to fly into Dakar, Senegal and travel from there overland to Njawara. All the above concerns and questions were answered but a small hiccup in fundraising occurred leaving a distinct possibility that the students will not be able to raise enough to make the trip.

The reason being the major source of funding for the trip fell through. This left all of us jittery but Tom and his students were in no mood to change their plans to travel to the Gambia in May 2005. On the same day 15/02/05 I received the following from Mr. Jay Walterriet, Director of Public information for Alpena Community College. It stated that he was asked to contact me for more photos of myself and the clinic at Njawara. He wanted more information regarding the Leadership planned trip to Gambia.

I was told that the local television station would like to do a segment on the Leadership class and their trip. As part of the segment photos were needed. I sent all photos that were relevant to enable the reporter to do his TV-segment on the planned Leadership trip to Njaswara, Gambia.

Mr. Jay on the 17/02/05 emailed thanking me for providing the requested photos and assured me that ACC has received good deal of interest from the local media regarding the Leadership class trip and both he and Penny Boldrey were trying to provide all of the information they could. My e-mail was given to reporters who might want to contact me for more information.

The entire twenty students could not enlist for the final take off to Africa. So Thomas Ray and 11 students took on the venture of their life time to the Gambia as guest of Manding Medical Centre at Njawara village. On 17 February 2005 Tom sent me a copy of the final letter he sent to the commissioner and the local authority at the Lower Badibou district spelling out their intentions and wish while guests of the Manding Medical Centre for a two weeks duration. Here it is.

Thamos P. Ray

Alpena Community College

666 Johnson Street

Alpena, Michigan 49707

17 February 2005

Dear Commissioner Batala Juwara,

I am pleased to inform you of our plans to visit Njawara on behalf of the Manding Medical Centre. I am the advisor and instructor for a group of college students from Alpena Community College in Michigan in the USA. We plan to visit Njawara in May and hope you will help us find lodging with local families during our stay. Our plan as of now is to fly out of the US on May 6th to Banjul via London and to return on May 19th 2005.

During our stay in Gambia, our hope is to provide any assistance we can to the community on behalf of the Manding Medical Centre. We would like to visit the school in Njawara and tutor the children and share stories and activities with them. I also hope that we will have the opportunity to visit the important centres of the community and learn as much as we can in our short stay about the people and life in Njawara and Gambia. I have communicated our plans with Dr. Alhasan Ceesay, who has kindly extended the invitation to us on behalf of the Manding Medical Centre.

Sincerely

Thomas P. Ray

English Instructor

This letter was acknowledged by the commissioner and the district authority in the Gambia. Now that I was certain of the trip I set to inform my board members in like manner. The certainty of the trip was concretized by the following sent by Tom on 10 March 2005.

It simply updated me on the progress made regarding the trip; that the students have raised half the money needed to travel to Gambia. He affirms the fact that everyone concerned is working hard on the remaining sum. The arranged inoculations and are preparing to apply for visas to Gambia.

He said they were all enthused and has used my address in Gambia for the visa information requirement. Again, I was delighted for things are now heading the right direction for the historic and unique trip to Njawara.

I am now certain that more doors to boost ours and the centre's goals for the Gambia will be open by this simple friendly act of ACC. Here finally is my despatch the board members of Manding Medical Centre at Njawara village.

MANDING MEDICAL CENTRE/NJAWARA

UNITED KINGDOM CONTACT

245 GREAT WESTERN STREET

MANCHESTER, M14 4LQ

ENGLAND

E-MAI:alhasanceesay@hotmail.com

Tel/Fax: 44+161-342-0854

Date: 25/03/05

DEAR BOARD MEMBER,

I am pleased to bring to your attention about American guests to Manding Medical Centre at Njawara. Mr. Thomas Ray along with 11 Alpena Community college students will be visiting the Gambia as our guest in May 2005. They will be leaving the USA for the Gambia on May 6th, 2005 and depart for United States on the 19th, of May.

I would be most grateful if you give some of your time to meet them and make their visit memorable. There are many benefits to be accrued for the centre and the Gambia. I am at present arranging in the form of scholarships or placements in various fields of study at my previous college in Alpena Michigan.

I have been in constant contact with Commissioner Batala Juwara at Kerewan and I would like all of you to brain storm and make this an ongoing link between us and Alpena Community College and other Michigan cities I am now in negotiation with. Alpena city has developed interest in our project.

I am also happy to report that my former college, Alpena Community College has awarded me, "Distinguished 2005 Graduate." Find enclosed correspondence from Mr. Thomas Ray, in behalf of the Leadership class of Alpena Community College, to Commissioner Juwara and Sefo Fafanding Kinte. I look forward to your understanding and participation to help open up the Pandoa's Box of goodwill for the Gambia. This is a onetime opportunity for the Gambia that would make our two people linked for good goals and noble courses for generations of Gambians.

My regards and keep in touch.

Yours truly,

Dr. Alhasan S. Ceesay, MD

Founder/co-coordinator

Cc: Mr. Ousainu Darboe

Mr. Fafa E. Mbai

Dr. Dawda Ceesay

Dr. Ayo Palmer

Mr. Saim Kinte

Mr. Sambou Kinte

Mr. Mustapha Njie

Mr. Maja Sonk

Mr. Dodou Ceesay

Mr. Sisawo Ceesay

Mrs. Mbee Sonko

On April 7th 2005, Tom updated me stating that the visa applications were going well and that most of the students have received their visas. In addition let me privilege you the reader with some of the reactions emailed to me about the pending trip and what it would mean to them. Alison Jane Smolinski said: "Hello Dr. Ceesay. I am one of the students in the Leadership class at Alpena Community College.

I am really excited about the service trip, only a couple more weeks. Right now we are trying to prepare for the trip, just getting the basic necessities and what we should be packing. I just read about how you are building a bakery at Njawara.

Even though our resources are limited, is there something we could do to help out? I thought we could help in some way. I also just wanted to say thank you for the wonderful experience you giving to us. I realize it will be truly an eye opener. I feel as if I could never be able to repay you for these two weeks that you about to give us. Thank you Dr. Ceesay!"Another email from Brittany Postumus simply stated; "I am one of the students from Alpena Community College that will be coming this May to help.

After learning all the things that you have done I must say you are an inspiration and the world can use more people who care as much as you do. I can't wait to come to Njawara. I am very excited to be able to help and thank you for the invitation." Lastly, Ms. Grace Schimitz sent in the following before leaving for the Gambia. "I am a member of the Alpena Community College class that will be assisting you this May at Njawara.

I am greatly looking forward to my visit to the Gambia. Thank you so much for the invitation! The Friends of Manding, a charitable Trust at Colchester had the following in its web site about the trip to Njawara, the Gambia. It read as "News flash 12 American visiting:" "A class of 11 students and their instructor Mr. Thomas Ray from Alpena Community College, Alpena Michigan, will be visiting the Gambia as guest of Manding Medical

Centre from the 6th to 19th May 2005. They will be visiting communities and tutor at local schools. Alpena has developed interest in project Manding Medical Centre at Njawara. We are negotiating to have this exchange as an ongoing affair between Alpena and Njawara." As time drew near to the flight to the Gambia Tom contacted the Commissioner on several occasions to clear last possible huddles that may surface. None the less preparations went smoothly and Thomas Ray and his ACC Leadership class left America on May 10th 2005 via Madrid and then Dakar, Senegal before embanking at Banjul, the Gambia.

As fate would have the team instead hired a bus from Dakar to Hamdali village in the North Bank which was nearer to Njawara. I learnt they were given a VIP escort from Hamdali via Kerewan to Njawara village. As expected, I called the Mayor of Njawara, Mrs. Hadi Panneh enquiring about the American visitors. She told me they were fine and housed at the village centre, a semi motel used for foreign guest to Njawara. Tom and I spoke at length along with Sefo Fafanding Kinte.

Sefo Fafanding reassured me that everything possible will be done to help make "our guest comfortable and likewise a memorable visit in due course. I spoke briefly to the commissioner the next day to get a feedback from him.

The two week flew fast for the students most of who did want to leave at the time for kindness rendered by the villagers. It is said that good thing never last long and this the experience of the student who went to Njawara in May 2005. Here is the reaction of Americans after the trip to the Gambia. The ACC students started sending their report and experience as guest of Manding Medical Centre, Njawara, The Gambia. Starting with Alison Jane Smolinski reported as bellow.

"Hello Dr. Ceesay: The trip to Njawara was incredible! I did not want to leave. It was an experience of a lifetime that I will never forget. Everyone in the village was very kind and helpful. I have never met such kind people in my entire life. I found the villagers doing everything possible to make their lives better. I realized that many people work together to get a job done or finished. This is absolutely wonderful.

Everyone was so helpful in the village. The people of Njawara gave us such wonderful hospitality. The food and shelter was more than we deserved. Also your wife, Mrs Fatou Koma-Ceesay, was all too good to us. We had a remarkable time with her at Bundung/Serekunda. Her cooking was excellent. And the gifts she gave all of us, we did not deserve. Your family is wonderful and was too kind to us.

I would like to thank you for the incredible experience you have given me. I could not have asked for anything more. I immensely enjoyed myself. I want to go back one day. I also want you to know that I will do my best to help in whatever way I can. I realize that action are louder than words and hope I can prove that to everyone. Thank you Dr. Ceesay."

Another reaction came from Grace Schiminitz. "I really enjoyed my time in Njawara. The people treated us very well and it was a pleasure to spend two weeks with them. Your wife is a wonderful person and was very hospitable to us. I will always be grateful for her kind treatment.I hope to make another visit to Njawara in the future. It is a wonderful place.

It was an eye-opening experience. The people were absolutely marvellous. They treated us as their own family and welcomed us with open hands. I had no idea that they would be that hospitable. I really miss walking to the river and spending time with the children. It was my first experience in Gambia and hopefully it will not be my last. I hope I can return their kindness.

I would love to see how the kids have grown up." The last but not the least came from Mr. Thomas P. Ray, English instructor at ACC. It read; "I want to thank you for the opportunity you provided my students on this trip.

The entire experience was enjoyable and valuable as a means of teaching my students something about the responsibility that comes with the privileges they enjoy here. Everyone was kind to us on the trip and the students came away with many great souvenirs and memories. I have many digital photos and am working on producing a CD of them to send out.

I also plan to type up a version of my journal for posting on the internet and I will send parts of that to you. I plan to call the village this weekend to extend my appreciation to everyone. Do you know anything about the proposed potential sister city relationship between Alpena and Njawara? I would like to start making some local contacts here to help that process. I am also hopeful that future trips will be possible for my students.

-Mr. Thomas P. Ray-

As you know very well man proposes but God dispose things. Tom took over the running of the department and with that came a hand full challenging responsibilities. He was not able to provide the CD until 11th of October 2005 after several reminders from me and those visiting my Website (www.Friendsofmandinggambimed.btck.co.uk). Finally, Tom contacted me on 4/11/05 to let me know he had the college mailing office send the CD of photos and other material registered delivery to me. Then he made donation of $1000(one thousand us dollars) in the name of Friends of Manding, a Charitable Trust at Colchester Essex organising fund raising activities for Manding Medical Centre at Njawara the Gambia, West Africa. This cheque was duly received and forward registered mail to the Secretary of the Friends of Manding for depositing into our account at LLyod's Bank in Colchester Essex County.

Tom asked about the state of the proposed sister-city program between Alpena and Njawara. Yes, this was one of my goals for inviting the Americans to my village in the Gambia. I just believe that unveiling the false masks and stigma others have about Africa will create harmony in its unique way. People need to accept differences in the cultures. I transmitted all reactions presented by our American visitor to the Commissioner, the chief, and the village heads especially Hadi Panneh of Njawara village.

ALPENA: THANKS FOR TWINING WITH US/SISTER-CITY PROCLAMATION.

Having now been recognised as Distinguished 2005 Graduate by Alpena Community College I made a proposal for a twining relationship or sister-city status between Alpena and select villages in the Gambia.

I, you guessed right, contacted Mathew Dunckel as a sound board or trial balloon for the above idea. He replied that it was a sound idea and suggested my contacting the Alpena City Council members on the subject. He gave their web site thus:

http://www.alpena.mi.us/council/members. In addition he gave the names of Councilman Dave Karschnik and Councilwoman Carol Shafto for me to initiate direct contact with the Alpena City Council. He told me that the mayor was John Gilmet and the City manager was Mr. Alan Bakalarski.

Armed with all this information and more I made my first push through Mrs. Penny Boldrey, Executive Director at Alpena Community College. I had no doubt if I get her interest in this unique wish she would do all within her power to not only contact the right people to make it eventually happen but would open up more doors for my villagers and our health project at Njawara.

Penny Boldrey upon hearing from me linked with Councilwoman Shafto on the June 14th, 2005 thus; "Hi Carol, from one Distinguished Grad to another….. I received the enclosed message from our 2005 Distinguished Graduate, Dr. Alhasan Ceesay.

I' m wondering if perhaps you can help me with his inquiry regarding the possibility of twining between Alpena City and two villages in the Gambia, West Africa." Penny in turn informed me that she had contacted a good friend, Carol Shafto, who is a member of Alpena's City Council and also an Alpena Community College Distinguished 2003 Graduate, regarding my request for twining between the above communities. She enclosed Councilwoman Shafto's response to the idea.

My reaction was swift and my message to Councilwoman Carol Shafto ran thus:-"Hello Councilwoman Carol. Mrs Penny Boldrey sent me correspondence she had with you regarding a proposal I made to the city of Alpena. My initial e-mail kick starting a twining proposal between the city of Alpena; Njawara and Kinte Kunda villages in the Gambia West Africa was sent to Mayor John F. Gilmet, Dave R. Karsctunick, Mike Polluch, Sam Eller and Carol Shafto.

It read, "I'm pleased to write and inform you that I am deputized by village heads of Njawara and Kinte Kunda to contact you and initiate a twining/sister city status proposal between Alpena and the above two villages. Njawara is my home village and Kinte Kunda is where I attended primary school in the early fifties.

Tom Ray and the Leadership students visited both places during their two weeks stay in the Gambia. They met the chief of the district, Sefo Fafanding Kinte, at Kinte Kunda. Kinte Kunda has been the seat of many chiefs of the region and Fafanding is the most recent of several from this village. Njawara is historically a trading centre connecting Gambia and the Northern part of Senegal. Today she has become a tourist destination. One can easily log onto information about Njawara village on the internet.

It boasts of lots of female education oriented projects. In addition it has an agricultural training centre."The contact was made in behalf of the village heads of the above and the local authority at the North Bank division of the Gambia. This twining would be a very rewarding interaction and educational for both yours and the villagers. The people are eager to make worthwhile friendship with America.

The chiefs and village heads have urged me to initiate their wish for the twining between them and Alpena or any city willing to go into such relationship with the villages. You can link up with Mr. Thomas Ray and his students for feedback on their experience as guests of Manding Medical Centre at Njawara village, the Gambia. The villagers and I would be most grateful if given the chance to link up with Alpena City.

Carol Shafto sent in this hiccup. "Dr. Ceeasy, I cannot proceed with any more discussions with the City Council of the City of Alpena until I am much clearer about what a Twining proposal entails. Could you please describe to me what you have in mind? Although we may be supportive of your work at Njawara and Kinte Kunda in the Gambia; we cannot really act on your request until we know what we are agreeing to.

Could you send me a brief outline of what you are seeking from the City of Alpena?I will be happy to act as a liaison between you and the City, but cannot do so until I have a clear idea of what I am advocating for. Thank you most sincerely."

–Carol-

On July 13, 2005 I sent the required clarification to Councilwoman Carol Shafto as follows. Hello Carol, I am glad to hear from you. To be simplistically clear, twining means a sisterhood relationship between two cities for the mutual rewards of those involved. Hence it is a friendship like affair where people from Alpena can be part of and likewise the villages involved but at no cost to either party.

For example Councilwoman Shafto can choose to spend two weeks in Gambia helping reorganize or create a more functional administrative system or even learn from the villagers.

In brief it is a two way international relationship. Or cultural dance -troupes from the Gambia villages can be coming to entertain Alpena, possibly more cities, during the summers. This will help raise funds for the city, the villages, like wise for our health project at Njawara. It will provide much awareness and understanding of the two people merged in friendship.

It is like adopting each other and opening up rewarding human adventures at no cost involved. In a nut-shell, it means ratified friendship between Alpena and the two villages. I hope this makes it palatable for Alpena to want to be part of such endearing relationship. I thank you in behalf of the Kerewan local authority, the villagers and Commissioner for North Bank Division, the Gambia. God blesses all of you." –Dr. Ceesay-

Needless to say Councilwoman Carol Shafto was very pleased with the above clarification and appealed to Alpena City Council to consider the idea of twining in behalf of the Gambian villages. Hence, Carol on the 13/7/05 sent me this e-mail following the receipt of the above message to the councilwoman. It simply states that, "I have forwarded this information to the mayor and city manager and offered to be the liaison if the City should consent to comply with this request. I will keep you posted with any development."

I updated the Commissioner and all concern at the Lower Badibou district regarding progress of my initiative with Alpena City few weeks after hearing from Councilwoman Carol Shafto. The Commissioner and the local authority sent me the bellow covering letter in support of my push for a twining relationship with Alpena City Michigan, USA.

Njawara/Kinte Kunda

Lower Badibou District

North Bank Division

The Gambia, W. Africa

E-mail:njawaranato@yahoo.co.uk

November 5th, 2005

To: Dr. Alhasan Ceesay

Manchester, England

Subject: Twining of Njawara, Kinte Kunda & Alpena Michigan

Dear Dr. Ceesay,

Your first letter dated September 23rd, 2005 has been received and the content of which is understood, both the Commissioner, the Chief and the Alkalos (village heads) of Njawara and Kinte Kunda are very much interested in having Njawara, Kinte Kunda and Alpena City twined. The Communities of both villages met and discussed the issue and they are very much happy about the lofty ideas. Njawara and Kinte Kunda are located in the Northern part of the Gambia. They are just about 60 kilometres away from the capital City Banjul, the Gambia. Kinte Kunda is just 2 kilometres away from our administrative headquarters Kerewan where both the Commissioner and Area Council stay. Whereas Njawara is located 9 kilometres away from Kerewan. Regards

Sincerely

Aja Hadi Panneh (Alkalo)

Alh. Fafanding Kinte (Chief Lower Badibou)

Cc: Mr. Batala Juwara (Commisioner NBD)

I replied to the above support with this note despatched immediately to the village Akalos, the Chief and Commissioner North Bank Division at Kerewan village.

245 Great Western Street

Manchester M14 4LQ

England

16/11/05

A BIG THANK YOU TO ALL

Dear Commissioner,

I'm profoundly grateful to you, Sefo Fafanding, the local authority (area Council and chiefs) and especially Alkalo Arfang Bah and people of Toro. Lastly but not the least a big thank you goes to the people of Badibou, Njawara and my sister Hadi Panneh Alkalo of Njawara village. I am very happy for support and understanding given to Manding Medical Centre.

I'm pleased to inform you that I have initiated a twining process between Alpena and the villages of Njawara and Kinte Kunda. I have forwarded your note of 5/11/05 to the Alpena City Council. Copies were also sent to Mr. Thom Ray and the college.

Again, thank you for making our American friends happy and welcomed to our beloved country. God bless all of you. I will continue working for our development.

Sincerely

Dr. Alhasan S. Ceesay, MD

Director/Founder

Manding Medical Centre.

I then sent Carol Shafto the letter from the district authority plus this note urging action from her end.

245 Great Western Street

Manchester M14 4LQ

England

8/11/05

Mrs. Carol Shafto

Councilwoman

Alpena City Council

208 North First Avenue

Alpena, MI 49707

Dear Mrs. Carol Shafto,

The enclosed is reply to your last e-mail dated 25/9/05 regarding the twining proposal made to the Alpena City Council earlier on by me in behalf of Njawara village and Kinte Kunda, the Gambia, respectively.

The enthusiasm about having this relationship with Alpena is immeasurable. The villagers are looking forward to a warm and fruitful relationship between the two people. They all pray that you would be as eager to consummate it as they have already done in their wishes and hearts.

Finally, may friendship and human kindness be an everlasting link between all humans. God bless you and we look forward for a positive reply soon.

My personal regards and thanks to the City Council and all of Alpena.

Yours Sincerely

Dr. Alhasan S. Ceesay, MD

It was not until September 21, 2005 that I sent Councilwoman Shafto the following reminder and follow up note. "Hi Carol, I hope you had an enjoyable summer. This is a follow up of that lofty idea of twining Alpena City with Njawara and Kinte Kunda villages in the Gambia.

Has there been any movement forward at the Mayor's Office about the proposal made to the city? Is there anything I or the district authority in Gambia need do to bring this to fruition? I have not heard anything about it since your last email of 14/7/05. Again, regards and thanks. I bank on your continued interest. God Bless."

–Dr. Ceesay-

The next day God smiled onto our dream to befriend America. Councilwoman Mrs. Carol Shafto sent me the following reply to the inquiry about the status of my dream for America and the Gambia.

It rang in the most melodious and cherished message I ever had for a long, long time after my being admitted into medical school and upon treating my first patient in the villages. Here is Carol's email to me. "Good morning Dr. Ceesay: I appreciate your persistence in accomplishing this goal. Without that it surely would have failed. I do apologize for this delay.

I have just returned this week from a wonderful month long tour of the UK and Ireland. My last communication, before I left, with the City Manager was that this was a good idea, will be good for public relations, and that we should go forward with the idea. The Mayor is also in favour. So there is absolutely nothing standing in the way of this happening.

I am willing to do the work of it, but I honestly have no idea what to do. Do you know procedures or paper work or any such thing from your end? Is it as simple as a proclamation? I would like to have more information about your village, your people, and why you are interested in twining with Alpena – what connection there is.

I would then put together a presentation for the City Council and ask them to decide that we are sister-cities (the term used here, although I know the UK and Europe use "twining) with the villages of Njawara and Kinte Kunda.

We could erect a sign at the City entrance, etc. If you have any idea or directions for me, please let me know. Also any information you can provide on your village would be helpful. I will continue to work with you on this until it is accomplished.

Your friend in Alpena – Carol Shafto –

This was followed by my forwarding the bellow addendum to whatever had reached the Councilwoman's desk. Being the architect of this union much was expected from me. And so I never relented supplying as much information as many times as I can afford. My phone bill sprouted to a Warping £600 etc. Most important was this addendum bellow.

SYNAPSIES OF NJAWARA/KINTE KUNDA VILLAGES

Njawara is a 350 years old market village situated on the bank of the Miniminiyang bolong, a creek of the River Gambia, in the Lower Badibou District of the North Bank Division of the Gambia. Njawara has a population of a thousand residents and is 95 kilometres from Banjul, Gambia's capital City.

The village lies close to the Senegalese border and has been the trade links between Gambia and Senegal during the colonial days. Njawara was established and founded by the Panneh family of the Wolof tribe and initially called "Panneh village."

The elderly still fondly refer to her as Mpanneh. Among the residents of now Njawara are Mandingkas, Fulas, Sereres, Jolas, Konyanginkas, and Mabara tribes. All of whom are farmers, with few serving as petty traders, growing Peanuts, Rice, Coos, and a variety of vegetables. The nearest government administrative post is 9 kilometres away at Kerewan village. Njawara lacked modern luxuries of electricity, proper telephones, sewer system, pave roads but water is now pumped from a nearby borehole.

The village has a thriving school and a dynamic citizenry working hard to improve their lot and the future of the younger generation.

KINTE KUNDA village has been the political base of Lower Badibou District for decades. It has provided us with several chiefs in the past and Sefo Fafanding Kinte is the most recent contribution. Kinte Kunda village comprises of mostly Mandinka tribes men and women. It is the home of venerable late Sefo Njako Kinte who, in the 30s ruled the district with and iron fist. It was he who imposed one of his brother, Almami Kinte, to take over the administration or village headship of then Njawara (Mpanneh).

None the less he was a respected chief. Kinte Kunda was the first village that had a school in the entire Lower Badibou district and I am told that he chief insisted that

the school be built in his home village leaving a row that lasted through his rein. The village is now a smaller population than Njawara and the current appointed chief of the district, Sefo Fafanding Kinte resides there. Residents of Kinte Kunda are all farmers eager to improve their lives and those of their children.
They are friendly, peaceful, charming, descent hard working people who contributed a lot to growth of the Lower Badibou District in the North Bank.

These two villages along with the entire Lower Badibou District yearn for this twining/sister-city status to come to realty. Hence, I enclose relevant messages regarding the proposed twining from the district authority as per fax from the Gambia. The villagers and I are interested in twining with Alpena Michigan n an effort to open up the Pandora's box of friendship, goodwill and more understanding of the people and cultures that would allow us relate in this shrinking globe we all share. There is a lot we can do for each other once the ugly veil of ignorance, misunderstanding and fear is removed. And this can be done only learning and interacting with one another.

I am sure the students, who went to the villages, can tell how much warmth and friendship they received from the villagers they met. Exchange visits and whole host of beneficial programs to both parties can be organized within the framework of this twining. Once again, I personally appeal to the Mayor and City Council of Alpena to give this desire of the villagers a chance of fruition for Alpena City and the above villages in the Gambia. BY DR. ALHASAN S. CEESAY, MD

In short while, I received the following reply from Councilwoman Carol Shafto of Alpena City Council letting me know of the final details, date of the be proclamation for the sister-city relationship between our villages and Alpena Michigan. Without further ado I present the message as sent on the 17th of November 2005.

"Good Morning Dr. Ceesay,

After many months of communication with you, I can finally announce a DATE for our Twining/Sister City Resolution! The Alpena City Council will adopt a resolution to establish a Sister City Program with Njawara/ Kinte Kinda on December 5th, 2005.

I am going to be personally preparing the resolution. Since it will be a part of permanent records for both the villages and the City of Alpena, I would like be sure all of the information is accurate. Penny Boldrey suggested that I email the text to you after I complete it. If you are willing, you could read it for any factual errors or omissions before I send it on to the City. If you are willing,

I will send that via email when it is ready, sometime next week. Meanwhile I am meeting with Tom Ray from the college who led the Leadership Class expedition to the villages. He is VERY enthusiastic about this proposal and is going to give me information and even share some pictures. We will be meeting next week.

Finally, I have invited several people to come to the City Council meeting to provide testimony and support for this proposal. Both Penny Boldly and Tom Ray will be there. Also they are inviting some of the students who went to the villages to also be present and speak to the issue. So it would be a very nice presentation and will be more than just a formality.

Also, if you would like, I can arrange to have a tape of the meeting sent to you. Our meetings are videotaped and played for the public on the public access television channel several times a week, between meetings. I can make a copy of the tape of the meeting and have it send you or to the village officials or both if you would like. Also, the resolution will have an official seal of the City of Alpena and the signature of the Mayor.

I will have as many copies as you need made and will laminate them so they will be preserved. I will send those to you and/ or whomever you designate. I will get several if necessary.

I am so pleased to finally be able to bring this to completion. I know it must have been frustrating to you to have this take so long and to have us seen to be so unresponsive. I hope this totally enthusiastic ending makes up for all of that!

Your friend in Alpena:

- Carol Shafto –

On the day of ratification or passing of the resolution for sister city relationship between Alpena and the two above villages several speakers were heard. These included, among many, Penny Bodrey, Mr. Tom Ray, two student representatives who visited Gambia in May 2005 and Dr. Avery Aten. This was buffered by loop of fifty photos of the villages taken by the student while in the Gambia. At the end of the presentation Mayor John F. gimlet read into the record the above proclamation and vote was tabled to pass it.This Sister City proclamation between Alpena with Njawara/Kinte Kunda, Lower Badibou District, the Gambia was moved by Councilwoman Carol Shafto, seconded by Councilman Karschnick, that the proclamation to establish a sister city program with the villages of Njwara and Kinte Kunda be approved. The move was carried by unanimous vote. A copy of the sister City Resolution passed by Alpena City Council on December 5th 2005 is reproduced for your pleasure to read.

Chapter 18

PROCLAMATION TO ESTABLISH A "SISTER CITY" PROGRAM WITH NJAWARA AND KINTE KUNDA, LWER BADIBOU DISTRICT, GAMBIA, WEST AFRICA

WHEREAS, the City of Alpena recognises and supports the concept of global cooperation and community; and

WHERAS, the villagers of Njawara and Kinte Kunda, through their local leaders and Dr. Alhasan S. Ceesay, have reached out their hand in friendship and goodwill, and

WHEREAS, relationships were established by students and faculty of Alpena Community College when they were warmly welcomed to the villages for a service project earlier this year, and

WHEREAS, mutual understanding of our diversities as well as our similarities and the cultural exchanges that will result, will be beneficial to the citizens of both areas, and

WHEREAS, true global community is often established one person at a time, and one city and village at a time, leading to beneficial relations and programs for all;

NOW, THEREFORE, I, John F. Gilmet, by virtue of the authority vested in me as Mayor, **DO HEREBY PROCLAIM,** a "Sister City" Program with the villages of

NJAWARA/KINTE KUNDA

LOWER BADIBOU DISTRICT

GAMBIA

And urge all area citizens to extend the hand of fellowship and an embrace of genuine fraternity to their friends in NJAWARA/KINTE KINTE KUNDA and pledge support and loyalty as these communities of two great nations join together as "Sister Cities" Signed at Alpena Michigan, United States of America, on this 5th day of December, 2005. Councilwoman Carol Shafto read the following reply from me to Council and residents of Alpena City.

ALPENA, THANKS FOR TWINING WITH US

Honourable Mayor John F. Gilmet, Alpena City Council and residents of Alpena; please allow me convey heartfelt thanks as well as greetings from the Commissioner, NBD, Kerewan Area Council, the Chief of Lower Badibou, the Alkalos (village heads) of Njawara and Kinte Kunda. I am today full of joy and gratitude for twining resolution ratified by the Alpena City Council.

I am speechless as one of my dreams for the villager and America has now materialized in this twining resolution passed by Alpena. We are two good people now merged in good will for humanity and friendship. This coming together will archive a lot for both of us.

There is a lot for us to gain as well as learn from each other and generations to come will thank us for having taken the first footsteps of bringing people of diverse cultures and understanding together. Enclosed is message from the Gambia in response to the most welcomed news in your last email. This is the top of the iceberg for there is lot more benefit in this act. In addition, as long as I am alive Alpena and Gambia will not only benefit from this unique venture but will smile yearly for having dreamt along with me.

Let me, in passing, mention with thanks the first harbingers of this day. They are Mr. Thomas P. Ray and his Leadership team of students from Alpena Community College who visited Njawara village in May 2005. Thomas Ray and the students laid the marvellous foundation we today concretize.

Mrs. Penny Boldrey and Mathew Dunckel deserve our appreciation for remaining interested and in constant contact with me. The Gambia, the district authority of Lower Badibou and villagers remain eternally grateful for giving us the chance of twining with you. A Huge thanks Alpena City, the Mayor of Alpena and Alpena City Council for work well done. Councilwoman Mrs. Carol Shafto who relentlessly steered the twining proposal to completion also deserves our profound gratitude.

The villagers and I are eternally indebted to all at Alpena. In addition, we look forward to working hand in hand for the reward of all parties. Finally, I would again like to pay tribute to past and present friends at Alpena who helped me reach this pedestal. All of you helped make my sojourn to America a remarkable success. I would like many more of my friends to be like you at Alpena.

I hope you will believe, as well as join me, in my dream of providing modern medical aid to the Gambian villagers. Thanks a million and God bless America!

Signed: DR. ALHASAN SISAWO CEESAY, MD

FOUNDER/COORDINATOR

MANDING MEDICAL CENTRE

NJAWARA, THE GAMBIA

Two weeks later I received three copies of the "sister City Proclamation" along with a video tape of the Alpena City Council Meeting of December 5, 2005. Also enclosed were the Alpena news and copy of Alpena Public Notices showing minutes of the City Council meeting which carried ratification of the sister city proclamation by a unanimous vote. I must confess exhilaration in my heart for Alpena City Council having done so much for my villages without reservation and accomplished with great speed.

I sent the following communiqué to the current representative to the Gambia, Ambassador Joseph D. Stafford in preparing them for the arrival the package from the Alpena City Council for forwarding to the Commissioner of the North Bank Division, the Gambia.

MANDING MEDICAL CENTRE

245 Great Western Street

Manchester M14 4LQ

Email:alhasanceesay@hotmail.com

Date: 10/12/05

Ambassador Joseph D. Stafford

Embassy of the United States of America

Kairaba Avenue

P. M. Box 19

Banjul, the Gambia,

West Africa

RE: Manding Medical Centre/Alpena USA Twining

Dear Ambassador Stafford,

I am Dr. Alhasan S. Ceesay from Njawara village and currently on studies in the UK. This is to introduce the above self-help health organisation at Njawara as well as kindly request favour of your good office's service in behalf Alpena Michigan and the villages of Njawara and Kinte Kunda, the Gambia. I pioneered the above centre, after graduating as a doctor and upon returning to the Gambia in 1992. It became an NGO in 1994 after being fully registered by the Justice Department and recognised by the Ministry of Health in 1993. In addition, we are now a registered Charitable Trust, as Friends of Manding, in England and Wales by the Charity Commission of the UK. Our website is:

www.friendsofmandinggambimed.btck.co.uk. It will show our home page as "Friends of Manding." Alternatively, one can used a short cut by typing in "Manding Medical Centre, Njawara" and click search. The same home page plus lot more will appear. I have also written two books and a hefty portion of proceed from the sale of both books is earmarked to help support Manding Medical Centre at Njawara and our goal of providing medical aid to the villager, especially children. More information about my work and commitment to providing much needed medical service to the region in conjunction with the Gambia Ministry of Health can be seen in our website as above. Finally, I am more than delighted to report that Alpena City, Michigan, USA has just ratfied a sister city program with my home village Njawara and Kinte Kunda village in **the** Lower Badibou District, North Bank Division, the Gambia.

Hence, I have asked the Alpena City Mayor's Office to send five copies of the final proclamation declaring the sister city status between Alpena and the above two named villages in Badibou to you for your office to kindly deliver the documents to the Commissioner North Bank Division at Kerewan.

Thank you for taking time to assist us in the above matter. Please feel free to contact me any time convenient to you. Best wishes for good health and achievement in the coming year. Regard to your family.

Yours Sincerely

Dr. Alhasan S. Ceesay, MD

Founder/Coordinator

Manding Medical Centre

Njawara, The Gambia, West Africa.

This letter was followed with two telephone calls to the Embassy of the United States in the Gambia to verify receipt of the package sent from Alpena to Joseph D. Stafford. The Secretary to Mr. Stafford, in the last phone call let me know it usually take a month or more before none official mail arrives at their desk.

He assured me that the office will do as request whenever the package reaches the Embassy. I called Sefo Fafanding Kinte and Alkalo Hadi Panneh and told them to check with either Ambassador Joseph Stafford directly or one of the officers in the know at the office for their copies of the sister city proclamation of which the villagers are unsung heroes for having received the ACC students who visited Njawara in May 2005 with open hearts, hospitality, generosity and warmth.

It was not until Thursday, February 16th, 2006 that Ambassador Joseph D. Stafford and team where able to deliver, in person amid tumultuous reception and celebration, the sister-city proclamation between Alpena City, Michigan USA, with Njawara and Kinte Kunda villages in the North Bank of the Gambia.

I made it clear that the brief ceremony at Njawara on the 16/2/06 marked the end of phase one of the sister city relationship between us and Alpena Michigan. I suggested the following four areas for food for thought by all concern. They are:-

1. Education

This already started in earnest as some in Alpena have expressed desire to sponsor worthy candidates at the primary level for an experimental period of one year. Higher levels, such as college education and nursing training and or other relevant skill areas will in due course be included.

2. Health

A lot is planned for health oriented programs and Manding Medical Centre will be enhanced to a much functional status. There will be training programs for health personnel etc.

3. Tourism: I am studying ways of creating tourist attraction with facilities erected in due course to the region.

4. Cultural: Exchanges entailing having cultural dance troop(s) from the Lower Badibou District travel to Alpena Michigan, and other cities in the USA during the summers to display our fabric of entertainment, history and arts. These are few ideas in the pipeline. Feel free to add yours to enrich the program. This is by no means binding or final but seeking more suggestions on how to benefit both parties in this unique twining program just approved by Alpena City. Let me make it crystal clear that there is no financial commitment from Alpena.

However, the cultural show can raise lot of money upon performing in America. I thanked the Commissioner North Bank, Sefo of Lower Badibou, District Authority and Kerewan Area Council for having worked so hard with me to provide this excellent opportunity to our people. I promised that more is on the way.

Three weeks earlier I received this e-mail from Councilwoman Mrs. Carol Shafto announcing the good news of her efforts. "Dr. Ceesay, we have sent five copies of the proclamation to the America Embassy- which you provided the address for. I also have three copies of the proclamation for you as well as a copy of the tape of the meeting; a copy of the newspaper where the action appeared; and a copy of the newspaper with the official minutes. I will get these out to you today.

It was a most wonderful evening as you will see on the tape. Five people, your friends old and new, spoke in favour of the proclamation. This included Dr. Avery Aten who I have now spoken with and who is very enthusiastic about working on the medical aspect of things with you. He will be in touch with you by phone he said. But you will be able to see him and hear what he had to say during City Council meeting of December 5, 2005.

Also speaking where two students who have visited the Gambia; Tom Ray and Penny Boldrey. (And me, of course). I read your wonderful letter for the record. We also had a loop of over fifty slides showing on the screen during the presentation. It was the nicest sister-city ceremony we have ever had-by far! Usually we just read the proclamation and that is it. I think this ends my part in all of this-except for one thing.

My sons and I were going to "adopt" a family through Save the Children. This involves sending a letter each month and with an amount of money. We would be happy to adopt some children from your village instead if there is an easy way to do this. We would need a name and address and what form we could make our donation in (money order?).

We are not really wealthy- but could send $20 -$25 a month for at least a year to a deserving child. Of course; we would hope that they might send a note now and then... but this all up to you.

I hope you are pleased with all that has happened.

I remained your friend.

Carol Shafto.

In reply I sent my friend Carol Shafto the following.

Hello Carol; Now I am able to response to your email. First, please accept our eternal ineptness' for having worked so hard to bring the twining into reality. Only God can reward your efforts. Please kindly extend our heartfelt gratitude to the Mayor and your fellow Councillors at Alpena. Send me the Mayor's telephone. I need to convey our appreciation to him. I had a long chat with the village and they were in cloud nine about the approval of the sister city program.

I will be forwarding the names of deserving school children you might want to sponsor/adopt. I will cal you, before forwarding the names, about it when I get the list that the parents and headmaster promised to send me. Thanks a million and God blesses you and yours. Best wishes for good health and successful 2006. I look forward to our travelling to the Gambia soon. Regard.

Sincerely

Dr. Alhasan S. Ceesay, MD

In the mean time Mrs. Penny Boldrey was also busy doing a story for the ACC Alumni News. In addition Carol was able to have a feature about the just approved sister city program done by the local news paper. She was very happy about it as the email bellow from Carol shows.

"Good Morning Alhasan, "our story" is headline, above the fold, in the Alpena News today! It is wonderful publication for your project. I will send you copies but you can read it on-line today only at www.thealpenanews.com. It reads "Alpena's sister-city-ACC graduate initiates partnership with Gambia villages." And there is a wonderful colour picture of one of the ACC students with village children. I hope you enjoyed the story and are pleased with my efforts for publicity.

The news reporter, Sue Lutuszek, will do a follow-up story about people "adopting Children for education purposes", like I am doing with my son(s).

It is a good day for celebration. Check the website.

Your friend

Carol

Here is one of several features about the twining between Alpena City with Njwara and Kinte Kunda villages in the North Bank Division, the Gambia.

ALPENA NEWS MICHIGAN, USA

SISTER CITY PROGRAM HAS TIES TO

ACC STUDENT OF 1960s

A link dating back to the 1960s has helped Alpena establish a sister city program with Njawara and Kinte Kunda, Lower Badibou District, the Gambia.

The program was initiated by Alhasan Ceesay, MD, an Alpena Community College of the 1960s and the 2005 Distinguished Graduate who lives in the Wes African country. He was assisted by ACC staff and Councilwoman Carol Shafto.

"He feels this is his American home and villages in Gambia are his African home and wanted to link the tow together." Carol Shafto said.

When Penny Boldrey of the ACC Foundation first put Ceesay in touch with Shafto for assistance in the venture, Shafto was leery of his intentions. "I did not get it," she said. "I wanted to know what we are going to gain?" the whole idea is simply to put out information on the situation in those villages in the public eye, Shafto said Ceesay's dream is to build a medical centre to serve the villages, since care is many miles away and roads in and out of villages aren't passable by ambulance.

Currently patients are transported out of villages without ambulances for distances to health centres from their homes. Avery Aten, MD, of Alpena also has become involved with the project. "The medical aspects of this relationship can be long-term," he told city council members. He said so medical statistics regarding the area, such as the average life expectancy is 53 years old and 85 out of 1000 children die during birth.

According to Shafto, some of Aten's hopes include sending medical equipment which is no longer used here to the villages and even possibly having nursing students experiencing practicing there. "I just see all kinds of goodwill things happening," Shafto said. "For us to have the opportunity to lead about a totally different culture is good for us."

"One aspect Shafto highlighted is the opportunity for elementary classroom in Alpena to communicate with the village school. Although she assisted in having the proclamation made, Shafto gives credit for making it happen to individuals at ACC.

"My part is minor compared to what ACC has done," she said. "They are the ones who really got this started." During the trip the students met with various village leaders who showed them what projects they were working on and where the greatest need was. In addition, the students taught some short classes on the United States.

One day the group helped with the construction of a mosque. They also visited the agricultural centre and health centre. Ray said the trip "contributed greatly" in making the sister city proclamation a reality "because it gave people in Alpena a connection to the village." "The Gambia District Authority of Lower Badibou and villagers remain eternally grateful for giving us chance of twining with you.

Huge thanks to the City of Alpena, Mayor of Alpena and Alpena City Council," Alhasan wrote. "The villagers and I are enternaly indebted to all at Alpena. In addition, we look forward to working hand in hand for reward of all parties."

-Sue Latuszek: The Alpena News 2005-

The first hatchling of this merging of diverse hearts is as follows:-

Njawara Basic School

Lower Badibu District

North Bank Division

The Gambia, W. Africa

19/01/06

Dear Sir/Madam

RE: To whom it may concern.

These students are promising students whose parents are not able to fully support their educational needs. As a result, we would be very grateful if a concern person(s) can assist the students and their parents in taking care of some of the financial difficulties they are encountering to earn education. These include school fees, uniforms, book bills and other school needs. Thank you and in anticipation, I remain,

Yours Faithfully

Lamin K. Juwara

Principal

These where the initial list of needy student who would have benefited from what was going to be the Manding Medical Centre/USA scholarship grants.

NAME	AGE	CLASS	PARENT
1. Ismaila Ceesay Njawara	14yrs	8B	Dodu Ceesay
2. Edrisa Barry Njawara	14yrs	8B	Adoulie Barry
3. Alieu Dem Njawara	12yrs	7B	Modou Dem
4. Mamud Panneh Njawara	12yrs	7A	Ousainu Panneh

Turning the impossible possible

NAME	AGE	CLASS	PARENT	
5. Adama Jallow	12yrs	7B	Assan Jallow	Ker Ardo
6. Kally Bah	13yrs	8B	Saikou Bah	Ker Ardo
7. Njammeh Bah	12yrs	7B	Musa Bah	Toro Bah
8. Hammed Dem	12yrs	7B	Musa I. Bah	Toro Bah
9. Ebrima Kanteh	15yrs	7B	Baboucar Kaneh	Toro Bah

10. Mustapha Jawo   15yrs   8A   Omar Jawo   Toro Bah

11. Modou Touray   11yrs   6A   Sohna Jaw   Panneh Bah

12. Nuha Krubally   10yrs   5A   Modo Krubally   Samba Musu

13. Matarr Panneh   10yrs   4B   Bora Panneh   Njawara

14. Modou Loum   14yrs   7B   Bintou Jammeh   Ker Jebal

The above list and letter were faxed to Councilwoman Carol Shafto on the 23/02/06. The fax simply read:-

Hi Carol,

I hope you are okay and back at work. I hereby forward a list of school children from Njawara school needing sponsorship. Feel free to contact those you think would like to participate in this educational project. The first three candidates in the list are earmarked for you and your son(s). See names 1 – 3 in the list.

Send all monies via Western Union in the name of Aja Hadi Panneh, (Alkalo of Njawara village) to any Gambian Bank that Western Union deals with in Gambia. Then email me stating amounts, date sent and for who. I will follow up by contacting the Principal of Njawara School, the parents and the chief of the district to ascertain prompt and proper distribution. In addition, I will have Aja Hadi Panneh (Alkalo), the parents, Headmaster and were possible the recipient students to write acknowledging the amounts received. Please feel free to contact me if you have any questions or ideas to promote the above noble educational commitment. Once again, thanks and we remain grateful for your stand.

Your Friend

Dr. Alhasan S. Ceesay, MD

Alasan Mbalo and Roeyata Ceesay

Chapter 19

Manding Medical Center

When God wants to destroy someone, He first made him an unusual dreamer. So Gandhi had his dream of people solving social deference none violently and Rev. Martin Luther king, jr. held onto his admirable dream of children of Jews and Gentile, black and whites holding hands and living in harmony spearheading peaceful cause for mankind. There are the Albert Schweitzer's and mother Theresa's of the world dreamers who spent their lives believing in their dreams for mankind.

My dream, since 1956, was the simple goal of providing medical aid to those far and in remote villages. The villager, who is forced to walk miles on end to seek medical aid for his already dying child, wife or friend, deserves a better health system. Something I saw in 1956 left an indelible mark in my mind and I have since then asked and prayed that God help me bring part if not full to the kind of tragedy that was passing right before me. I was hopelessly unable to give relief except to comfort those involved.

In 1956, while on my way to Saba village, I met an anxious father carrying his son and his almost dead pregnant wife on the back of donkey heading for the health center at Kerewan village, another three or more miles from where I met him. The child was vomiting yellow stuff, he was sweaty, his eyes were reverted backwards and the pregnant lady groaning every time the mule moves. There was some greenish fluid dripping off her lapper. She could barely hold the ropes controlling the donkey.

I went to Kerewan later that evening and asked about the status of that family, only to be told that the boy passed away half a mile to the dispensary and the lady was referred to the central hospital in Banjul but the family had no money to pay for her transportation nor was the River ambulance available as it was undergoing maintenance at the Dockyard.

To cut a long story short, both child and mother died because of lack of medical facilities or modern medical aid to the villager. One or all of those lives could have been saved and remain beneficial to the country than the fate that befell them. I prayed and grieved with the family for months and redoubled my efforts at school in other to solve such development in future.

I committed myself to medicine from that day on and never regretted making such a challenging decision in my life. Hence, when on the day I was taking the Hippocratic Oath, I not only swore to uphold all therein but to make sure that God help me not to ever deviate from my commitment and promise to be part of the solution in the health services of the Gambia, to foster health education for the villager, and to complement the existing medical facilities in the Gambia as well as ease the shortage of medical service personnel. To many, except the dreamer, such Erewhons leads to failure as they turn to be white elephants.

Some friends tease me by flatly promising to rise from their graves on the opening day of such an Alice in wonderland project. Let me make it crystal clear that I had no illusions about what was needed, or to be done and that the building of the hospital would indeed be a lifetime challenge I am fully ready to grapple with. There would be a lot of well-wishers but very few will ever want to join until the opening day ceremonies. So first things first,

I met an attorney friend Mr. Ousainou Darboe, a villager like me, on September 24, 1992, and pleaded for his assistance with the legal aspects of setting up a charitable foundation, Manding Medical center at Njawara village in the provinces for the sole purpose of providing much needed medical aid to the villager. He was very obliging and requested no payment in return for his services. In the mean time I got a board of governors elected while he prepared the memorandum and articles of association of Manding Medical Centre at Njawara village.

Also, I met with the Lower Badibou district chief, Kitabou Singateh, who by the way was my primary school class mate at Kinte Kunda from 1953 to 1957, the District Authority, Commissioner and the kerewan Area Council. All of whom were more than delighted and did all they could under the law to help me set up a grassroots local advisory committee, which was headed by the commissioner, to assist the board and also let the villagers feel being part of the ongoing project.

At my home village, Njawara, a group organized itself and formed a pioneering committee to formally ask the Alkalo (village head/mayor) and the people of Toro Bahen village to donate the earmarked land between it and Njawara for the sole purpose of establishing the Manding Medical Centre on it.

The land issue was partially cleared by the first week of the appeal. In October 1992, Alkalo Omar Koi Bah of Toro Bahen, along with alhaj Musa (Njabi) Bah and Sirimang Bah called my brother, Doudu Ceesay, the elders of Toro Bahen and I to officially inform us that the earmarked land of two plots have been donated to me for the sole purpose of erecting a medical center and hospital facility for the villagers of the region and Gambia. We thanked him for his foresight and kindness towards future generations.

I went back to my lawyer, Ousainu Darboe who by then had finished all work needed for the registration of Manding Medical Centre. We are forever indebted to Alkalos Omar Koi, Arfang Bah, Musa (Njambi) Bah and resident Sirimang Bah, and the people of Toro village. Lastly but not the least our venerable able lawyer Mr. Ousainou Darboe, without whose kindness and legal mind the registration of Manding Medical Centre would have taken longer that it did assisted me.

I also express profound gratitude to the Hon. Chief of Lower Badibou district, Kitabou Singateh, the commissioner, and the local district authority for their understanding and willingness to contribute positively towards our goal and growth. I submitted the registration application material to the Attorney General's Chambers at the Justice Department, Banjul, on October 22, 1992 and Manding Medical Centre was officially registered as an incorporated charitable organization under the companies Act, 1959 by the 27th of October 1992. Manding Medical Centre' certificate of incorporation is number: 224/1992.

With the completion of the paper work and registration of the center, I embarked on a blitz of letter writing informing philanthropists and organizations worldwide about Manding Medical Centre and the need for assistance or donations of medications, equipments, medical videos with which to teach our cadre and villagers to become health worker or evangelist, or nurses and to help us build the center. To complete the establishment process, after the land was officially ours, I wrote to the following letter to the Ministry of Health informing them of the formation of Manding Medical Centre, a self –help health organization at Njawara, Lower Badibou, North Bank Division, the Gambia. Our temporal address was at 5B Ingram Street in Banjul, capital of the Gambia.

Manding Medical Centre

5B Ingram Street

Banjul, The Gambia

March 2, 1993

Permanent Secretary

Ministry of Health

The Quadrangle

Banjul, The Gambia

West Africa

Dear Permanent Secretary,

Re: Application for the establishment of a Medical Centre at Njawara in the North Bank.

We are pleased to bring to attention the setting up of a self-help Health organization in the North Bank Division at Njawara village. The directorates and members of the organization would be more than grateful if the Ministry of Health would allow us establish Manding Medical Centre at Njawara village, Lower Badibou District of the Gambia. Manding Medical Centre, when fully operational, will provide medical, surgical, gynecological and obstetrics, Pediatrics and other facilities to the villagers.

It will also help ease the shortage of medical facilities in that region. Manding Medical Centre will have health education secessions in the villages as an effort to enlighten our youths. Again, thank you for taking time to consider our application and we certainly look forward to a positive recognition of the need for such a center in the rural sector of the Gambia.

I am anxiously waiting to hear from your office at your convenience. Regards

Yours sincerely

Dr. Alhasan S. Ceesay, MD

Director/Coordinator

Meanwhile the villagers grew more enthused and throngs of them attended our monthly health field trips or clinics.

The attendance grew so large that we ended up listing the villages to attend in turn of nine villages per trip. This usually totals to a bit above 1,000 patients at a given visit. I normally go on weekends with three doctors and at times four volunteer doctors along with Nurses aid Mrs. Mbee Sonko and Ida Njie to assist us do the job. The field trips/clinics start with an announcement by Radio Gambia giving the names of villages expected to attend and at which village health center.

The clinic day starts with an early morning breakfast by the team and then a ride to the village health center where we would find the villagers and their sick ones assembled. Every occasion starts with the offering of prayers and then the various village heads, in attendance help us in organizing the flow of people wanting to be see by one of our team doctors. In most cases the day goes trouble free but at certain localities the political tension does make it very difficult to have such large groups of people without little arguments.

Thanks to the Commissioner (s) for deploying the police or making them available to quell trouble and help us maintain order during these clinics. Commissioner Lamin Koma can tell you how rough things can be at some of these clinic centers.

He was trapped in one of these bad moments of people rushing to be in the front line of the queue to see one our doctors. The Ministry of Health finally sent us the following affirmative reply as thus: -

Ministry of Health & Social services

The Quadrangle

Banjul, The Gambia

Ref.P510/289/01(95)

Dr. Alhasan Ceesay

Manding Medical Centre

5B Ingram Street

Banjul, The Gambia

RE: Application to establish a Medical Centre at Njawara

I acknowledge receipt of your letter of the 2nd March 1993 on the above-mentioned subject. I wish to inform you that this Ministry has no objection to your application to establish Manding Medical Centre at Njawara. This initiative is in line with our national health policies and we would render our support in our joint efforts to improve the health of the people.

Signed: N. Ceesay (For Permanent Secretary)

After several more field trips it was suggested we apply for a None Governmental Organization (NGO) status. It was believed that if we become and NGO, help would come our way quicker. I went to work on this suggestion and arranged for Tango Secretariat Centre to send one of the United Nations voluntary program officers to come and evaluate our performance relative to the objectives of Manding Medical Centre.

This was accepted and a field trip was set up for September 12 to 22, 1995. Radio Gambia made the announcement well ahead of the time for our arrival and the following was the outcome of that august gathering of September 21 &22, 1995.

Chapter 20

TANGO SECRETARIAT TRIP REPORT ON MANDING MEDICAL CENTRE, SEPTEMBER 21 – 22, 1995

A field trip to Kerewan at the North Bank Division was organized by the Manding Medical Centre Executive Director Dr. Alhasan S. Ceesay in conjunction with Tango Secretariat Centre to see the organization's activities and meet the members before recommending the organization as a member of Tango.

On September 21, 1995, two meetings were organized in two big centers where members gather to air their views and experience from the organization. Alkalos, chiefs, imams, women, men and youths attended these meetings. The key leadership from five villages in their speeches showed interest and support for the project and organization. Alkalo of Toro Bahen Omar Koi and chiefs donated the land for the constructing of Manding Medical Centre, the hospital and its ancillaries. The two meeting were highly attended and successful.

The Tango (UNV) program officer Mr. Muloshi on behalf of Tango gave a keynote speech on Tango's operations and activities as an umbrella organization and urged members to work hand in hand with the organization in their efforts to develop their villages and North Bank area.

The three meetings with the commissioner during the field trip on our courtesy call were successful and encouraged the executive Director of Manding Medical Centre, Dr. Alhasan Ceesay, to cooperate with the strict, especially the commissioner who is one of the advisors in the local committee.

The commissioner thanked Tango for making the purpose of the mission clear to him and promised that he will try by all means to cooperate with Tango in the area of Technical advice and institution capacity building. Clinic day was organized on September 22, 1995 at Njawara and 150 people attended and got treatments.

RECOMMENDATION

Looking at the caliber of leadership and development activities compared to some NGO tango members in comparison to Manding Medical Centre, the organization need consideration since they have already activities with a promising future.

Looking at the composition of the Board, they have people with a great vision. They have strong membership and backup at the grassroots levels. The organization has chosen to do what is right at the right time and their concentration in one area is vital and a good starting point.

Any success achieved by any organization depended on good leadership and discipline. Manding Medical Centre has quality leadership and deserves NGO status.

Signed: M. Muloshi

UNV Program Officer

We were delighted by the recommendation made by the United Nations voluntary Program Officer in the Gambia. We redoubled our efforts to contact organizations seeking help worldwide. In between letters and monthly field trips to different select health centers we were blessed with visits from interested friends and groups or representatives of similar organizations in the globe. I had several telephone calls to Dr. Edward Brown, an official of the World Bank in Washington, D. C. responsible of the bank's health affairs at the time.

He was very receptive and had several added discussions with Dentist Melvin George, then Director of Medical and Health Service for the Gambia, on how the bank could help in the financing of the building of Manding Medical Centre.

These talks went on well and Dr. Edward brown gave me his promise and personal commitment to helping the project and that we have to start in a small scale and the building will have to be done in several well planned phases. Dr. Sidi C. Jammeh, a former Armitage School colleague, promised to help me by constantly reminding Dr. Brown of the need to help us with the project. This kept the momentum at the World Bank alive for Manding Medical Centre. Among our guest were a couple from Colchester, Essex, UK, Lorna V. Robinson and husband Keith Robinson were very impressed by our project and enthusiasm of the ordinary villagers about Manding Medical Centre.

They fell in love with the idea and objectives of the self-help health organization and promised to help as much as they could. We had by this time submitted application for NGO status and ACCNO Secretary replied thus:

ACCNO Secretariat

Dept. of Community Development

13 Mariner Parade

Babjul, The Gambia

September 12, 1994

Ref.CD/ACCNO/Vol3/(183)

Dr. Alhasan S. Ceesay

Director/Coordinator

Manding Medical Centre

P. O. Box 640

Banjul, The Gambia

Dear Sir,

RE: application for an NGO status within the ACCNO framework

Please find enclosed a self-explanatory letter from the Ministry for local government and lands concerning the approval of your application for NGO status. ACCCNO Secretariat congratulates your organization for successfully completing the registration process and wishes you a fruitful relationship in the field of development.

Thank you for your cooperation

Yours Faithfully

Musu Ngujo

For: ACCNO desk Officer

Cc: file & R/File

Replies from our worldwide appeal letters did not pour in money nor did they materialized beyond promises to help in due course. Hence, I decided to open up a pharmacy at my expense at my residence in the Bundung area of Serekunda using the proceeds from its sales to finance the health field trips and activities of the organization. This meant spending an extra three to fours at the pharmacy daily after eight hours at the RVH before rejoining my family.

All drugs used for the treatment of patients at our field trip clinics were purchased from sales I made at the Bundung Pharmacy. A local agency, known as IBAS, lent me D8000, interest free, which was used in buying drugs and paying for transportation for the project's activities. The loan was completely repaid well ahead of the allowed sixteen months period given by IBAS. We are obliged and grateful to Aja Ndey Oley Jobe and management of IBAS for their kindness to assist us at the time.

Just when things were about to be financially complete for us to start the first phase of building the various sections of the hospital, came the unexpected coup d'etat of July 22, 1994. The reaction from would be our donors and supporters or sponsors were swift and equally unexpected.

All those who were considering giving the project a chance sited likelihood of sudden national unrest and instability as reasons for their withdrawal of promised aid and participation while some suggested my waiting until after the transition phase of the coup d'etat before they would reconsider reopening our files with them. Again it resorted to legend or case of the chicken the egg, which came first as no one, knew when the transition would end and we kept our fingers crossed hoping that daylight will be ours in not far distance. It was a severe blow to our hope and for getting the type of interest and support that was engendered for Manding Medical Centre would be difficult to match after such crisis that occurred in the Gambia.

Many were acting in conjunction with their governments, which were not sure of what the future under military rule would be for the Gambia. All prospective and possible international sources earmarked for Manding Medical Centre were either frozen or evaporated into thin air with the coup leaving me floating in the middle of the ocean of despair without a life jacket except God's merciful hands. I knew the villagers would grow restless if nothing happens in the direction of building the center.

I called an emergency general meeting with members from most of the villages and told them of the new challenge and development and this information not only fell on deaf ears but left their spirits dampened.

Interest waxed and waned at some quarters but I kept on trying my best not to be despondent like the others have shown. I kept the organization alive under very limited funds raised from the pharmacy at Bundung until my trip to the UK in January 2000.

Before leaving the Gambia, the Commissioner for north Bank Division and chairman of the local advisory committee for Manding Medical Centre, Mr. Lamin Koma, gave me the following letter to assist me in my fund raising drive while in England and possible other European countries. It read thus:

The Commissioner

Kerewan Village

North Bank Division

The Gambia, West Africa

June 15, 1998

TO WHOM IT MAY CONCERN

I hereby write to testify and confirm that Manding Medical Centre is a self-help health project situated at Njawara village, North Bank Division.

As the Commissioner of this division I was elected as the Chairman of the local advisory Committee of the

Manding Medical Centre. As I am concerned, I am aware of this self-help project since it took off the ground, by the able hands of Dr. Alhasan S. Ceesay, a born citizen of Njawara village.

The purpose of the establishing of such a medical centre is to provide medical attention/care to all Gambians irrespective of religion, tribe, nationality or gender and age within the country and sub-region.

It is in these regards that this office writes to seek for your assistance in providing support in cash/kind to make this medical center a reality. I look forward to your continued support and cooperation.

Signed: V. Baldeh

For Commissioner

North Bank Division

The new millennium started with good omen for Manding Medical Centre. I have been invited to go to Europe and America on a fund raising trip for the center but could not because of my commitment with the Royal Victoria Hospital (RVH). I needed a longer vacation period to be able to travel and keep my job at the same time.

Above all my family needed the monetary support, which would fade away if I lost the post at the RVH.

Hence, to my delight and greatest timely occurrence I heard from my long-standing friend in Colchester, Mrs. Lorna V. Robinson, inviting my wife and I to come to the UK to attend the wedding of their younger daughter on January 9th, 2000. Coincidentally, I had just started my annual leave, which was to finish on the 26th of January 2000.

The excitement mounted when we received a fax from the visa officer at the British High Commission in the Gambia requesting that we report to the visa processing office with our passports on Tuesday 8.30 am January 4th, 2000 for processing of our visas for our pending travels to the UK.

This took me by surprise because of the casual way we had discussed the possibility of such a trip. So when we got the telephone call followed by the said fax from the visa section I was caught off guard and had to rush through all the preparations for my wife and I to travel to UK without a second thought on whether adequate arrangements were being made for my eventual pursuit of a postgraduate degree (MRCP) in internal medicine.

Hind side has it that I needed to discuss this aspect with the visa councillor and request for eventual student visa status or leave to remain until my completion of the post graduate degree I wanted to pursue.

Miss Famatanding Ceesay, Daughter

God's ways and timing are best for every occasion. I was yearning to get a way out of the financial limbo the center ran into since the change of government in the Gambia. Now that opportunity was suddenly thrown on my laps by Lorna Robinson's open-ended invitation for my wife and to attend their daughter's wedding ceremony in the UK.

Interested donors started being weary about Military rule and possible restlessness that may ensue. Hence, Manding Medical Centre literally lost all its prospective overseas support as well as sponsors most of who had cold feet after the July coup d'etat of 2004.

I ended up running the center from my meager salary of D1500 or seventy-five pounds sterling per month and of literally hard labor with long hours at a time. The other source was from what little I could make from sales at the Bundung pharmacy.

To cut a long story short we were granted visas to travel to the UK. We left the Gambia on the 6th of January 2000 on a new footing and challenge to bring back some life into Manding Medical center while in England. I got on the ball as soon as the wedding ceremony was over. I obtained a three-year study leave from the Management Board of the Royal Victoria Hospital in Banjul.

This gave me all the time I needed to try to rekindle interest in the center and thereby inject into Manding Medical center cash flow it needed to help us meet or our targeted goal and objective for the farming community in the North Bank Division of the Gambia. It was more like a miracle entering this new concrete and direct ways. Help from my host Lorna Robinson of Colchester, Essex, UK further anointed my hands.

Lorna and I wrote several letters to various places, including celebrities and organizations, most of who replied in the negative because of perception they had about the political climate in Gambia since the coup d'etat of July 22nd 1994.

Nonetheless some hinted being interested at a later date, meaning when the solders return to camp. A few donated small amounts plus hospital items. By now it became clear that we have to counter the perception most, on this side of the isles feel or had about the Gambia at the time.

This dreadful start did not alarm me much for I am fully aware of the wrong information about the average African in the village, who like most, is just a descent human being trying to earn an honest living for himself, family and community. Villagers are least interested in all the political gimmickry shrouding and clothing their lives.

I do not at all blame the rest of world for getting sick and tired of helping and not seeing any tangible good come out of it and worse some African politicians and regimes show no interest in helping move the African people onto better and modern rewarding modalities of life.

They offer more lip service than opening avenues for progress. How many knew that the Ethiopian starvation was politically orchestrated by the then Mangestu regime? Genocide regime and the heartlessness of some African politicians made me feel sick.

To remove any possible sceptics regarding Manding Medical Centre and its objectives we decided to have it registered as a charitable organization in the UK under the name of Colchester Friends of Manding charitable trust. The Robinson knew a solicitor who would be so kind to help us with the legal aspect of the registration process with UK charity Commission.

They spoke to Mr. Bruce Ballard of the Birkett long Solicitors to come to our aid. This kind gentleman, like my lawyer friend, Mr. Ousainou Darboe, gladly agreed to help and sent us a draft of the Trust deed. After a series of changes were made on the draft he forwarded our request to be registered in the UK as a charitable organization helping its twin partner or parent group, Manding Medical Centre at Njawara village in the

Gambia, West Africa. Meanwhile, we concentrated our activities through media campaign effort to call attention to existence of Friends of Manding and their desire in building a hospital for Manding Medical Centre at Njawara, the Gambia. Again we ran into a very gentle heart in the person of Miss Helen Anderson of Colchester who was the Community website editor for Essex County. She went head over heels regarding the idea of helping others so far away when approached by Lorna Robinson.

Helen thought the idea wonderful and at the same time helped us have our own website and also had an article published by the Evening Gazette which had a large reader circulation. In the same vein I got the interest of Dr. Linda Mahon-Daly, Dr. Peter Wilson, Dr. Laurel Spooner, Dr. Richard Spooner, Dr. Philip Murray, Dr. Barbara Murray, Dr. Fredric Payne, who by the way was our Medical superintendent under who I worked at the RVH during the later part of colonial Gambia, along with many surgeries in the Colchester area.

These were my Good Samaritans of the day who worked acidulously to make Manding Medical Centre become a reality for the villagers in the Gambia. Dr. Linda Mahon-Daly helped distribute letters about Manding Medical Centre to nearly all her colleagues in the Colchester Borough and so did Dr. Laurel Spooner. Bless their hearts for kindness and job well done.

The news article published by the Evening Gazette brought us another very helpful and kind person, Mr. Malkait singh who is an ophthalmologist and had made several trips to the Gambia before knowing about the Friends of Manding. He was delighted to join Neville Thompson, Connie Thompson, Lorna Robinson, Keith Robinson, Loenard Thompson, Mark Naylor, Barbara Philips and others as pioneering members of Friends of Manding.

Mr. Malkait Singh and I grew to be very good friends and he had since given me lots of personal monetary help to cater for my exams and family back in the Gambia. I am very grateful for interest and kindness, and concern he showed about my family. A few months after the formation of Friends of Manding, Dr. Laurel Spooner spent a week in the Gambia vacationing and doing some fact finding about the center.

During which time she visited Manding Medical Centre at Njawara in the North Bank Division. The villagers were happy to meet her and thanked her about good work being done in Colchester regarding Manding Medical Centre. Everyone was happy about the news that people in the UK were poised to assist Manding Medical Centre goes forward in its drive to provide medical aid to villagers.

A meeting of member of the Friends of Manding was scheduled for the first week of February 2001. Mean while our solicitor continued pressing for registration of Friends of Manding, which is the arm and Manding Medical Centre's Colchester branch support group, as charity in the UK.

Dr. Laurel Spooner suggested we start with small-scale form of the center and then gradually expand as funds become available. This consideration would be studied in full and deliberated upon by the committee during the forth-coming February meeting.

Keith, Dr. Ceesay, and Mrs. Lorna Robinson

Miss Binta Ceesay, Daughter

Chapter 21

WHAT IS MANDING MEDICAL CENTRE?

Manding Medical Centre, located at Njawara village in the North Bank Region, Gambia, West Africa, is a self-help village health organization founded by Dr. Alhasan S. Ceesay. Its objective is to provide medical service to the villagers by providing efficient and affordable medical aid to all people in and around the Gambia, especially the rural sector.

We are dedicated to relieving suffering and ensure effective treatment for villagers and all attending Manding Medical Centre at Njawara, NBR.

ESTABLISHED

The Manding Medical Centre is founded by Dr. Alhasan Sisawo Ceesay, a native of Njawara village in 1992, because of sheer shortage of medical service to the region and the preponderance of premature deaths by children from Malaria, malnutrition, diarrhea, and worm infestations. These childhood maladies account for almost 25% of Gambian children's death before the age of five years.

The Gambia Ministry of Health officially recognized the Centre in 1995 and prior to which it became a None Governmental Organization (NGO) on September 12th, 1994.

In addition, the Manding Medical Centre now has Friends of Manding Charitable Trust, Colchester, Essex, UK as its arm and liaison in the UK and the European Union countries. The Friends of Manding is a registered charity in England and Wales. Its registration number is 1088136 since August 21, 2001.

In similar development and purpose, Dr. Avery Aten heads the Friends of Manding Alpena Charitable Trust, Alpena, Michigan, UAS since May 2005.

MISSION STATEMENT

Suffering in another human being is a call to the rest of us to stand in fellowship. It requires us to be there and it is a mystery, which demands the spirit of caring, sharing and our presence. Our duty as healthcare professionals is providing medical care, which is a fundamental right of all human beings.

This village health organization is dedicated to providing medical aid to the rural sector and farming community in the Gambia. It will compliment the health service in the Gambia in addition it will promote preventive medicine in the hinterland of the Gambia.

MEMBERSHIP

Well over twenty thousand villagers, comprising of farmers, village heads, and chiefs, the Kerewan Area Council, Commissioners and local District Authority are now fully active enthusiastic members of Manding Medical Centre.

All are welcomed to join the endeavors of the center. People from the rest of the globe are more than welcomed to participate or share with us our dream in bring much needed medical service to people in desperate state because of lack of medical facilities.

ACTIVITIES

Manding Medical Centre tries to alleviate some of the above mentioned health problems and situations by having bimonthly health field trips/clinics to villages teaching them about health, preventive medicine and hygiene that would help reduce the number infected and the vectors responsible for these diseases.

We encourage antenatal and postnatal attendance of clinics by mothers and we treat the sick amongst them with minimum charge to not so elderly and pregnant young ladies.

The service is free to children, the very elderly, and the indigent needing emergency treatment. The rest pay amounts well below tat in private practice.

Money accrued is subsequently used to buy drugs with which to treat the patients and for other projects of the center. When in cession the center treats well more than 1000 patients per field trip to the villages. We provide free information and advisory service on aids and sexually transmitted diseases (STDs) to the young, all patients, their relatives and friends. We also plan to have a Nursing School in due course to augment not only staff but also the government health centers when the need arises.

IMMEDIATE GOAL AND APPEAL

The villagers are very enthused about the center and Toro Bahen village, next to Njawara village, has donated two plots of land for the building of the center and its ancillary units, which is now leased to manding medical center for ninety-nine years. More than 2000 children die tragically from malaria and other childhood ailments stated above for shortage of health services.

We are eager to start building the children' and maternity wings of the proposed Gambia General Hospital at Manding Medical Centre and do need raise the required 900,000 pounds sterling to accomplish our goal. Ten bags of cement cost thirty pounds sterling or $60 (sixty us dollars). Also we would be most grateful if we could be assisted with medicines and equipment to facilitate our work.

Hence we implore you to kindly support our yearning to build the children' and maternity wings of Manding Medical Centre. We are dedicated to providing medical aid to the villager, especially children. We are investors in people and you are invited to join the endeavors of Manding Medical Centre at Njawara village, the Gambia, West Africa.

Help us make a difference and beacon of hope for the villagers. Please give generously. Today's hope can be tomorrow's reality. We want to contribute positively towards the health services of the Gambia, and with this center in place it will create greater health awareness and privation by the villagers. Cash contributions of any amount should be sent in the name of Manding Medical Centre, to the Friends of Manding charitable Trust, 82 Finchingfield Way, Blackheath, Colchester, Essex, CO2 0AU, and England.

It is vital to be certain that Dr. Alhasan S. Ceesay is informed of your contribution via email thus: alhasanceesay@hotmail.co.uk. Your kindness and humane consideration to help save lives will always be deeply appreciated and grateful for by the villagers, the Gambia and I.

OVERSEASES LINKS

The Friends of Manding in Colchester, Essex County, UK, is formed by a local group of residents, doctors, and nurses who regularly visited the Gambia and is in support of Manding Medical Centre. Manding medical center through the auspices of the Friends of Manding recently received recognition and registration by the UK Charity Commission.

They serve as support and our liaison in the Europe Union. The Friends of Manding in behalf of Manding Medical Centre at Njawara has been entered in the central Register of charities with effect from August 21, 2001; the registration number is 1088136 for England and Wales. Also, a similar charitable trust, the Alpena Friends of Manding Charitable Trust of Michigan, USA, has been established in Alpena, Michigan in June 2006.

It's headed by Dr. Avery Aten a resident physician chairman of the Women and newborn of the Alpena region Community Health along with the medical community of Alpena.

Ntoro Bahen village, Badibou, NBR, The Gambia

Chapter 22

MANDING MEDICAL CENTRE MILESTONES

Manding Medical Centre has been in my mind's drawing board since the early 1950s but it took off in earnest when I returned to the Gambia, after graduating from medical school in 1992. The Centre is registered as a charity with the Attorney general's Office, Department of Justice, Banjul, The Gambia, since 1993. The Gambia Ministry of Health also recognized it in the same year. Toro Bahen village, Lower Badibou, NBD, Gambia, donated two huge plots of land for the location of the center in 1993.

Our non governmental (NGO) status was approved in 1994. On September 21, 1995 Tango Secretariat sent a United Nations voluntary program Officer, Mr. Muloshi on field trip to evaluate the organizational and extent of support for Manding Medical Centre at Njawara village. Mr. Muloshi's recommendation after two days field trip to the region stated thus; "Looking at the caliber of leadership and development activities to some NGO Tango members in comparison to Manding Medical Centre, the organization need consideration since they have already activities with a promising future. Looking at composition of the Board, they have people with a vision.

They have strong membership and backup at grass root levels. The organization has chosen to what is right at the right time and their concentration in one area is vital and good starting point. Any success achieved by any group or organization depends on good leadership and discipline. Manding Medical Centre has high quality leadership and deserves NGO status".

It was not until my travels to the UK in 2000 that the Friends of Manding Charitable Trust was formed and registered as charity in England and Wales by the UK Charity Commission. Friends of Manding is the extended arm of Manding Medical Centre at Njawara, The Gambia. They serve as our liaison in the UK and the European Union. Please browse on our website thus: http://friendsofmandinggambimed.btck.co.uk, to learn more or for further information about our work and organization.

We are still on fund raising activities to earn enough to enable us build the children' and maternity units of the hospital at Manding Medical Centre at Njawara. In May 2005, 11 American students and their instructor Mr. Thomas Ray visited Manding Medical Centre at Njawara. Additionally, input from has now resulted in Alpena City, Michigan, USA, twining by proclamation with Njawara and Kinte kunda villages in Gambia respectively on the 5th of December 2005.

In June 2006, Dr. Avery Aten, Chairman of the Women and Newborn of Alpena Region Health Community along with the medical community of Alpena commenced processing application for a charitable Trust to be named Alpena friends of Manding Charitable Trust, Michigan, USA.

This will soon be finalized and up and running to help Dr. Alhasan Ceesay in the provision of medicine and educational assistance to schools in the Lower Badibou district, the Gambia, West Africa.

In August 2008, Dr. Alhasan Ceesay and the Badibou Cultural Dance Troupe will visit Alpena and other cities in Michigan for fund raising drive to enable the building of the Manding Medical Centre children and maternity units at Njawara village.

Dr. Richard Bates, an Obyng, and a number of medical professionals involved in obstetrics and gynecology at Alpena, Michigan joined Manding Medical Centre's crusade on 17/08/07.

Chapter 23

TEMPLATE FOR REGIONAL DEVELOPMENT

Manding Medical Centre became a template for districts elsewhere and villagers to nurture, develop further and handover to the next generation. This None Governmental Health Organization epitomizes a developmental watchtower for the region.

Manding medical center is a pulsating source of hope, jobs training and superb medical service at Njawara village the Gambia. Everyone knows that government alone does not move things fast enough. Society must be radical and pragmatic to pitch into its development.

We know all too well that the developed world got where its because private efforts were self prophetic and projects like Manding Medical Centre goes long ways to initiate and stimulate community to work together for a positive agenda for its people.

Hence after many years of foot dragging and vicissitude by society I decided I will build the hospital if I have to single-handed. I worked years receiving no government assistance and without grants from the great of the Gambian community.

Manding Medical Centre is a positive good that help our regions to cross the road to a better healthcare delivery. We thank everyone for making it possible that our center became a platform and guide in rejuvenating our regions. We now provide medical service to all Gambians and none Gambians domiciled in the Gambia. We will create more jobs as need arises. This was the reason why I gave my life's comfort for reward that will benefit most needy villagers. It came through determination and kindness of many people worldwide.

There are some things only governments can do but together communities through collective initiatives can achieve at least fifty percent of their developmental needs in addition to government effort. Today some see Manding medical centre as perpetual monument of good, an honor to the country and a general benefit to villagers and children in the North Bank of the Gambia. Manding medical centre is an inspiration and cause for thankfulness and celebration.

Miss Roheyata Ceesay, Daughter

Chapter 24

AN APPEAL TO INTERNATIONAL COMMUNITY

Dear Readers,

The above information about Manding Medical Centre is included in this work only hoping that it will help spread the word more extensively and draw awareness to a greater community of people and readers of my work. It's my belief that lots of good people out there may want to participate or give to the cause and goal of the center should they be aware of its existents for the villagers.

Hence, I am appealing for help and participatory support from all able to extend their hearts to make this much needed medical endeavor to come to fruition for the rural sector of the Gambia. Who knows you might even end up coming to bask in our beautiful seaside and relish Gambian generosity. Music for me is reaching out to help others and my patients are yearning for your kind participation and donation in cash/kind. Thanks a million for considering our appeal.

God blesses your heart(s). I write with believe that by it money can be generated to provide a much needed medical service to the rural sector. Writing about the Manding Medical Centre may course some Good Samaritan and any wanting to leave foot prints on the sand of time for a good cause to come to our assistance to help us meet the goals of the center at Njawara village, the Gambia, West Africa. My head, heart and soul are devoted to my family, the Gambia and Manding Medical Centre. It is not a God given calling but a mere conviction that our rural folks deserve better health service than currently available and hence human calling to want to contribute positively to bring resolution of some of our rural health service inadequacies.

I never had an angel come down to me nor have I ever heard the voices of God saying, "Ceesay, you must do so and so" as many mocked Manding Medical Centre emanated from sheer conviction that it is a dutiful way of doing the right thing for curbing premature deaths of children before reaching 5 years of life from malaria, water born diseases, and warm infestations; and in the same vein providing both pre and postnatal care to the pregnant. Hence, portions of proceeds of sales in all my work go to help meet the center's operational costs and in providing scholarship to indigent indigenous rural candidates due course return to serve rural Gambia wishing to read for a medical degree or agriculture and Medicine.

Signed: Dr. Alhasan S. Ceesay, MD/Email: alhasanceesay@hotmail.com

Chapter 25

LORNA ROBINSON, AN ANGEL OF MERCY

Keith, Dr. Ceesay, & late Lorna Robinson

There are certain moulds God broke them moments after He finished making them. Mrs. Lorna V. Robinson was one of these unique, caring, sharing and rare angels of mercy. Mrs. Lorna Robinson and I met through her job as general nurse at the then Essex County General hospital in Colchester, Essex County in 1990, when I was a trainee doctor at the hospital.

She and husband Keith Robinson became my friends as far back as in the 1990s and one of their annual pilgrimages is visiting my family in the Gambia, West Africa. This benevolent couple has since been my Colchester if not my England.

Together we set to catch a dream of providing medical aid and service to Gambian villagers. I left at the end of my training to serve my country in 1992. In December 1999 Mrs. Lorna Robinson sent an invitation for my wife and I to attend wedding of Miss Fiona Robinson, her younger daughter, to gentleman Reeves.

We have since 2000 worked acidulously to make the above goal come to fruition, especially for those in the rural sector of the North Bank Region of the Gambia. It was Lorna's joint effort with, nurses, Doctors Laurel Spooner, Barbara Murray, Richard Spooner, Phil Murray, Linda Mahon-Daly, Peter R. Wilson, Malkait Singh and residents of Colchester, which lead to the formation of the Colchester Friends of Manding Charitable Trust.

It was registered as a charity in England and Wales in 2001. The charity number is 1088136. This charity acts as liaison in the European Union countries for Manding Medical Centre at Njawara village in the Badibous of the North Bank Region, the Gambia. Since its conception, the Friends of Manding Charitable Trust had busied itself on weekly or bimonthly Gambi-barzaars in an effort to help raise money for building of both the children and maternity units of the center.

Mrs. Lorna Robinson spent countless week-ends either selling material such as toys, coats and anything she could lay her hands on as long as she believes it will generate money for the building of the children and maternity units of the center. She spent most of her retirement time organizing activity for the center to help promote our cause. She sent books, spectacles, pens and pencils along with medication for the center's use.

The influence of this Good Samaritan group in Colchester reverberated and lead to the formation of a similar charity group in America, which is lead by Dr. Avery Aten, Alpena Friends of Manding Charitable Trust, Michigan, USA, was formed in May 2005.

All this came about because Mrs. Lorna V. Robinson, the lady of mercy behind the wheel, would not rest while the indigent goes without the most basic things in life. Here is how Lorna views her part during one of many conversations we had about the need to share worth and ourselves with other less fortunate than us.
She simply said, "Ceesay, I feel delighted and warm at heart in helping others, like the villagers. I strongly belief good used could be made from my work and experience I had at the NHS over years. I will try to recruit as many retired nurses to our cadre as long as they listen to my please.

The other secrete is that such activity keeps me young, participating and contributing to the needy. I feel alive and forever growing. In life we most extend our hearts to others and with compassion reach the needy." This tit bit tells about the unselfish nature of Mrs. Lorna V. Robinson who through the years since her retirement gave her all to help others, especially the villagers, breathe a sigh of relief and to have hope and knowledge that someone far away they never met cared about them.

Lorna continued saying, "It brings joy to my heart when I share the little I have with the needy. It helps to uplift the despondent. Millions suffer needlessly for not having means of proper health care, clean and safe water, good shelter and chance to attend schools. I want to help you get the villagers from a downward spiral of deepening health deprivation. I certainly take hope in people like you and your stand to help your folks back home in the Gambia."

It was this unique caring angel that I lost on the 3rd of March 2010 for she returned peacefully to her maker on this day. The above was my Lorna and now I cry, when shall we be blessed will another like her? Losing Lorna Robinson left me feeling that I lost the best person, outside of my family, I ever known.

She was a kind soul of unswerving determination to share the little She had with the little guy needing her help. She stood by my cause in thick and thin moments of my stay in the United Kingdom.

Dr. Alhasan S. Ceesay graduating from the American University of the Caribbean, West Indies, 1992

The provision of medical care to villagers is more than a responsibility; it is a sacred trust for me. I will not the villagers or memory Mrs. Lorna V. Robinson down because I believe in looking to the well being of the less fortunate.

One carries on trying on reflecting on all the children and villagers who need this health care. Hence no trepidation will hold me back. My family, the villagers and I miss and deeply mourn her premature departure from mother earth. May she rest in peace with her maker and may we the living without fail or fear able to follow the high shining examples of indefatigable Good Samaritan she was in life.

I hope you will join me to keep her memory and legacy alive for other to copy while we continue taking medical aid to villagers in rural Gambia. Lorna V. Robinson thanks a million and goodbye for now.

Signed: Dr. Alhasan S. Ceesay, MD

Manding Medical Centre, Njawara

The Gambia, West Africa. E-mail: alhasanceesay@hotmail.com

Chapter 26

MY SAMARITAN MEN OF GOOD WILL

Every successful person had Samaritan angels who Offered their shoulders for him or her to stand on and see further than most. Compiled herein are my Samaritan men of goodwill. Hence, I beg leave to indulge in a bit of sentimentality about a few rare human angels who played major part in today's success and help for my villagers. Believe me their moulds, as you will soon find, are beyond those of simple people.

These men help me reach today's pedestal. In medicine for the villager, I profiled ladies who championed my cause. Now, bear with me for just a few lines on the Samaritan men of goodwill. They like the previously mentioned ladies al not only believe in my dream and objective for the villager but also gave all they could to help make that dream come to fruition.

These men gave unparalleled needed help and friendship to me when I was distressed and in utter despair and darkness. Some even shed a few tears with me because the pain and set back certain roadblocks caused my goal. One of these was the day I received GMC' e-mail of the 17th June 2008 recanting recognition of my primary medical qualification based on frivolous website enter.

Hell brewed to its hottest temperatures, as it took time to unravel the misunderstanding, before GMC rectified the error. However, with your indulgence let us start from the beginning of the geneses. It was with God' anointing hand in conjunction with Sisawo Bajo Ceesay, alias Sisawo Salah) that my twin partner I landed on this Garden of Eden. Father gave us love and good guidance throughout his life with us. He and I had deferent perception about western Education and culture but we reconciled after my completing primary school at Kinte Kunda.

My father's experience from the hands of colonials made him never to entertain idea of his progeny deviating from the farmers' mold. Nor would he allow me pursue Western Education and ideology, which at the time was alien to my father and his peers. He once told me: Son, my wish for you is to be a hard working good farmer and not indulge in the quagmire and sleaze world of spin-doctors. I do not want you tinkering with ideology that would infuse into you wrong philosophies about life and God.

My father came from a different generation with totally different perceptions about invaders ruling them. Let us for a moment step into their shoes to find out why the resistance for their progeny to attend school.

In my father's days men believed in God, the sanctity of life and peaceful coexistence of the communities they lived. About the invading longhaired men he calls devils, father said: "Son the way these men, meaning the colonialist, took over our countries can only be the work of the devil. They came from the blue sea and seized our land and minerals, and remaining on the best parts while leaving us the worst places to farm and for our animals to grace.

To pour oil on fire they requested that we change our religions and ways to their dark and indiscipline life styles. To top up, our people were forced to live under laws promulgated by the invaders on top of which we must pay to learn their languages while they make systemic concerted efforts to distorted and destroy everything that was dear to us.

They massacred, disgraced, and dethroned all our kings and chiefs. These shameful acts were reinforced with policies of divide and rule by pitting tribe against tribe and even bribing those bad elements willing to do their dirty work. Wages paid to workers were not worth the coin they were minted on. They made certain no organization, political or professional civil service existed in our countries". He said, "They filled the jails with those of us who refused to be indoctrinated or accept the supremacy of the foreign invaders.

So Son, because of kind-heartedness and gentled nature of the African our ways are undermined and thrown out by invaders who replaced it with greed, unkindness, spin-doctoring, and lack of respect for man and nature. He concluded by saying, these are just a few reasons why I would not let my blood attend school".

The above is a pinhole view of father's radicalism and patriotic views. He did recap late later in his old age and finally gave full blessings to my efforts and future goals. He passed away peacefully to his maker in 1991 while I was a trainee doctor doing my clinical clerkship rotation at Colchester General Hospital in Colchester, Essex County, England. Notices no matter how simple were just bundles of scribbles on worthless paper to the farmer. The illiterates who cannot decipher the prints are cheated of their rights and land.

I was not going to be among those who cannot decipher the print and hence found my way to Kinte Kunda Primary School where I met with the head Master, Mr. Louis Albert Bouvier, who hails from Banjul, our capital city. This benevolent teacher was my first real contact with Western Education and we gelled instantly and became inseparable. He allowed me to stay at his home and treated me as his own son.

He was kind and firm and wasted no time teaching me about life and on how to compete without strangulating the competitor.

Dr. Alhasan S. Ceesay holding Africa

He told me repeatedly that competition was a healthy fund and stressed that one must be honest and have integrity and tolerance in life. He counseled hard work at everything one did. Above all, it was incumbent on me to have faith and to serve God daily, if not more but never less. Also he allowed me all the freedom a growing child needed without pampering me.

He did lay certain straightforward and simple rules for me. I was to study at a designated time, return home in time whenever I went into town, unless given an extension by him, and to be in bed by 10:00 pm, with lights off whether sleepy or not. He insisted that I perform my five daily prayers as expected of my religion even though he was devoured Catholic.

Mr. Bouvier would only help with my homework when he felt that I have done my best at it and that I was not trying to have him do the work. Otherwise, he would let me go and make a fool of myself before the class before I deserve his coveted help. Hash you think but this strict beginning or treatment, as you would call it, made me do well at school and do things with confidence independently at very tender age.

I remain profoundly grateful to Mr. Louis Albert Bouvier for being educational springboard, for being a sincere and true friend and mentor. Something said by Francis Farmer summed up the relationship between L. A. Bouvier and me. She said, "To have a good friend is the purest of all God' gifts, for it is a love that has no exchange of payments. It is not inherited, as with family.

It is not compelling, as with a child. And it has no means of physical pleasures, as with a mate. It is, therefore, an indescribable bond that brings with it a far deeper devotion than others". Mr. L. A Bouvier continued to help and mold my academic life until when I started Armitage School in 1957. Leaving a friend like Mr. Bouvier was difficult and emotional for both of us. We have become one and are now to say farewell and perhaps separate forever.

He prepared me well but like any parent or true friend he worried about the difficulties that lay ahead. I just wished they had transferred him with me to Armitage. On the day I boarded the land rover to Armitage tears rundown Mr. Bouvier's cheeks and mother turned her head away to hide her own.

L. A. Bouvier was my best friend, after the loss of my twin brother, fate had it that I was now about to be far away from all I knew and loved. Mr. L. A. Bouvier kept cautioning me to, "keep your head up and do your school works. You have never been a failure, and even if such a sad experience occurs, keep trying over and over to overcome it.

We send you to Armitage with prayers, pride and above all with our deepest love. May God keep you in good health. Goodbye, Mr. Ceesay."

It was very moving for this was the first time he addressed me as Mr. Ceesay. We boarded the Land Rover and as it started to move Bouvier followed for some distance exhorting me not to fear to ask for help when need arose. He kept saying he would gladly help or would ask my parents to pitch in whenever possible.

Mr. L. A. Bouvier and I kept in touch despite the distance poor mail service of those days. The link continued while I was in the USA. I lost my friend in a motorcar accident, six year before returning from America in 1974. His vehicle is said to have ran off the road went over a hill. Another part of me went with him. The evil that men do lives after them and the good is interred with their bodies.

Well rest assured that L. A. Bouvier's good deeds did remain alive and intact on earth. At Armitage it was a newly qualified teaches from Kaur, Mr. Keko B. A. Manneh, who then doubled as our class' English and Mathematic teacher that filled in gap left by my leaving L. A. Bouvier at Kinte Kunda.

He was soft-spoken Chaucerian, a nickname we gave him because he crammed the entire work of Chaucer. He too loved me and was a good guide at Arbitrage. I am grateful for encouragement and help he gave and for really being there when I needed an honest person to open up to about difficulty or academic aspiration.

I left for New York on the 24 August 1967 and arrived at Alpena Michigan 1:30 Am on the 25 August 1967. Mr. Henry V. Vali, a counselor and foreign student advisor at Alpena Community College, was at the bus station to pick me. After the formality of welcoming to Alpena he drove me to 251 Washington Avenue the home of Mr. Howard Riggs where it had been agreed I stay until start of the semester in September before moving to Russell Wilson Hall at the Alpena Community College campus. Not surprising Mr. Vali and I became friends and remained so ever since.

Mr. Howard Riggs and family welcomed me home as late as it was on that glorious day when I set foot in Michigan. They were all delighted to have me in their lovely home and they gave me princely meal to nourish my body and milk to quench my thirst.

Howard owned Ice-Cream Pallor down Town. He was very modest, delightful man and above all a very generous person. Soon Mr. and Mrs. Riggs became mom and dad throughout my American stay for their overwhelmingly kind people deserving such salutation from a poor villager. Howard's warmth and generosity to other made his family unique company to foreign students coming to Alpena. The Riggs were the ideal Americans to me.

They were average working family who readily shared the little bit God gave them with others less fortunate. I remained grateful to these kind-hearted friends. Mr. Vali and Mr. Thomas Rither, Director of Foreign students at Alpena Community College, and I met several time to discuss my financial nightmare. Mr. Rither was too concerned that the college might face INS censor if he allowed my staying without a sponsor or means to pay fees and cater for myself.

He was adamant and made it very clear to me that failure to get help for the first semester will leave him with no other option but to advise the immigration to consider deporting proceedings against me. He gave a week ultimatum for me to sort things out before our next meeting 18 September 1967. Copies of letters from my would be sponsor, Mr. Isdor Gold, never move or evoke sympathy from him as he epidermises a true inelastic bureaucrat.

Mr. Henry V. Vali convinced Mr. Thomas Rither to hold on while get in touch with some residents about my case. He was on the telephone to different would be possible sympathizers to my cause. Most of who agreed to contribute toward the cost of my first semester at Alpena Community College.

Vali also spoke to the president of the college in my behalf to prevent Mr. Ritter from hastily and unilaterally contacting the INS for frivolous fears in his head. My plight soon became a house whole affair and many residents pitched in to help resolve the case.

The appeal by Mr. Henry Valli and Mrs. Viola Glennie snowballed letting me start my first semester at Alpena Community College, Alpena, Michigan. Fr. John miller at St. Bernard Rectory in Alpena not only lent me $250 but evangelized my state in every sermon for three weeks netting me much needed financial help. God bless his heart. He left Alpena before my transfer to Olivet College in Olivet Michigan in 1979.

Judge Philip Glennie was head of the 26th circuit Court of Michigan at the time. His wife, Mrs. Viola Gennie, was professor of foreign language at Alpena Community College. Both not only contributed substantial amounts towards my tuition but also became my adopted parents in Alpena. They continued to link with me like wise support my goal until their return to heaven in the late nineties.

I remember these friends with joy mingled with sadness that they are not here to share reward they showed but also I remember them with intense gratitude for role and kindness shown me while a student at Alpena Community College, Alpena, Michigan, USA.

In another vein Alpena Community College gave me part time job at the Library and a summer job at the Salmon Experimental Fish hatchery. Thanks to grand efforts of Mr. Henry V. Vali and residents of Alpena I was able to overcome the financial crisis of my first semester at the college. I met Mr. Cloyd Ramsey while seeking a summer job at the Medical Arts Clinic in Alpena. He was then manager of the unit at the time. Upon hearing my plight he promised to see what he could do even though the clinic itself had no jobs openings for that summer. I left him impressed and very moved by what he heard.

He too became an integral part of my time and sojourner in America than any through contributions and loans he took from the Alpena bank in my behalf to support my studies throughout my stay in the USA and short stay in Liberia, West Africa. It was through kindness of Mr. Ramsey and his sponsorship that enabled Michigan Technological University at Houghton to accept me do a Masters program in Biological Sciences from 1971 to 1973.

L – R: Dr. Alhasan Ceesay, Prof. Sulayman Nyang, Mr. Clloyd Ramsey and Prof. Francis Conti

It was Mr. Cloyd Ramsey who came to my rescuer when things went very bad and unbearable and practically unsafe for me after the military coup d'etat against William Tolbert' administration of Liberia in 1981.

He provided a round trip Air ticket to the USA and supporting it with invitation for me as their guest at Sandusky, Michigan December 1981. The invitation secured me a B-2 Visa to Detroit, Michigan. I arrived in New York 1:15 pm 20 December 1981. I prayed on disembarking and I was grateful and thankful to God and Cloyd Ramsey having set foot once more on US soil. I thank Cloyd ceaselessly in my heart for having helped me escape to America despite the ignominy of being in exile and to seek asylum soon.

I caught my flight to Detroit, Michigan around 3:45 pm same day. The Ramseys were at the Detroit Metropolitan International arrivals terminal waiting to receive me. They must have noted the fatigue in my face, if not the sorrow of leaving my beloved Gambia and people behind for an indefinite time. They welcomed me graciously and we headed for Sandusky, a small village in Michigan. I therein and then became part of the Ramsey family.

Life has it that when some of us were created the mould broke. Most give their time and money to their own families or to work that brings them some happiness and some money. Cloyd Ramsey is among a few who give themselves wholly and unselfishly to others. I can never be able to repay or tell how devoted Ramsey is in sharing life with the needy unless you meet him.

In brief, Mr. Ramsey and wife Narrate fed and sheltered me when I needed food and place to stay until I get my feet back on earth. He was my salvation voice in the wilderness of life's rugged road. I stayed as their guest in Sandusky until it was time to seek asylum at the Immigration and Nationality Service (INS) in Detroit. There was no other situation less tense and so empty of hope than this next phase in my life.

Life became an abyss of despair which only God and good friends, like the Ramseys, pulled me out from underneath. Shakespeare said, "Between the acting of a dreadful thing and the first motion; All the interim is like a phantasm, or a hideous dream. The genius and mortals instruments like to a little kingdom, suffers then the nature of an insurrection."

Indeed an insurrection has been going on in my head during those horrible days of the coup d'etat of April 15th 1980 I became aware of the need to muster courage, strength and endurance to prepare myself for the coming exile days and form it may take. Again, Mr. Ramsey contacted the Gambia several time to no avail to verify and correct a possible misunderstanding that may have occurred. Several friends and legislators Ramsey contacted advised that I seek asylum from the INS. Senator Carl Levin sent us a package of three copies of Form 1-589 for my use on 6th January 1982.

We took the bull by the horns, completed the forms and Ramsey and I proceeded to INS office at Mount Elliot Street, Detroit, Michigan on the 22nd February 1982, were I was subsequently interviewed separately and told action will be rendered in four months earliest. If wishes were horses beggars would gallop to heaven for it took well more than eight months before any reply came and only after numerous INS court hearings did we get some semblance of partial positive direction. The final act was left with the State Department and vice president's office.

Things were so delayed and difficult that I asked Ramsey to take me to the Catholic Mission for me to seek Sanctuary or more public help and support. We landed at St. Paul's' Cathedral, Diocese of Michigan, where Hugh Davis led me to the refugee office of the Diocese. On hearing my story the refugee co-coordinator, Mrs. Patricia Koblinsky called rev. Hugh C. White, advisor to then reigning Bishop of the Diocese, Bishop Coleman Mcgehee Jr. The Diocese received and let me stay at 44 Ledyard Street in Detroit. In the mean time Ramsey sent the following appeal to the INS office at Mount Elliot in Detroit, Michigan:

TO WHOM IT MAY CONCERN

This letter is to acknowledge my association with Alhasan Ceesay, over a period of fifteen years.

During that time I have found him to be a young man of very high ideals. His only interest in life has been to obtain an education and return to serve his home country and help his people. I have personally invested thousands of dollars in Alhasan Ceesay because it seemed to me to be a very efficient way to help the impoverished people from his country that has had a great deal less than I have.

If anyone were to follow the course of his life, he would see that his motives most certainly were not to simply escape the futility of his home country and live that, good life here. There is no doubt in my mind that the dangers that he describes do exist for him. Even if these were less than perfect proof, would you like to take the chance of being wrong and find out that he had been imprison or worse killed for no reason at all?

Please save this man. If you cannot do it for his sake, then consider the investment made by concerned individuals, other organizations and myself. Thank you for your serious considerations of this matter.

Signed: Cloyd Ramsey, Sandusky, Michigan, USA

My next Alpena Samaritan and brother in Chris as well as profession was Dr. Charles T. Egli, who I met almost about the same time I did with Ramsey. He was a Surgeon working for the Medical Arts Clinic at the time of our meeting.

He came into the radar after a speech I gave to the Alpena Medical Association. He too has contributed prominently and was instrumental in having the medical Association comes to my aid with a donation of $400 towards my second semester fees at Alpena Community College.

By this miracle I was able to complete payment for the second semester at college. Charles, as he prefers being called, is a surgeon and devoted Christian who also became very close friend and had done a lot to encourage my efforts.

His rallying for assistance continued through out his days at the Medical Arts Clinic. For you to note Dr. Egli's closeness here is a letter he sent in my behalf during my petitioning for asylum in the USA. It read:

Medical Arts Clinic

Alpena, Michigan

November 14, 1986

RE: Deportation Notice on Alhasan Ceesay

Dear Senator Levin,

Alhasan Ceeesay was a college student in Alpena many years ago when I first met him and was very much impressed by his sincerity and enthusiasm. He went onto graduate school at Michigan Technological

University in Houghton, Michigan, in hopes of getting into medical school. He tried very hard to get into medical school in Africa. He was receiving no support from his own country because it considered him a political agitator and tribalist. Alhasan Ceesay on his own initiative was able to get into medical school in Monrovia Liberia and succeeded in taking two years medical education before he fled for safety to the USA. He later sought political asylum in the USA for fear of persecution due to the aftermath of an attempted coup in July 181.

It has always been his desire to complete his medical training and return to the Gambia when the climate warrants. For almost five years now, Alhasan has been trying to receive asylum, during which time his chances at medical school are affected. Most recently he received a letter from INS judge ordering his deportation. The deportation of Alhasan Ceesay back to the Gambia would result in his certain death or imprisonment and would constitute another tragedy in the way our government handles people like Alhasan. In a country where there are so many illegal aliens it seems that there must be some place for one more refugee. I beg you to personally consider Alhasan's case.

Sincerely

Dr. Charles T. Egli, MD

Mr. Homer Shepard, resident of Flint Michigan, was also very kind to me while at Flint. He offered to lodge me during the summer of 1969 on securing a full time job at the St. Joseph Hospital on Flint, Michigan as nurse assistant. Homer and wife offered to help defray rent expenses, which were taking a quarter of my earnings. With this help I was able to return to Alpena Community College at the end of the summer and pay my dorm and food bills and still had some pocket money to buy pens and other sundries during the semester.

God blesses his heart. We lost contact since my return to Africa. All letters to his address were redirected, as addressee no longer leaves here. Bishop Coleman Mcgehee had already blessed efforts of the hastily formed CEESAY COMMITTEE. It became the Adhoc committee and my Pegasus wing.

Like any normal human gatherings we had our different ideas as to how to approach the asylum problem but all of it steered towards or sought better ways to meet the challenges and enigma about to end all that I stood for and worked hard for in life. The brain storming sessions were very pragmatic if not practical and well-intended discussions. One of the exploratory searches for solutions led us to Mayor Harvey Sloan of Louisville, Kentucky.

I met Mayor Sloan in 1976 when I was trying to get into medical school at the University of Louisville. Also we used to write each other while I was in Monrovia, Liberia, West Africa. I was invited to his office early February 1983, and was given opportunity to talk with key aids at the Louisville City Hall while he attended other state affairs.

His executive aids, Sharon Wilbert and Mrs. Blanche reviewed my case along with information already in my file open in my name. They concluded that I did deserve help and I was asked to speak to Mrs. Joyce J. Rayzer, Director, and Health Affairs for the Mayor. Joyce contacted the Dean of the Medical School and gave him an in-depth briefing of my background and precarious situation I was faced with. Two weeks later on February 28th 1983, I received the following letter from Joyce in behalf of Mayor Harvey Sloan. It read thus:

Office of the Director of Safety

City Hall

Louisville, Kentucky 40202

28 February 1983

Dear Mr. Ceesay,

It appears, as the old saying goes, that I have good news and bad news. I have been in contact with the University Of Louisville School Of Medicine with regards to your admission at the fall term. I have spoken to Dr. Donald Kemetz, Dean of the Medical School, and Mr. Harold Adams, Special Assistance to the president of the University of Louisville.

Both of these administrators upon reviewing the information you sent me feel that you are a very good candidate for the minority admission program.There is however, one issue, which must be resolved favorably before your admission to medical school, or the financing and packaging necessary to begging this endeavor can be given serious considerations. The issue, which must be resolved, is the financial determination base on whether you would be granted asylum in the country.

Without the asylum being granted and hence financial aid the university cannot proceed with your request for admission this fall because your legal status would be too tenuous for them to invest hard cash in your future medical development under such nebulous state.
It appears that you must begin medical school anew. The two years completed at Liberia, cannot be accepted for transfer.

You will start as freshman upon being granted asylum in USA. Again, try and find resolution to granting you asylum. I have been assured that everything that can be done for you will be done immediately upon a favorable notice of your asylum. Every body in the Mayor's office says hello, and we are sending you our prayers.

Sincerely

Joyce J. Rayzer

Director, Health Affairs

This was the impact Mayor Harvey Sloan had. In addition Mayor Harvey Sloan sent the following directly from his desk to the INS pleasing for them to grant me asylum.

City Hall

Office of the Mayor

Louisville, KY 40202

November 7, 1983

Alhasan S. Ceesay of the Gambia has contacted this office in an effort to gain political asylum in other to complete his medical education at the University of Louisville. I know that he is dedicated individual and is more desirous of providing needed medical aid to his fellow man.

Mr. Ceesay petitioned for political asylum in February 22, 1982 due to a purge, which followed a failed coup in the Gambia. The Medical school at the university of Louisville is currently processing his application for the 1984/85 academic years. It would be most helpful if you could assist him in expediting his papers.

He will not be admitted unless a written statement confirming his residency status is available. Since he has already lost two years awaiting residency confirmation, it would be deeply appreciated if you could assist this young man in any way possible. If my staff or I can be any further assistance in the matter, please do not hesitate to contact this office.

Sincerely

Harvey L Sloan

Mayor Louisville

Let us for a moment revert to Bishop Coleman McGehee at the Episcopal Diocese of Michigan in Detroit Michigan. Below is letter sent to the INS director, Edwin Chauvin at Mount Elliot in Detroit, Michigan.

Office of the Bishop

4800 Woodward Avenue

Detroit, Michigan 48201

24 October 1983

Dear Mr. Chauvin,

As Bishop for the Episcopal diocese of Michigan, located in Detroit, Michigan, I write you this letter on behalf of Alhasan S. Ceesay, a petitioner for political asylum in the United States. As you may note from the file Mr. Ceesay seeks political asylum base on his fear of political persecution and danger to his physical safety and well being by the government, were he to be returned by the INS to his country the Gambia. Mr. Ceesay's life will disclose to you, he was active opponent of the political regime in the Gambia. After protesting incarceration of his friends, Mr. Ceesay was placed on a list of individuals who were allegedly involved in criminal activity and who were involved with the Movement for Justice in Africa (MOJA) and were sought for interrogation by the Gambia government.

The Gambia government has singled our Mr. Ceesay because of his political opposition and has prevented him from continuing his medical education in Liberia by cutting off his financial assistance and by asking the Liberian government to return Mr. Ceesay to the Gambia. I am personally acquainted with Mr. Ceesay, and believe him to be an individual who is worthy of support of the Episcopal Dioceses of Michigan.

I feel that it took great courage for Mr. Ceesay to stand up for human rights and to publicly oppose the political regime in the Gambia. I am convinced that Mr. Ceesay is an altruistic individual who deserves to pursue his medical training to benefit, both in the United States and perhaps elsewhere, those individuals who might be helped by his medical ability.

Mr. Ceesay has already establish his medical science aptitude in his studies at Medical School in Liberia, and he has applied to and been accepted by the School of Medicine at the University of Louisville, Kentucky, with tuition to be paid by that institution, upon his authorization to remain in the United States.

Mr. Ceesay has also sought authorization to engage in employment pending the outcome of his asylum request, he proposes to assist in medical research at the university should his employment authorization be granted by your office. Therefore, on behalf of Mr. Ceesay as well as the members of my Diocese, I would urge you to give favorable consideration to Mr. Ceesay's petition and expedite his request for employment and his political asylum petition in every possible way so that his efforts to enter the University of Louisville School of Medicine may not be delayed any longer than may be necessary by legal and administrative procedures which you office follows.

Please feel free to contact me if I can be of any assistance in helping you to reach your determination on this matter. I fervently believed that, upon your investigation of Mr. Ceesay's case, you would reach the conclusions that he would be an asset to the United States, and that his fears as to his persecution and personal safety should he return to the Gambia, have firm foundation in fact.

Very truly yours

(The Rt. Rev.) H. Coleman McGehee, Jr.

Bishop of Michigan

The Bishop of Michigan, H. Coleman McGehee followed the above with a letter to then vice president George Bush Sr. Who sent the following tars reply.

The Vice President

Washington, D. C

April 25, 1984

Dear Rev. McGehee,

Thank you for your recent letter concerning Alhasan S. Ceesay. It was thoughtful of you to write and I appreciate your having taken the time to bring Mr. Ceesay's case to my attention. I have asked the State Department to review all asylum cases and human rights violations, which are brought to my attention.

I have, therefore shared your letter and the enclosures with officials at the Department of State and asked that they review Mr. Ceesay's request and write to you directly. I have also asked that a copy of their response be forwarded to my office. With best wishes.

Sincerely

George Bush

Bishop McGehhee, Bishop Mason, Rev. Hugh C. white, Rev. David Brower, Rev. Bill Woods, Rev. Virgil Jones, and Rev. Mark D. Meyer all touched my heart in similar fashions Hence here is my collective feeling and experience in a nut shell about these devoted men of Christ.

All of the priests lived in Detroit, Michigan except Rev. Mark D. Meyer, who lived in Plain view, Texas, USA. I lived with Rev. Mark Meyer in 1989 after hurricane Hugo devastated our campus at Montserrat, West Indies. The rest of the above I met while trying to defray deportation notice from the INS. Those were challenging and nerving political moments for m family and I.

These men of God never docked when told about my nightmare. These true believers became unique brothers I would like to share few outstanding things they did in style engraved in simple devotion to Christ's dictum. I write because these men impressed me in their interpretations and devotion to the Gospel of Christ. Hence forgive me if I became a bit sentimental in relaying help they gave to me at various challenging times of my life. They were personal pastors for me. These were the beacon of hope and faith that stood by me when it was all doom and gloomy for me.

They were simple people, humble ones at that, I can confide with, debate with, and had shoulders on which to cry my heart out without being embarrassed and above all expect a little prayer at the end of it. Then guess what? We would be on tract trying to get hold of friends of theirs and people that might lighten my burden.

Their devotion to justice and fairness was magnanimous and are my brothers in Christ. Rev. Mark Meyer, on being told the hardship I endured in Montserrat from hurricane Hugo gave me a room and gifts more than ten thousand u.s. dollars to help me complete my pre-clinics at the American University School of Medicine.

I learnt from these men of God that there is a special strength that can sustain us through almost any difficulty. That strength comes from God and from kind hearts like these Samaritans of good will. The strength comes from partly within but even more, it comes from faith and love of those close to us.

These men gave themselves wholly and as unselfishly to others in need when I met them at the Episcopalian diocese of Michigan. They devoted time to my cause and dropped selfish interests aside to help me fight my case against the INS while I was up to my neck in legal and political mud.

I found nothing in these men but admirable integrity, honesty and unswerving commitment to leading life devoted to God, the Bible and in helping the downtrodden. I always feel elated whenever I get chance to speak to these kind hearts from afar. Meeting them makes me feel reunited with my best friends. I rather have a million more like then than multi millionaires that do not care about the plight of the common man. Again, I applaud contribution and friendship these men touched my heart and life with. God blesses them.

My family, villagers and I are extremely indebted to them. These men translated their concerns, and love of humanity and continued to be my good Samaritans and a bridge over trouble waters. These believe in the worthiness and sanctity of life. And above all they ascribe to the power of knowledge and justice over ignorance.

We look forward to the day we can serenade them amongst us in the smiling coast of the Gambia. We pray they keep fit to be able to join us in the opening ceremony of the Manding Medical Centre at Njawara village, the Gambia, West Africa.

These men translated their deep faith, concerns, and love of humanity. I opted to do my clinical rotations in Colchester, Essex, UK in 1990 and chanced to meet the Robinson's. Keith Robinson vested my newly born baby girl, Famatanding Ceesay, at the Colchester County Hospital, which marked our first meeting.

This slightly shy bloke impressed me a lot. He was all smiles and fund. He titled the little ears of my daughter and told her not to be as bad as her daddy. We all laughed over it. We from that moment liked each other and he became one of my inseparable unique Brits. Keith and wife would visit the Gambia and my girls loved them to bits.

Not for the presents he takes to them each time but because of his amiable personality, altruistic, very caring human he is. He had spent boxes of monetary aid towards my NGO, Manding Medical Centre at Njawara village, and the Gambia. On the forming of the Friends Manding Charitable Trust, he was unanimously voted chairman of the charity by the members.

He had since inspiration of the Friends of Manding Charitable Trust worn the cap admirably and did a job well done for the charity. Also he had been instrumental in the Gambibazaar held every fortnight in Colchester to help raise funs for Manding Medical Centre's goals back in the Gambia. He is committed to seeing the center come to fruition for the villagers of the Gambia and any that would need its service.

Personally, he and his wife had been my lifeline and support. They have always come to my aid the call of expectation and I remain profoundly grateful to him and his wife Lorna V. Robinson. Ten years ago I was on the verge of preparing becoming a consultant and return to serve the Gambia.

Today an untold anguish my life went through in these years was dampened by kindness of Lorna and Keith Robinson and many other kind and generous Brits. They are my Colchester Samaritans and Njawara villager's angels with golden hearts. We are working hard to seeing that Manding Medical center transcends the dream it was to reality for the Lower Badibou region. Its service is much needed by the villagers. God blesses their hearts. In Manchester many helped but few match Elhaj Asfaque Ahammed, Neville Brown, Kofi Awudo and Ahmed Nizami.

Elh. Asfaque Ahammed is proprietor of Punjab Collection located at Wilmslow Road in Manchester. A lot has already been revealed about the kindness and generosity of this gentile heart and family in my first book, "The legend again all odds."

Asfaque Ahammed has since my early days in Manchester to today been benevolent towards me. He gives me food and money any time he thinks or feels that I am on the brink of collapsing because of joblessness, hunger, and worries about the state of my equally beleaguered family back home. Only God can reward such humble good people.

I first met Neville in Montserrat, West Indies, while I was a medical student at the American University of the Caribbean. We have ever since been cordial and upon finding me out in Manchester he had steadfastly kept that friendship ablaze. He in various ways would come to my aid with small but significant donations at the time.

He even helped in securing a job at Belfry House Hotel at Hands Forth in 2006. He is kindhearted fellow and my Montserrat. Kofi Awudo is Toggles gentleman I also met through his link with Neville Brown. He turned to be very kind and generous to me. He bought me shoes and shirts to allow me start work at the above hotel.

Years later on my return from Glasgow, Scotland he was the one that lodged me free of charge for three winter months. He is of exceptional quality and humane person. I remain grateful both fellows. I met Mr. Ahamed Nizami in 2008, an angel in human flesh, at Waseem's work place in Manchester. This lawyer turned Editor and I gelled from that hour to today. He is currently the Chief Editor of the Khalish Magazine, an Urdu language magazine in UK and worldwide. He also doubles as one of the Pakistani group leader in Manchester. On knowing my predicaments his benevolence surfaced.

There nod then he promised to help me with some the problems pulling me down and also indicated interest in helping my NGO Manding Medical Centre get financial aid to get a head start on the provision of its goals for the villagers. In addition he proposed a fun raising idea using his medium and other avenues that may come to light.

We tentatively initiated, depending on approval and provisos set by Keith Robinson, Chairman of Friends of Manding Charitable Trust in Colchester been met, formation of the Manchester manding Medical Center Annex to be office at 9 knowley Street in Manchester. To further demonstrate his kindness and interest in my goal Ahmed Nizami donated fees for all three PLAB exams I took in 2009. Gentle hearts like Ganem Hadied and others felt sorry that my life became an unkind and rough ride for me. He said, "Ceesay, I wish I can help more to get you out of the limbo you found yourself. Just believe in God and this pain will one day pass like history."

Mahmud Adam also marched Ganem's effort by collecting money from the Liverpool mosque. Both monies were used for my exam fees and for which kindness I remain eternally grateful to all donors. Mohamed Salam of Greenhey business in Manchester was another Good Samaritan that came to my aid when I was left to sleep in cold weather at Alexandra Park. Upon contacting him he kindly offered me room in one of his flats in Manchester.

He was very kind and generous towards me. We have many times prayed together for my eventual breaking out of nightmarish bad luck life had been to me in recent times. Last but not the least is Sami Bati from Algeria who I stayed with at 245 Great Western Street and who relentlessly called and ask people and friends to come to aid. He raised a bundle to help me pay school fees for my daughters in the Gambia and feed my bones.

My brother Abdullah Hashim and wife Asiya Qadri were very kind Bangladesh cum Pakistani couple I met during the most challenging times of my life. Their kindness is yet to be matched by their peers. I met the couple while sleeping rough in the street of Manchester as Mohamed Salam' offer of a place came to an abrupt end.

The place was rented to a family leaving me homeless with no place to go except spend the nights at cold and treacherous Alexandra Park. It was very risky but being jobless it was the only option left to me. Hence, it was a miracle when this God fearing Good Samaritan couple came to my rescue.

They not only lodged me temporally at their other flat at 2 Sway field in Manchester but also continued to shower me with gifts and food. I certainly look forward to hosting and having my villagers and family serenade this unusually kind and generous couple from Bangladesh. Yankuba Samateh and dear friend Abdal Nasser deserve a mention with gratitude and thanks for kindness and generosity they showered me with during these dark days and for constantly reminding me that I am more than capable of bringing my dream to fruition for the villagers.

Mrs. Roheyata Corr-Sey, a cousin, remained the most supportive and one that kept encouraging me more than any family member had done during this sojourn of mine. God blesses her and her family. I look forward to being able to thank her in person for insisting that blood is thicker than water and for being with me in thick and thin of this murderous trail.

I just have to have continued faith; confidence to do it and the universe will cooperate to justify these days difficulty. My life being as mythical as Pelebstine fever, it was full of ups and downs and again it was Ahamed Nizami who offered to lodge me when I was asked to leave my previous address where I was renting. His kindness is phenomenal and transience's mortals.

I look forward to him being my guest in the Gambia. Worth mentioning is Abdullah Shahim, a young Bangladeshi fellow who practiced his believe that we are all God's children and do need to help the miskin whenever we can. He has graced my life with kindness and brotherhood that any human being yearns to get. He and his wife Asiya Padri have been one of the bright experiences of my UK sojourn. God bless their hearts. Asiya is a shining beauty and sunshine of Abdullah Shahim.

Each day became a specific thrill that lead to that exhilarating moment of victory for mankind. It was a hard challenge and a march placed before me. It is a march I will pursue towards the day I would once again be able to serve the Gambia as a physician.

Friends such as Lorna Robinson, Eliza Jones, Mahmud Adam, Ganem Hadied, Abdinnisir, Faisal, Yusuf Ali, Ishfaque Ahmed, Ahmed Nizami, Abdullah Shahim, and countless angels all suffered my pain and felt way into my heart through compassion as I plied through financial inadequacies. Angels like Faisal, Abdul Rhaseed, Abdinnisir, Yusuf Ali, and Mahmud Adam deserved to be classed as paragons of kindness.

These Somalis are among many who refused to let me bit the dust because of foot dragging visa problem. They encouraged by sharing food and they had with me and made certain that I persevere for a bright day for family and country. These are people who help lift my feet when my wings could not remember how to fly away from hardship.

Faisal would on weekends prepare hot and well spiced Spaghetti and meat, or buy food for me from the next door restraint. Abdinnisir Hassan in almost tearful manner would push me into going to get food. On top of this generosity these folks let me stay in their flat at 284 Great Western Street, Manchester while my lawyer fight not only to untangle but to get the Home office act on change of status request I made to that office back in 2004.

I feel favoured, if not blessed having to face these inhuman challenges without losing my sanity. Being in the belly of a ferocious beast is more comfortable than life I am currently saddled. I feel like being at the interface between Purgatory and hell on earth. Simply put, my experience was no domain for the weak. The dilemma in this life remains ceaselessly changing.

These few, this band of altruistic brothers kept me going through many a dark hour of my life in America and Great Britain. They stood tall for me among many in caring for the plight of those who they never met in poverty stricken parts of the world. Friends like these are angels who lift us to our feet when our wings have trouble remembering how to fly.

In this almost inhospitable life friends like these are a great gift indeed. Tinged with trepidations for what the future can sing I picked up courage and inspiration knowing that good comes out of fighting for what one believes in. Life has taught me how to look after myself and that things do not just happen, people make it happen.

And so the villagers and I appeal for your help and participation with Manding Medical Centre.
Together we can walk on water and make this dream of providing medical aid to villages become worthy cause for generations.

I have learnt not to rest on my oars else I fall into a deep and turbulent sea of troubles. I have to keep running in order to be with the best or where I am. I will continue to not only learn to improve my performance but to work hard to see that this dream of providing a much needed medical aid to villagers is brought to fruition.

Dalliance said, "Say of me what you will and the morrow will judge you, and your words shall be a witness before its judgment and a testimony before its justice. I came to say a word and I shall utter it. Should death take me ere I give voice the morrow shall utter it. That which alone I do today shall be proclaimed before the people in the days to come."

Mrs. Fatou Koma-Ceesay, Gambia 2014

Chapter 27

I REST MY CASE

Paul in a letter to Timothy 2 said, "I have fought a good fight, I have finished my course, and I have kept the faith." I hand this work for publication for you to be judge of the ravages of the years and how my life was that of extreme ups and downs.

In reality, I am very grateful to God even though my life met with various misfortunes, the most unbearable being the delay in my becoming a physician.

My life as witnessed in these pages was an assembly of trials and tribulation emanating from roadblocks placed on my path by inhuman laws and unfortunate dark circumstances.

Life has taught me to submit to divine decrees, whatever they may be from God. I feel on the whole overly rewarded and delivered even though I had no family here in England nor was I as lucky as others who can feel and experience the warmth of their wives and children on daily basis.

I succumbed to it as the way things were going to be for me and lived with this state of affairs while in Manchester, England. I experienced various turns of fate, enough for ten elephant loads, while on the little moat of the silver sea called England.

With my travels I was able to see Europe, the Americas and have learnt a great deal from it as well as experienced numerous unforeseen adventures thrown on my path. My life in England was pain; fear of deportation, hunger, extreme poverty due to joblessness, solitude and missing my wife and children I loved dearly.

I had a huge sense of duty in relation to the villagers and was not ready to fail them because of personal comfort or pleasures. Consequently Manding Medical Centre and benefits to be accrued from it became my most if not the only occupation and direction in life. Here is Manding Medical Centre if managed well it will do justice to rural health service for the next generation of Gambians to build upon.

The medical centre is now a recognized charity in both the United Kingdom and America. I am committed to serve the villagers so that life of the children and young people would be better than mine when I was young. I hope Manding Medical Centre becomes a model testimony of the boy from Njawara village who doggedly struggled to become a doctor and despite various twists of life is able to provide medical aid and service to villagers in rural Gambia.

May be this will strengthen some other fellow to strive to do better than I did to bring health and happiness to the region. I hope my adventure persuades youngsters that man is capable of a lot more than he thinks he is capable of. Our footprints must be inspirational to give heart to new coming Gambian generations. Twenty years ago none would dream of thinking me becoming an author or to challenge powers as I did in this little frame and life of mine.

I met a beautiful Maraka girl while I was in Monrovia, Liberia, West Africa. Fatou Koma is daughter of Elhaj Ansuman Koma and Jalian Ture of Kindia from Guinea Conakry. Her positive attitudes towards me lead our meeting on weekends at Cousin Sainabou Jobe's home. We started going out together and very soon I had the courage to ask her hand in marriage.

There was no bone of contention with regards for my love for her. She was the darling of my heart at first sight and I was not going to let a fly land on her from that day onwards. We had a simple wedding because her father did not quite approve of me because of fear for his uneducated but very pretty daughter being dump at one stage of the marriage for another educated city girl.

I, in the long run, allied his fears and he ended up being one of my best friends and confidants I had up to the day he went to his maker. Fatou Koma-Ceesay and I are blessed with three beautiful daughters namely, Princesses Famatanding Ceesay, Binta Ceesay, and Roheyata Ceesay. All of who, unlike me, had their schooling start at the age of five. The elder girl is aspiring to become a doctor and had been admitted to start her premed courses at Alpena Community College in Alpena, Michigan, USA.

Together Fatou Koma-Ceesay, the children and I went through all the tragedy of hunger, poverty and other sad experiences my sojourn in the quest of the Golden flees for the villager brought to us. Fatou Koma-Ceesay initially hated Manding Medical Centre for she felt it consumed me and took me away from her and the children. The call got me entangled in a web of unfortunate circumstances and laws.

The marriage had at one point almost spiralled to its end as wife' move became questionable. Nonetheless she remained a good mother and wife who took care of the girls in my absence. My mother in-law was battered by confusion and as to why Fatou stuck it out with me under such immense hardship. Love is stronger glue!

We loved each other and so we were able to stand by the other in good or bad times and my trip to England was the worse ever in our connubial life. It caused great turbulences in the marriage but I stuck with it for love's shake and the children who I love dearly. Today, we are back together as family under the same roof while planning and supporting future of our darling girls.

God bless Fatou Koma-Ceesay's heart and be reassured of endless love I have for her.

For now Dalliance said it best for me when he said, "Say of me what you will and the morrow will judge you, and your words shall be a witness before its judgment and a testimony before it justice.

I came to say a word and I shall utter it. Should death take me ere I give voice; the morrow shall utter it. That which alone I do today shall be proclaimed before the people in days to come." I wrote with the hope the life enshrined herein will serve not only as an inspiration to the despondent but a lesson never to allow this sort of experience it passed through this planet.

 I wrote in the hope that life enshrined in my books will serve not only as an inspiration to the despondent and downtrodden but a lesson never to allow this sort of experience it passed through this planet. I wrote because I felt that my life has something worth revealing to the world to engender tolerance and understanding between people and their governments. I risked revealing today for all of us to learn from it and move to a better and rewarding future.

Among the forces of life is one that stands a certain lofty peak a few is endowed with or able to explore its heights. Ambition urges us to leave the lower surface of earth where the ordinary people live and ascend to heights that pierce the heavens. This mission has led to numerous Erie paths but for me this Pell-mell towards a better medical service for the neglected villager was a worthwhile adventure.

I am profoundly grateful and indebted to my wife Fatou Koma-Ceesay and our daughters, princesses Famatanding Ceesay, Binta Ceesay and Roheyata Ceesay for enduring all the pains that we went through in thick and thin times during my sojourn to America and England.

Also my deepest gratitude goes to Cousin Yata Sey-Corr for helping keep my family hopeful. God bless her heart eternally. I forgive my own brothers and sisters who refused to cater for my family in my absence. Hello, hats off to Sey kunda!

Dr. Alhasan Ceesay, holding Africa

Chapter 28

MY ENDEARING LIFE & FATE

For a while in my native innocence all I had was erudition and wit, which always misfired. Everything I touched came to nothing but failure, whatever I tried to achieve came crashing down on my head. At any given moment some mishap befalls me and nothing surprised me any more. **I took my current plight with stride and smiled as fate taunts me.**

I remain poor but my in extinguishable strong will enabled me face life squarely and took me through these dark days. The twist of fate abated but my age had advanced beyond retrieval. The above apocalyptic life is indeed trying moments for my family and me. The only passion I have is providing medical service to villagers through Manding Medical Centre.

My dream spawns better future health service for future generations. I never set to write a bestseller but to inform and share ideas. Also I enjoy reading it as it's not found in any bookstore. It is hoped that in writing another will be spared of experienced I endured before being able to provide medical service/aid to Gambian villagers. Browse: http://friendsofmandinggambimed.btck.co.uk **or contact** alhasanceesay@hotmail.com

To view/purchase books: Google search Dr. Alhasan Ceesay/ books.

Rohey Ceesay, Manchester College Uk 2015

Chapter 29

THE WAY OF A DREAMER

Back in the Gambia a friend decried my efforts as nothing but a dream that I persistently chased. I let such observers know that it only takes time before my dream become fruitful. Here are a few examples: I left the Gambia in 1967 as a nurse and returned; after insurmountable roadblocks as a medical doctor. While practicing in the Gambia I further created two worthy entities, namely (1) The Gambia Health Credit Union, which today provides needed financial assistance to all health workers i.e. Nurses and Health Inspectors country wide. (2) In addition I created NGO Manding Medical Centre at Njawara village, Lower Badibou to help provide a much needed medical aid and service free of charge to villagers who could not afford to pay private clinics. With the help of visiting doctors the centre has treated more than 9000 villagers free of charge since its inception in 1993.

On returning to the UK, I again with help of resident nurses and doctors in Colchester Essex setup the Friends of Manding Charitable trust in Colchester UK. This was recognized and registered as a charity in England and Wales by the UK- charity Commission in 2002. In the midst of which I published my first book 'The Legend Against all Odds' and now has published more than thirty eight novels. To further cement my goal for the villager I was able to convince the Alpena City Council to form a sister city link with Njawara and Kinte Kunda villages in the Lower

Badibous of the Gambia in 2005. This was made easier after my being awarded on May 5th, 2005 'Distinguished Graduate Award' by Alpena Community College. My web site: friends of Manding gambimed continues to lure people to Njawara to see what help they could give the villager. Today, I am not only an author of several books; Google search: Dr. Alhasan Ceesay/books to view of purchase as contribution to rural healthcare; portions or sales from these books go to support goals of Manding medical Centre at Njawara.

I am indeed a dreamer and will continue to dream fir my people. If the above is dream then here is another step to help see through me. I am humble to let you know I am now a Publisher and my company in the UK is 'PUBLISH KUNSA LTD' and one can have their work published by logging on to our web site; www.publishkunsa.com. Again two pounds sterling from any book published by my company goes towards scholarships and rural healthcare as stipulated in terms of contract we would work on manuscripts.

Dreams must be activated and not wasted. I cannot fly without wing but can make artificial wings to let reach higher hits that loafers never can dream of. Allow the dream to force you into action. Yes, I too have a dream, which is simply that every hamlet in the Gambia be bequeathed good healthcare, safe drinking water, enough food and chance to a solid education for every child.

Yes. Education is power and a mover. I sacrificed my life to endure depravity, humiliation and solitude in other to bring medical aid to villagers. With all these I am busy trying to get more medical skills and experience before heading to Gambia, home , sweet home. With this tit-bit I can freely and willingly encourage you to dream but not to let it remain at that. A life with trials or challenge is like an orchestra without conductor and it very defeating if not boring indeed. One must act for the good of self and any community we find ourselves.

An old village sage once advice that 'A good person and at best a leader never yield to failure but only learns from it to move forward. Grand Pa Bajoja Ceesay told me that; "One willing to do good should not expect people to remove obstacles or stones from their path; but such leaders must accept it calmly in the event these place more boulders on our way."

This is what a dream turns out. At first it becomes a lonely avenue full of heartaches, which eases gradually as the good things unfold from one's relentless efforts to make the dream becomes fruitful and rewarding.. Simple its life 99.9% very hard work full of stumbling. Do not we all dream of going to heaven? Well the path to such respites need challenging theological and spiritual discipline. Hence we earthly dreamers dabble with ideas of landing on Mars and eventually colonizing it. So allow me ask, what is your dream for mankind, especially Africa?

Can Africa ever be free of ignorance, self subtenant, corruption and misuse of the tribe? These just few multipronged toxic dragon heads African must dream to remove from our midst. With better education and discipline Africa can overcome and progress. Dreamers are doing utmost to slay the pestilent dragon hindering life in the villages of rural Africa.

We must remove the monster of retro ration for the shake of the future generation. Again grandpa Bajoja Ceesay advices that we stay the good cause and never be taken by detractions. I am no millionaire but have a million dreams worthy of pursuing for my people. Would you dream along with me? Glad to let you know hard work yields rewarding fruits.

Dream and be in control of not only your own life but be a source of hope and inspiration while contributing positively to your community. Do not be carried along by current get rich quick and live selfishly. Life is to be shared even with dreamers. Time is not mine and life will continue for the villager. Success comes slowly and brings with it contagious hope that serves as blue print for other.

The fate of mankind is up to each of us. Do not succumb to idleness. Use youthful opportunity to develop out of ignorance, and corruption by having courage to bring change to the people. Be the change you want in others. Expect resistance on your path to bring change. A useful proxy in fulfilling a dream is not letting it wane away. Always think it possible and work hard at its realization.

Be warned to think what could be done and not that which cannot be archived. Matrix of success lies in hard work with guided ski full knowledge. I will work on my dream and morrow will be my judge along with benefits accrued from it. I hope my last footprints of my journey on earth will inspire people towards doing well and sharing their worth with others. From one villager to another may this wish be true for rural Gambia.

Ismaila Baba Sallah Ceesay, (brother) Gambia, 2017

Chapter 30

Mourning Mother America!!

Alhasan Ceesay (alhasanceesay@hotmail.com)

The Editor

Alpena News

Michigan, 49707

Dear Editor

I am Dr. Alhasan Ceesay, native of the Gambia and alumni of ACC 1979. I write seeking permission to shed tears, offer prayers and express my condolence on passing of my American mum. The sad news reached me a few weeks ago. I write with a heavy heart for loss of Mrs. Rita Elizabeth Riggs. She today joined her maker and I like to reiterate my sincere gratitude to her, her family, and Alpena residents.

In 1967 and on arriving in Alpena, almost dazed for never having left the Gambia mum Rita and Dad Tubby Haword Riggs brushed my fears aside to the wilderness by showing such human kindness I never expected from someone so distant and different. Yes they opened their home and hearts to me and remained my friends.

God bless them and America!!!

Rita and I have always been in touch and I am certain she is hovering above admonishing me to keep on fighting for downtrodden Gambian villagers. In this vein I also want to remember other friends such as late Viola Glennie, Judge Glennie, Magreett Cruise, Bill/Richard Cruise, Tubby/Howard Riggs, and Dr. Strom of ACC etc.

Yes, most of those who hosted me in Alpena have left. May their kind souls rest in peace at the best place in Heaven.
Today Gambian villagers, my family and friends bow in gratitude and in sadness for having lost a very exceptional lady. Yes, my 91 year old lady has left me. Tobby and Rita have been ambassadors of American kindness and rare breed ready to share the little they have with others despite origin, creed or believes.

They only saw humans like them. Hence Rita's life is one we need to celebrate and learn from it for the silent good she gave to many setting foot in Alpena in the 1960s. She gladly housed Gabber from Ghana, Emanuel from Peru and many more including me Dr. Alhasan Ceesay from the Gambia. In short my villagers and I will always remember Rita as icon of goodness. God bless to all of you. Regards
Dr. Alhasan S. Ceesay, MD
Email:alhasanceesay@hotmail.com

In our journey through life we once on a while come across some human angels like the above American adopted mum of mine. She always had broad beaming smiles anytime I visited her home. She would rush to the

Kitchen and bring the most delicious dish or cake she had for me to fill myself.

This was not all for she normally donates to help in payment of my fees at ACC when I got stranded in 1968. She became mum to me on day one I set eyes on her. She was sincere and not aloof and loves listening with empathy to our home stories.

On one of her visits to the ACC Fish Hatchery, where I worked party she said, "Son, this is not weather for a tropical fellow. Come to the house. I will prepare hot soup and some matting's and thermal wear for you." Such was her kindness and concerned for others. On transferring to Olivet College, this lady would call every two weeks checking how I was faring and if I had friends to help when needed. She spoke to a friend of theirs who had a gas station in Marshall City, Michigan and pleaded with them to offer me summer and where possible week end job to help supplement my financial needs.

She took me just as she did for her own. I will never forget her and way Mrs. Viola Glennie help me since setting foot in America. Glennie continued being in touch even while at Medical Schooling at the University of Liberia in Monrovia, Liberia, West Africa. These twin sisters are angels that never for one moment rest on their laurels when it comes to me.

I now have lost all of them but vow to keep their good work indelible and cherished. William Shakespeare reminds us that evil men do lives after them and the good is interred with their bones. Never have I been touched by so many all of who wanted nothing in return. Their acts were predicated on helping the downtrodden in Africa and contributing to my success meant fulfillment of that dream. Big inspirational foot prints indeed!

IN LOVING MEMORY

Rita Elizabeth Rigg
1920-2013

Chapter 31

Remembering Golden Hearts

William Shakespeare said, "Evil that men do lives after them and the good is interred with their bones." Greatness and good that follows venerable men and women did in their life time is endearing. Let us start where it all began. Back in the 1950s daddy introduced me to a very quite easy going gentle man in our capital city Bathurst, now Banjul. Daddy said; "Son this is your uncle Yunus Amadou Sey, also known as Sherif A. Sey. He is not only my relative but my heart and trusted friend in the city of Bathurst. Do not ever fail liaising with him when situation arises."

Smiling Mr. Sherif Sey walked towards me and gave me a firm but the most welcoming hand shake I never forgot. We jelled instantly and he soon was telling me his boyhood days and how daddy used to chaperon them while they navigate their way through bush country. Our acquaintance was short lived for he had a scholarship to the United Kingdom to be trained police bandmaster.

Mr. Sey is son of Amadou Sey whose father is Abdoulie Sey; a great and renowned marabou who settled at Toro Bahen in the late 1800s. Yunus Sey aka Sherif Sey joined the Gambia Police Force in 1949 and served to rank of Band Master on returning from studies in the UK in 1959.

Mr. Sey remained in this post until 1965 when he left on volunteer retirement. It would be years before he returned and took over the management and ceremonial services of the Gambia Police Band. We renewed contacts and he became my guide in Bathurst. I have such high esteem for this gentle heart because he treated me better than his own children. He would drop by to visit me at raggedy place I rented at Allen Street.

On leaving he would drop at least five pounds, which in the 60s was a huge amount of money, for me to buy food etc. He was privileged to reason why I went into nursing instead of accepting the Secretary Yard's plan to training me with offer of nine months course in the UK to become senior civil servant in the clerical division.

I told him that sheer lack of doctors and healthcare delivery in rural Gambia warrants my sacrificing my youth to bring medical service and relief to deprived villagers. I never missed the police band's activities and renditions it gave to guests or dignitary visitors to the Governor later the Prime Minister of the day. Mr. Sey was guest of honour at my nursing graduation ceremony in 1960 and he relished every speech and accolade I received. He was happy and surprise on learning that my dream to become a medical doctor had started on course and I would be flying the United States by August 15th, 1967 to start my premed classes at Alpena Community College Alpena, Michigan. He was instrumental in helping convince dad that my travels were worthy sacrifice for the Gambia and villagers. Dad never denied request Yunus sey asked because they have been one and good friends that stood for each other since days of yore. Mr. Yunus Sey was among a few relatives and friends who came to see me off at Yundum International Airport on that historic day of my life with me heading to the United States of America via Dakar, Senegal. He gathered all who came and asked that they pray for my venture and that I return to fulfil my ambition for rural Gambia. The passenger list was only five flying from the Gambia to Dakar that day and I was last to board because of Sherif and others wanting to hold me and give personal prayers for me. Mr. Sherif and shed tear once he let go of my hand. I look back to have last glimpse of him all the way to the plane on the tar mark. I sat by the window hoping for chance to see him on the ground but the plane flew too fast and passed the terminal in a minute. While in USA after a day's stay in Senegal, Sherif Sey was one figure I could not removed from my mind because he was so good to me in Bathurst, the Gambia. Hence we exchanged lot of letters as I update him about my progress. In the mean time legend gave us chance to meet in Guinea Conakry as Mr. Sey was there deputizing for dad, who was in his nineties and very frail, to officiate in my marriage to Fatou Koma-Ceesay in 1987. Several years with lot of hardship and roadblocks passed before I finally returned as medical doctor serving my homeland. Sherif Sey lodged me at his home in Fagi kunda until when I was able to afford place to rent. He then urged me to bring Fatou koma-Ceesay to the Gambia. This I did despite fact that I was still fighting to return to the USA to do my Residency program in thoracic medicine. Nine year passed before Fatou and I were invited to attend wedding ceremony of a daughter of Mrs. Lorna Robinson, o ne our best friends while we were in Colchester, Essex, UK 1990-2. While the venerable Band Master and humanitarian Yunu A. Sey aka Sherif A. Sey passed away peacefully. Late Sherif Sey was unique and kind person who had passion to help others he came across. He had ever been missed by all family and friends all over the

Senegambia region.

Sherif A. Sey, Gambia Police Band Master 1949 -1965,

Another icon of admiration was no one other that Dr. Ebrahima Malik Samba, MB Bsc, FRCS and Public Health Officer. He also was born in Bathurst and educated in Ghana, Ireland, Scotland, and Germany and later in the USA. He earned the MB BSc from Ghana, did law and diploma in European studies 1959- 1960.

Earned his doctor of Public International law from McGill University 1960-1961; another masters degree in Law from the University of California at Berkley USA 1961-1962. Venerable indefatigable Samba finally returned to the Gambia in 1963 as a Surgeon. It was during this time that, as clinician and Public Health expert he became recognized internally for his work as Director of the

Onchocerciasis control program which became show case piece in West Africa.

He later served as Director General of Health for Africa for several years before finally retiring to his homeland Gambia. Here he and colleagues built the Muslim School which today boost of lot of university and skilful tradesmen and women. In conjunction he was either chairman or one of executives of many local community organisations in Banjul. In addition to all this he was an elder at the mosque. Dr. Samba and grew to be friends from day used to teach anatomy and Surgery to our nursing class.

The second time this man came to my life was in 1991 while I was on my clinical rotations at the Colchester General hospital in the UK. Life had turned for the worse and I was about to be bounced out of the program because of tuition problem having exhausted money I brought to UK. Dr. Malik Samba came out of the blue to rescue me as stated below.

He is my Gambian Samaritan. It was during those frustrating moments that I decided to bite the bullet and called a long time Gambian friend of mine, Dr. Ebrahima Malik Samba, to come to my rescue. This he did by promptly calling his bank in London and authorizing them to send me three thousand seven hundred pounds sterling loan to help me complete the semester. I received it with gratitude and humility. Praises be God's for only through Him have miracles been happening for me.

Two weeks later the same bank sent another equal amount allotment from Dr. Samba. In my acknowledgement letter I thanked Dr. Samba for the two disbursements and told him that the University had already debited them to my accounts to clear the outstanding bills. Later that week the bank called and wrote to say they made a mistake by sending me the second allotment from Dr. Samba's account and that I should return the money forthwith. At the time all monies sent to me had already been applied toward my fees at the American university of the Caribbean.

Dr. Ebrahima Malik Samba kindly intervened and blamed the bank for the mistake and let me now owe him Four thousand four hundred pounds sterling instead of the original approved three thousand seven hundred pound sterling. No other Gambian would have acquiescence other than this angel friend of mine. He proved to be true and true real friend in need and in good times. I will reimburse him all monies I owe him whenever my earnings improve. This saga allowed me to sail on through until November 11, 1991. The great Doctor and philanthropist slept away peacefully to his maker on the 28th of July 2016.

Dr. Ebrahima Malik Samba, MB BSc, FRCS etc

Another former Gambia Samaritan and tutor was Dr. Sam Palmer, a gynaecologist and head of maternity unit at the Royal Victoria Hospital, Banjul the Gambia.

He was one very interested in my case and donated £50 towards cost of my travels the United States. He even gave me names of Gambian I might liaise within the even unforeseen difficulty.

We kept in touch until my return to the Gambia in 1993 but he had retired and travelled out of the Gambia. I left for UK and was sadly told of his passing by Dr. Ayo Palmer a paediatrician and one of his daughters manning the children unity at the Royal Victoria Hospital.

In loving memory of Mrs. Patricia Koblinsky
Diocese of Michigan

Dear Editor,

I wish through your paper to express sympathy and sincere condolence to Mr. Bob Kolinsky, his family and the Diocese of Michigan for the untimely lost of our dear friend and Sister Mrs. Patricia Koblinsky. The departure of some leaves us bewildered, shocked and flushed. We ask why at this time dear God? Mrs. Patricia Koblinsky is now gleefully resting in the right hands of our maker.

We will miss her. For me, a part of me went along with her. She was a good friend and a true Christian heart that was dedicated to all of us God's children. Four years ago she cried with me and at that same time helped to wipe my tears. She gave hope of freedom and assistance to me and to entire villagers several thousand miles away.

Patricia Koblinsky knew none of them but like the rest of you she more than any was dedicated in seeing that we all breathe the air in peace and walk together side by side in freedom on mother earth.

Patricia: thanks a million for having lived a full Christian life and for all of us. Our profound gratitude and indebtness goes to you for being our Good Samaritan.

The only befitting legacy I have for you and my villagers is returning to serve rural Gambia and especially the villager you fought for during these last minutes of a full Christian and a wonderful life of giving to others. We will never, never forget you and May your soul rest in eternal peace by the right hand side of the Almighty God. Amen!!

Your everlasting Friend

Alhasan S. Ceesay

With Fatou Koma-Ceesay back in the Gambia I continued my scourged or blighted life at the condominiums. I stayed in Montserrat like an orphan working all day and studying up to 1.30 A.M every night for four good months before being join the rest of the students at the Wayland Baptist University in Plainview, Texas. In that interim I chanced to make a lot of friends at the condominiums.

Most rewarding of all was the bond that developed between Rudolf and Sophie Kurt; retired German couples who had come to make this nation island their home away from home. The rumour about a marooned American University of the Caribbean's student on the island needing urgent help spread in town and around the business community like a wild fire making me even more embarrassed to go to town. So on December 19, 1989, I decided to take a break from my studies and be with Rudolf and his wife Sophie Kurt for a chat before they retire for the night. I will come back to this day later.

Allow me return to the Diocesans of Michigan in Detroit. It is said that whosoever is delighted in solitude is either a God or beast. My friends at the Diocese not only helped me make the past year bearable but they made me certain I am invited to most if not all social functions and movies to avert my becoming lonely. Special thanks go to Rev. Hugh White and family for relentless efforts to keep me sane and mingling with Americans.

In a village no one goes lonely but in big cities like Detroit, the Latin adage "Magna civitas, magna solitudo" applies. Simply stated, the larger the city the greater the solitude. Rev. Hugh C. White championed social aspects for me throughout my stay in Detroit. The world would have turned into wilderness of solitude without true friends like Hugh White and his family. Meanwhile Mrs. Patricia koblyski, Rt. Rev. Bishop McGehee, Rev. Hugh White, Rev. Virgil Jones, Rev. David Brower, Rev. Bill Wood, Rev. Walter White, Mrs. Ann Kenzie, Mrs., Lois R. Leonard, John Cannon, Mary Hattle, Betty Howitson, Mrs. Shella Garner, Theresa VanGorder, Alexandra Manshour, W. Y. Gard, professor Francis Conti, Robert Duty, Beth Sax, and Bishop Mason and a host of Episcopalians translated their deep faith, concerns and love of humanity and continued to be my Good Samaritans and a bridge over troubled waters.

These warm hearts were led by the Rt. Rev. H. Coleman McGehee, jr., who was true believer in God, the sanctity of life, and power of knowledge and justice over ignorance, He, like me, defies authority that supplies swords to defend and strengthen ignorance and oppression. Today, when someone kills he must die but he who kills the spirit goes scotch free.

Should friendly oppressive governments continue to be left to cover crime with crime and more crime and not be answerable for their ugly deeds? Is this international law and justice for the beleaguered?

Bishop McGehhe's **weekly** radio commentaries are a clear picture of the spiritual force leading the Episcopal Diocese of Michigan in Detroit. I only wish that I lived long enough to take him and his people to be serenade in the Gambia. This bird's eye view of the Diocese suffices at the moment. On April 16th 1983, Patricia Koblyski came to pick me up from the cots at Trumbull Street. I was relieved to see her. We drove to the Diocese and continued searching for solutions to my problem.

She took me to the Renaissance Centre Monday where I met attorney Robert Duty. Mr. Duty turned to be very friendly and also eager to help me tackle my asylum problem. Again, as before, I narrated every aspect of my plight to him. He listened very attentively and would at time only interrupt by asking questions to clarify the picture as presented to him.

At the end he sent me back to the Diocese to write **out** all about my political activities from my undergraduate days to the very minute I came to see him. I went to work on the request the moment I reached the Diocese. Being a novice at typing I spent the better part of the day on the trying to type it until when Sue Coburn came to my rescue. She did a good job for which I am eternally grateful. However, before the Diocese closed for the day Mrs.

Patricia Koblyski had set up an ad hoc committee consisting of herself, Bishop McGehee, Bishop Mason, Rev. High C. White, Rev. Virgil Jones, Rev. William Wood, Rev. David Brower and Mrs. Lois R. Leonard, Editor of the Diocesan newspaper, the Record, to help me in my fight against deportation to the Gambia.

These ladies and gentlemen became the brains the brains behind my fight with the immigration courts. While gathering more evidence for the INS I took sanctuary at the Mariner's Inn on Ledyard Street. It was time to close and I was taken to the Mariner's Inn on Ledyard Street in Detroit.

Mrs. Binta Ceesay, elder Sister

Lois R. Leonard is the Editor of the Diocesan Record Newspaper at the Episcopalian Diocese of Michigan in Detroit city. Below is example of love and support Lois Regina Leonard had for me.

Alhasan Ceesay leaves our Santuary for Medical School
A word from Bishop Mason And Rev. Hugh C. White
You will be delighted to learn that Alhasan S. Ceesay was accepted yesterday (Tuesday, November 11, 1986) into the medical school of the American University of the Caribbean, Plymouth, Montserrat, West Indies. Alhasan is hoping to commence his studies at the medical school this

coming January 7, 1987. You know that Bishop McGehee and the Diocese have given Alhasan sanctuary for more than three years. Mariner's Inn has provided him with housing and sustenance. Bishop McGehee in his letter to Dean of the Medical School in the West Indies said, "I know Alhasan personally.
He is a person of integrity, intelligence, human sensitivity, and God knows, perseverance against formidable inequalities." For the past several weeks a small group of persons in the Diocese have raised $15,000 towards the $30,000 required for his medical training. You may wish to join in the support of Alhasan. The purpose of this memo is to give you that opportunity. You do understand that every dollar raised will go directly to his personal support.
You may make a monthly or quarterly pledge to be paid over the next eighteen months, beginning December 15, 1986 and going through to July 15, 1988. All monies received for this purpose are tax deductible.

Evelyn Bayer at the Diocese Centre (4800 Woodward Avenue, Detroit, MI 48201) will take your pledges or your money. We are confident that Alhasan Ceesay will serve all people wherever he is. He is personally committed to returning to the Gambia as a doctor to his people. Signed: Bishop Mason and The Rev. Hugh C. White
A copy of my letter followed for Editor of the Diocesan newspaper to print in The Record.

Dear Editor,

I will be most delighted if you would kindly publish this note in the next issue of the Record for me to extend deep appreciation and gratitude to the Diocese of Michigan, my support group, Mariner's Inn, and all who steadfastly stood by me to seek resolution of my intractable INS case. Thank you is awfully inadequate and words cannot aptly convey to you what the help you rendered meant to my villagers and I.

I take this opportune moment to express profound gratitude for your generous and the overwhelming support accorded me.

The fruits of your benevolence will be shared with the sick and needy in due course. To those not aware, I am pleased to report my being accepted at the American University School of Medicine in the West Indies effective January 7, 1987. Most relieving is the fact that I will be able to meet with my family in Guinea Conakry on my way to the Medical school.

All of this would have been impossible had it not been for love, encouragement and support you provided me during these difficult times of my life. Therefore, allow me to convey to you, in advance, sincere appreciation of my family and villagers for the kindness you always touched us with during my exile days or years.

We are very grateful and a million thanks to all of you who one way or the other contributed to make this chapter and day possible for my villagers. Thanks for being true friends of human rights and for being so kind and helpful to my mission and me. I will certainly return to serve the Gambia as soon as that is possible for me.

Thank you! My gratitude to this country (America and Americans) is immeasurable. It is here that life taught me how to forge ahead for my people and for nothing more I am thankful for the love and friendship of the people from whom I learn the true meaning of sacrifice and good will towards others.

The French capsule my feeling best in the saying, "Tout est bien, qui fini bien." All is best that ends well. God bless all

of you. "Au revoir Mon ami." Goodbye my good friends. I will see you in the Gambia. We certainly look forward to welcoming you in our villages to thank you for your stand in this unusual case.
Sincerely
Alhasan S. Ceesay

With this newfound relief I braced myself for the task that lay ahead. I got my little possessions, I had, all packed, bought my air ticket to Guinea Conakry via Amsterdam and the London and Antigua to Montserrat, West Indies.
I made my last pilgrimage to the Diocese of Michigan early on December 19, 1986, the day of my flight out of America. Everyone seemed to want to hug me and wish me well and a safe journey.
They were also relieved that life has now signaled progress for me and that the prospect of meeting with my family was super. The Bishop broke down, at his office, when I shook his hands for the last time. He and I have grown very close and are now parting for, possibly, for good.
I took a last look at him, with tears dripping on my cheeks, and walked out saying thanks, goodbye and God bless you sir. I heard his footsteps behind me up to the end of the corridor and I disappeared into Rev. High C. White's office who was then on the telephone making final arrangements for me at Detroit Metro Airport for a 1.00 pm flight from Detroit to Chicago for both of us. The scenery of well wishers repeated itself at the corridor where I met a throng of people wanting to see me for the last time.
I will never forget (The Rt. Rev) H. Coleman Bishop McGehee, jr, Patricia Koblyski, Hugh White and the Ceesay-Committee, Lois R. Leonard, Evelyn Bayer, Marry Ellen Robertson, and Rev. Walter White, executive director at the Mariner's Inn. Rev, Hugh C. White and I entered the

car amidst tears and cheers from those onlookers and good friends of mine.

This was the beginning of the closure of my life in exile and the Mariner's Inn saga. At the Metro airport and after the formalities, Hugh and I bought few soft drinks but none of us finished his because of the Erie feeling that we are now about to separate for long, long time to come, or perhaps forever. We arrived at O'Hare International Airport in Chicago two hours early.

This gave us time to browse around and renew our commitment not to lose contact of each other, especially the Bishop and my friends at the Episcopal Diocese of Michigan. Time flew rapidly and soon we had the PA announcing boarding time for Amsterdam.

The Rev. Hugh C. White and I shook hands for the last time at O'Hare International on December 19, 1986 and I broke down for the first time since I left Diocese of Michigan in Detroit. I have bid farewell to the last of the true friends I had in America. These were friends who uphold the doctrine of human rights and justice for all. We prayed together and I joined the boarding queues. Hugh too had a tear or two escape him. He stood watching for a while before he disappeared into America and I headed for Africa and the Caribbean. Very soon elation took over my sadness for leaving behind such good friends I made during the saga of my exile years. The flight was routine and went smoothly. I landed at Amsterdam, Holland, 5.00 am, the next day.

I could not believe that this time the sun has risen for me and that I am not in the Mariner's Inn but on my way to motherland Africa. The thought and feeling of relief I had at that December 20, 1986, can never be repeated. I made it to Guinea and in no time married one I loved dearly. I started classes at AUC and few weeks' later tragedy hit. My best friend Patricia Kobliski passed away.

The death of Mrs. Patricia Koblyski left me devastated and concerned. She meant a lot to me and her sincerity and determination to free me was unsurpassed by any other member of the Ceesay Support Committee. Her death was indeed a tragic loss to my villagers and me.

We pray and mourn her passing. Mrs. Lois R. Leonard's statement summed up my feeling about Patricia A. Koblyski when she wrote, "It still seems terribly strange to go in that building (meaning the Diocese) and not see Pat Koblyski." I missed her very much. Her death ushered in pain and a sense of great loss for me. May she rest in peace with God in Heaven.

Patricia Kolinsky was one of those who fought vehemently against the intentions of Richard Smith effort to stop my going to the Caribbean. Instead, Richard wanted me to do nursing because we fail to see eye to eye on most points he raised during our meetings. It was as though he felt a black should not challenge ideas he tabled.

This became great snarl between us with Lois enjoy the tug of war going on between Richard and I. Still determined to stop my getting help from the Diocese Richard managed to get himself selected to pay a surprise visit to AUC medical school in Plymouth, Montserrat, West Indies. He was eager come and check on my performance and to use any negative aspect of it to derail me. He now had the opportunity because some of the staff like David Breidenbach was not happy with me.

This was Richard's chance to drown me into oblivion to the bottom of the Atlantic Ocean. Richard led to the termination of Diocesan financial support of my studies at the American University of the Caribbean School of Medicine. To cut a long story short the committee under the wing of Richard voted termination of help I was giving. Here is what Lois R. Leonard told and explained in a letter to me.

Mrs. Lois Leonard felt that or explained her reasons for dissenting with the decision of the committee as follows, "My reasons for voting against the rest of the committee was that I felt that we had made a promise and we were not keeping it. We promised to send you enough for five semesters. And we stopped sending it before the time was completed." Lastly but not the least is late Dr. Joyce Inyang who I met early 2011 at the Hulme Library in Manchester, UK.

We jelled and had been best of friends until his passing away March 2016. We frequently visit each other to events or cook meals at my flat. We became twin brothers and Pan Africans constantly seeking solutions to healthcare delivery in our mother land Africa. His untimely departure left a void in my life for he was a true African and a kind gentleman I will never forget. May his soul rest in eternal peace with his maker, Amen!! RIP

In loving memory of a true friend: Dr. Joyce Inyang RIP

Chapter 32

ABOUT THE AUTHOR

I was born at Njawara Village, Lower Badibou District in the North Bank of the Gambia. I am a scion of a Mandinka and Fulani tribe and am one of five siblings. I had my education at Kinte Kunda, then Armitage High School, ending up as a registered nurse at the Royal Victoria Hospital, Banjul, before embarking to the USA on my medical degree quest.

I graduated from the American University School of Medicine in Montserrat, West Indies, in 1992 and returned to the Gambia to start setting up a self-help village health NGO Manding Medical Centre. The Gambia Government and the Badibou local authority register NGO Manding Medical Centre. The centre has treated more than 9000 patients free.

I am married to Fatou Koma-Ceesay and we are blessed with three beautiful girls, Famatanding Ceesay, Binta Ceesay and Roheyata Ceesay. Unlike me, all of them started school early without the roadblocks I had to cross in my early years. I am currently a medical officer at the Royal at the Royal Victoria Hospital on study leave. It is my hope that this work will inspire others and bring much needy help to providing medical service to rural Gambia.

You are urged to kindly log onto www.friendsofmandinggambimed.btck.co.uk, or www.publishkunsa.com to learn more about my work with villagers. Dear reader I hope you enjoyed

navigating through the piece of work I am contribute for all of us makes case for change in attitudes of government and the governed.

For now, Dalliance said it best for me when he said, "Say of me what you will and the morrow will judge you, and your words shall be a witness before its judgment and a testimony before its justice. I came to say a word and I shall utter it. Should death take me ere I give voice, the morrow shall utter it. That which alone I do today shall be proclaimed before the people in days to come."

I wrote with the hope the life and position enshrined herein will serve as not only an inspiration to farmers, the despondent but also a lesson never to allow these shameful international jigsaw games continue as experience to pass through this planet. I felt that it is worth writing about the above because it is something worth revealing to honourable men and women to engender change, tolerance and understanding between people and governments. I risked speaking out for all of us to learn from it and move forward to a better and rewarding future.

Have your manuscript become a book by submitting it for possible publication to acquisitions publishes Kunsa. Com

Please contact us to expose your work globally.

PUBLISH KUNSA.COM

How Publish
Kunsa works

Our
Services

Rural Scheme

Scholarships & eligibility

Our Publications

Why Publish Kunsa?

*At Publish Kunsa.com writers can get published free of all common hassles
from soft paperbacks, hard cover to e-book versions.*

Easy to Publish

1. Upload manuscript
2. make pdf format

3. convert to print ready copy
4. Book Cover Design

Leave a Legacy

Your publishing with Publish Kunsa will enable you help villagers and children have healthcare and be educated. It is a worthy legacy.

Scholarships

Empower villagers by educating their children by your work.

Worldwide Distribution

Your work is garranteed international exposure.

Donate

You can in addition donate in cash or kind to select areas of help you want to contribute to.

Excellent Support

Your work and queries will be given the utmost attention by very capable hands to make your work reach readers.

More about Publish Kunsa

Web design by Samson Web Design

-
-

© 2017 **Publish Kunsa**. All Rights Reserved.

www.ingramcontent.com/pod-product-compliance
Lightning Source LLC
Chambersburg PA
CBHW071310150426
43191CB00007B/576